THE EVERYTHING®
CLASSROOM MANAGEMENT BOOK

Dear Reader,

Thank you for your time, and congratulations on your foresight in buying *The Everything® Classroom Management Book*. Whether you're a new teacher or an experienced pro, you know that to succeed in teaching you need to get as much help as possible—not because you're less competent than other teachers, but simply because you want to be the best. This book will help you achieve that goal.

Here are my mentoring qualifications: I'm a veteran classroom teacher with twenty years' hard-won experience educating children in schools in the United States and in Great Britain (St. Julian's Comprehensive School, New-port, Wales). I've also won on *Jeopardy!* (1984), thanks to my broad knowl-edge of academic subjects; and I have a BA degree in English, and a Juris Doctor degree in Law. But most importantly, I've been in the trenches for two decades, perfecting my teaching artistry. Now I'd like to offer you my battle-tested strategies for managing your classroom, organizing your instruction, and becoming the superior teacher you were meant to be.

Thanks again for reading *The Everything® Classroom Management Book*, and may the torch of knowledge you pass on to future generations continue to burn brightly forever.

Eric Groves, Sr.

Welcome to the EVERYTHING® Series!

These handy, accessible books give you all you need to tackle a difficult project, gain a new hobby, comprehend a fascinating topic, prepare for an exam, or even brush up on something you learned back in school but have since forgotten.

You can choose to read an *Everything*® book from cover to cover or just pick out the information you want from our four useful boxes: e-questions, e-facts, e-alerts, and e-ssentials.

We give you everything you need to know on the subject, but throw in a lot of fun stuff along the way, too.

We now have more than 400 *Everything*® books in print, spanning such wide-ranging categories as weddings, pregnancy, cooking, music instruction, foreign language, crafts, pets, New Age, and so much more. When you're done reading them all, you can finally say you know *Everything*®!

E-QUESTION

Answers to
common questions

FACTS

Important snippets
of information

ALERTS!

Urgent
warnings

ESSENTIALS

Quick
handy tips

PUBLISHER Karen Cooper

DIRECTOR OF ACQUISITIONS AND INNOVATION Paula Munier

MANAGING EDITOR, EVERYTHING SERIES Lisa Laing

COPY CHIEF Casey Ebert

ACQUISITIONS EDITOR Lisa Laing

SENIOR DEVELOPMENT EDITOR Brett Palana-Shanahan

EDITORIAL ASSISTANT Hillary Thompson

Visit the entire Everything® series at *www.everything.com*

THE EVERYTHING®

CLASSROOM MANAGEMENT BOOK

A teacher's guide to an organized,
productive, and calm classroom

Eric Groves, Sr.
Foreword by Frederick C. Wootan

Avon, Massachusetts

*This book is dedicated to my patient and loving wife, Suzette;
my brilliant and talented daughter, Deborah; my kind-hearted
and ingenious son, Eric; my incredibly courageous mother-in-law,
Jovita; and my immortal and triumphant mother, Dolly.*

An Everything® Series Book.
Everything® and everything.com® are registered trademarks of F+W Media, Inc.

Published by Adams Media, a division of F+W Media, Inc.
57 Littlefield Street, Avon, MA 02322 U.S.A.
www.adamsmedia.com

ISBN 10: 1-59869-825-7
ISBN 13: 978-1-59869-825-1

Printed in the United States of America.

J   I   H   G   F   E   D   C   B   A

Library of Congress Cataloging-in-Publication Data
is available from the publisher.

This publication is designed to provide accurate and authoritative information with regard to the subject matter covered. It is sold with the understanding that the publisher is not engaged in rendering legal, accounting, or other professional advice. If legal advice or other expert assistance is required, the services of a competent professional person should be sought.

—From a *Declaration of Principles* jointly adopted by a Committee of the American Bar Association and a Committee of Publishers and Associations

Many of the designations used by manufacturers and sellers to distinguish their products are claimed as trademarks. Where those designations appear in this book and Adams Media was aware of a trademark claim, the designations have been printed with initial capital letters.

*This book is available at quantity discounts for bulk purchases.
For information, please call 1-800-289-0963.*

Contents

Foreword

Eric Groves, Sr., has impeccable educational credentials combined with over twenty years of experience working in the classroom. He leaves no stone unturned that could help in making sure you do the best, most professional job possible. He has an acute awareness of the elements of academic instruction, time management, discipline, relationship building, and job protection that form the basis of the teaching profession. His knowledge of the law and the fact that you cannot ignore living in a litigious world filled with passivity and unwillingness to accept responsibility, adds to his presentation. He does not miss any function of importance to you, the teacher.

The field of education, like other professions, experiences changing cycles of focus. Teachers respond best to these changes by properly managing their classrooms. Perhaps, for the sake of clarity, I should substitute the words "learning environment" for "classroom," and thereby eliminate any reference to class. The original educational meaning of class, "a course of instruction," has changed in today's vernacular, taking on its other definition: "a social network." *The Everything® Classroom Management Book* message makes certain that every new teacher has the tools necessary to plan, organize, manage, and control his or her classroom—making it a true learning environment.

Most of you joined this honorable profession because of your love for learning and with the hope of imparting knowledge to others. Becoming an outstanding teacher does not mean you dispense knowledge in the same way you might drop a scoop of ice cream into a waiting sugar cone. You must also instill in your students the need to ask questions with a sincere desire to find truth. The ability to think trumps any form of memorization, and it requires teachers highly skilled in developing a true learning environment for students to begin to think well.

The human mind has an awareness of everything going on around it, but it also has a built-in filtering system. You must properly guide those student minds toward acceptance of learning the subject matter while filtering out the distractions of the student-populated community in your schools. Remind yourself that students do not have the fully developed capability to understand the true consequences of actions. Therefore, the responsibility for managing that community to obtain the desired results falls upon you, the classroom teacher.

The subject matter will change just as certainly as student dynamics will change with the demands of our larger society. But, if you follow the well-tested ideas presented in this timeless book, you will readily adapt to the seemingly inconsistent requirements of administrators, parents, and even other teachers.

Do not tire in your attempts to develop your classroom into a learning environment. You will experience days when you wonder if you actually have the responsibilities of a psychologist, referee, friend, parent, coach, custodian, and, oh yes, teacher. When those days come to an end and the kids have left the building, take a deep breath and reread this book. You will find that it truly is *The Everything® Classroom Management Book*.

—*Frederick C. Wootan*

Acknowledgments

I wish to thank the supportive, professional staff of Grace Yokley Middle School, particularly Dave Bemowski, Tina Bombardier, Kim Burr, Danny Ciesla, Alanna Cooper, Marsha Folliott, Randy Garrett, Su Garrett, Karen Greenwood, Terre Gunkel, Craig Hansen, Glen Jensen, Kathleen Kay, Rama Kumar, Heather Mikalski, Angie Morales, Jeff Nelson, Michelle Posnikoff, Robert Quezada, Dale Rosine, Cari Sheridan, Patrick Taing, John Todd, Pat Trimmer, and Lynda Yassim. These dedicated men and women have taught me what sacrifice, service, and instructional excellence truly mean.

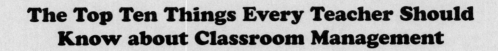

The Top Ten Things Every Teacher Should Know about Classroom Management

1. Be yourself. Teaching is an art, and you must be free to perfect your own artistic style, every day.

2. Dare to show mercy to a disruptive kid, whenever appropriate. Yes, maybe you're just delaying an inevitable punishment, but just maybe, you're brightening a kid's life forever.

3. Never let your students confuse your unfailing kindness with weakness.

4. By the same token, don't hesitate to impose appropriate discipline up front, when circumstances require you to do so for the student's own good and the good of your class.

5. Work extremely hard. If you expect your students to labor diligently, then you must do the same.

6. Keep on top of all required paperwork and grading, every day. If you don't, these crucial tasks will bury you.

7. You are not in the classroom to win the adoration of your students or colleagues. You are there to teach children and help them become lovers of knowledge and good citizens.

8. Never tell students, "I don't know what to do next!"; you are their leader. Stay informed and use your best ethical judgment to make intelligent decisions and resolve problems.

9. On the other hand, if you don't know the answer to a particular question, admit it, then promise to get the information as soon as possible.

10. Only insecure teachers bluster, shout, threaten, and bully. Keep your voice under control, apologize whenever appropriate, and model courtesy and compassion at all times.

Introduction

▶ WHAT DOES "CLASSROOM MANAGEMENT" mean? Renowned American educators Carolyn M. Evertson and Carol S. Weinstein define classroom management as "the actions teachers take to create an environment that supports and facilitates both academic and social-emotional learning." That definition's a little scholarly, but it's a good start. It just means that classroom management is a set of rules, words, and deeds that you, the classroom teacher, use to keep your classroom running smoothly so that you and your students can work, teach, and learn safely and efficiently.

That's what this book, *The Everything® Classroom Management Book*, is all about—helping you create a secure, productive classroom environment where kids can learn. This book will be your one-stop classroom-management reference, packed with strategies based on academic research and real-world experience. It gives you battle-tested tips on how to become an outstanding professional educator.

The Everything® Classroom Management Book will show you specifically how to understand and master the five critically important domains of classroom management: turn defiant students into stellar performers; transform unruly parents into loyal allies; make peace with difficult administrators; use teachers' associations to insure ethical and legal job protection; and create excellent classroom environments.

Also, by providing detailed strategies for teaching today's highly challenging students as well as minimizing disruptions and maximizing effectiveness, this guide can help prevent you from joining the 15 percent of teachers who leave the profession every year. Instead, *The*

Everything® Classroom Management Book is for you, the roughly 105,451 dedicated people who've recently chosen to become teachers.

After studying this book thoroughly, you should be able to effectively resolve a wide range of classroom-management problems, such as students who stand up in the middle of class and yell, "Shove it!" You should also be able to placate parents who storm in to dispute grades or object to your discipline strategies. Most important, you should be able to help students excel academically. *The Everything® Classroom Management Book* is meant to be an informative, entertaining, and indispensable guidebook for you, the teacher.

Even if you're a veteran teacher with years of experience, you'll enjoy this book because it's an invaluable source of new classroom-management ideas—such as combating cyber bullying, using the Internet, and mastering presentation software such as PowerPoint. You vets want to succeed as much as the rookies do, and you'll gather every resource necessary to attain success. *The Everything® Classroom Management Book* is a priceless resource for you because as teacher and author Memory Schorr has observed, "[E]ven veteran teachers need ongoing assistance. . . ." This book provides the ongoing assistance you've been looking for.

Indeed, with the total number of dedicated, selfless teachers now surpassing 6.2 million in the United States, and with 517,000 more teachers projected by the U.S. Census Bureau to join the profession by 2009, the need for a classroom-management tool such as *The Everything® Classroom Management Book* will continue to grow indefinitely. Good teachers will always need good ideas, and you'll find a wealth of them here.

Are you ready? Don't worry—with your own innate good sense and the information contained in this book, your students should soon become outstanding performers. Good luck, and remember the motto that the renowned American librarian John Cotton Dana (1856–1929) wrote for Kean College: "Who dares to teach must never cease to learn."

CHAPTER 1

What Is Classroom Management?

Think of classroom management as your personal toolkit of policies, actions, and words, which you use to keep your classroom functioning smoothly and your students working safely and efficiently. But to manage efficiently, you'll need to carefully study the basic concepts introduced in this chapter. Think of each concept as a tool in your classroom-management toolkit—a saw for cutting through confusion or a hammer for building comprehension and so on. As a teacher, you're only as good as your tools, so it pays to become familiar with them.

The Five Critical Classroom-Management Domains

The five critically important domains or areas listed below make up the broad topic of classroom management. Each domain is briefly touched on here, with more detailed discussions to follow, both in this chapter and in subsequent chapters.

- **Academic Instruction:** In this area, you must shine as a teacher because your students need top-notch instruction and because you must keep your job if you want to continue helping kids.
- **Time Management:** If you give in to the natural human tendency to be lackadaisical and sloppy, you're finished—and your students will never know how truly great you might've become.
- **Discipline:** You can't teach if your students are fighting and screaming in the classroom. Good discipline is a form of tough love, consisting of firm yet compassionate guidance.
- **Relationship Building:** To be effective, you must build professional working relationships with students, parents, colleagues, administrators, the school board, and the community.
- **Job Protection:** If you're not in the classroom, you can't teach. Don't lose your job and cheat your students because of avoidable mistakes.

Each of these domains is equally important and together they are critical to your success as a teacher. Think of these five domains as functioning collectively, like a well-built staircase carrying you safely upward to teaching excellence. Your daily teaching performance and the success of your entire teaching career will depend on how well you master the rudiments of each of these domains—academic instruction, time management, discipline, relationship building, and job protection.

Academic Instruction

Academic instruction is your primary duty as a teacher. You're in the classroom to teach effectively so that your students can progress to the next grade level with a good understanding of the academic material in your state's curriculum. Also, you're required to teach core values to students, such as tolerance, responsibility, and good citizenship. If you're not doing all that, you're not teaching. No, you can't always reach every student, but you must nevertheless consistently strive to deliver the highest-quality instruction possible.

ALERT!

According to *The Harvard Medical School Guide to a Good Night's Sleep,* by Dr. Lawrence J. Epstein and Steven Mardon, sleep deprivation, where you remain awake beyond the normal sixteen-hour wakefulness cycle, can cause dangerous "microsleeps," where you fall unconscious while performing conscious tasks. If you microsleep while driving to work, your students could end up deprived of your company—permanently. Get your eight hours.

One of the first tools you'll want to use in your classroom-management toolkit is the skill of effective lesson planning. A widely accepted formal lesson-plan model was developed by Dr. Madeline Cheek Hunter, Professor of Educational Administration and Teacher Education at the University of California, Los Angeles (UCLA). Consider using this format when submitting a formal lesson plan for administrative review or in connection with your ongoing teacher evaluations. Here's a version of Dr. Hunter's lesson-plan model:

- **Objectives:** Write a paragraph here about what students are expected to learn. Note any materials to be used, pages and exercises to be completed, and skills students should internalize.
- **Standards:** Access your state's website and match your lesson to one standard from the academic-content standards listed. If you can't match it to a standard, don't teach that lesson.
- **Anticipatory Set:** Explain how you'll motivate your students to participate in and benefit from your lesson by relating the lesson topic to the students' own lives and interests.

- **Teaching:** Explain how you'll teach the lesson. Give details on how you plan to use texts, supplemental materials, audio-visual aids, etc., to help students learn the desired skill objective.
- **Guided Practice/Monitoring:** State what work your students will be expected to complete, whether individually or cooperatively, and how you'll plan to actively monitor for understanding.
- **Closure:** Explain how you'll check for anticipated comprehension by asking your students to recap and recall the most important points of your lesson.
- **Independent Practice:** Discuss the homework you'll assign in connection with your lesson and how the assignment relates to the lesson.

The Madeline Hunter format is easy to use, self-explanatory, and straightforward. The following is a typical example of what such a lesson plan, following the Hunter format, might look like:

1. **Objectives:** Students are expected to analyze, in writing, the characterization techniques used in the novel *A Christmas Carol* by Charles Dickens, specifically in Stave 5 (Chapter 5), as it relates to the positive character changes and development of the novel's main character, Ebenezer Scrooge. Students should complete page 655, question number 1, "Literary Analysis: Characterization," in our literature textbook, *Prentice-Hall Literature: Timeless Voices, Timeless Themes,* edited by Dr. Kate Kinsella, et al. This exercise should engender in students an appreciation of the ingenuity used by the greatest fiction writers, such as Dickens, to create characters that are lifelike and believable.

2. **California Standard:** California reading Standard 3.3: Analyze characterization as delineated through a character's thoughts, words, speech patterns, and actions; the narrator's description; and the thoughts, words, and actions of other characters.

3. **Anticipatory Set:** Students can be asked to think about and verbalize whether they are exactly the same people now—with exactly the same attitudes, beliefs, and philosophies they have always embraced—or rather, if they have philosophically changed and developed over the years. Have any of their beliefs changed as a result of the new informa-

tion? Have their corresponding actions changed? After proffering various instances of positive developmental growth, students should think about the fact that well-developed fictional characters undergo similar developmental growth as a part of the process of making characters seem lifelike and believable.

4. **Teaching:** Input: Students can be provided with a textbook-based definition of characterization as well as examples of how Charles Dickens has utilized characterization to show how his main character, Ebenezer Scrooge, has grown and developed as part of the process of making the character seem lifelike and believable. Modeling: Students can be shown examples of various types of appropriate and reasonable written responses as models for answering the above-referenced page 655, question number 1, in our Literature textbook, *Prentice-Hall Literature: Timeless Voices, Timeless Themes.* Checking for Understanding: Students can be provided with an opportunity to practice writing some examples of various types of appropriate and reasonable responses to the above-referenced page 655, question number 1, in our literature textbook.

5. **Guided Practice/Monitoring:** Students are expected to demonstrate their grasp of the material by working in cooperative groups, assisted by the teacher, to help one another write a paragraph-long response to question number 1, page 655. The question is as follows: "Literary Analysis: Characterization: 1. By the end of the [novel], how has the character of Scrooge changed? Support your answer with three incidents that show this change."

6. **Closure:** Students can be cued to the fact that they have arrived at the end of the lesson and are now expected to work conscientiously, in cooperative groups, to complete the writing task that has been assigned as guided practice.

7. **Independent Practice:** Students are expected to complete independent practice in the form of an individual homework assignment, due the next instructional day following assignation, which will consist of the following: Page 654, question number 1, from our literature textbook. The question is as follows: "Review and Assess: Thinking about the Literature: Do you believe that people can really change completely, as Scrooge does? Explain your answer."

The example above contains a great deal of detail, and not every administrator will want or require quite so much information. However, sometimes it's better to err on the side of an abundance of caution. Ask for five minutes of your principal's time and briefly discuss the subject of lesson planning, asking for guidance on what's expected.

When it comes to lesson planning, you'll need to keep two sets of books, so to speak—formal lessons for formal occasions and a regular lesson-plan book for the daily job of educating students. Generally, your district will provide you with a plan book, or you can purchase one from a teacher-supply store if the district's book doesn't seem adequate. You can also download plan-book templates to your computer from countless websites. For example, one popular template is the Microsoft Corporation's "Planning Book No. 8," for use with Microsoft Word 2000 (or later) word-processing software, and which resembles most standard plan books. These planners generally use a similar format.

1. The top line of each page has a space to write your name and room number, plus a "Week Beginning" space to write the starting date for that week's lessons.
2. Each page is divided into rows and columns, creating large squares. Down the left, each weekday occupies its own full row, starting with Monday and moving down to Friday.
3. At the top of each column, left to right, write the name of each subject you teach. Secondary teachers might use only one column, but elementary teachers will use several columns.
4. In each square, note your lesson objectives, teaching activities, textbook pages and exercises to be completed, and special instructions for yourself (or a substitute teacher).

Keep your plans handy on your desk because you'll be referring to them constantly. Also, substitute teachers will find them invaluable if you're ever absent. Moreover, count on administrators occasionally visiting your classroom and asking to see your plan book. Keep it at hand so that you'll never have to admit, "Sorry, my lesson plans are at home." Such a lack of professionalism can have serious consequences, possibly the loss of your teaching position. Plan ahead for career success.

However, planning ahead doesn't mean chaining yourself to your desk and neglecting your health and your loved ones. Plan as far ahead as you can reasonably manage, but keep a balance between dedication to your job and attending to your health outside of the classroom. Get adequate rest, eat right, exercise, and spend time with friends and family. In this way, you'll become the teacher that your students need—rested, refreshed, recharged, and ready to provide the best academic instruction possible.

Time Management

Another important classroom-management tool is the skill of effective time management. American author and home economist Ann Smith Rice defines time management as "gaining control over what you do, when you do it, how you do it, and why you do it." In other words, your lifetime inevitably passes, minute by minute—and you aren't getting any younger. So if you want to achieve your goals, you've got to get organized, plan carefully, then act decisively.

The time that you're trying to manage falls into two broad categories:

1. Adjuvant instructional time
2. Instructional time

"Adjuvant" simply means, "in addition to." Your adjuvant instructional time is the daily time you spend in addition to your instructional time, before and after class, getting ready to teach and manage your students. During your adjuvant instructional time, you can engage in professional activities including:

- Planning lessons
- Grading homework and classwork papers
- Entering grade information into your classroom computer
- Filing students' papers in their portfolios
- Regularly preparing progress reports
- Providing instructional tutoring to challenged students

- Personally conferring with students, parents, teaching colleagues, administrators, and others
- Posting students' work and school information on classroom and hallway bulletin boards
- Procuring needed supplies, books, and equipment or setting up audio-visual equipment and materials such as transparencies, tapes, CDs, DVDs, etc.
- Accessing and studying students' cumulative files (commonly called "cums")
- Checking with school nurses on the medical status and requirements of certain students
- Checking with bilingual coordinators on the status and requirements of English learners
- Meeting with special-education teachers regarding disabled students' individual education plans (IEPs)
- Arranging logistical details for field trips
- Sponsoring after-school clubs and sports teams
- Attending seminars, completing courses, and sitting for examinations for professional growth

In contrast to adjuvant instructional time, your instructional time is the daily time you spend during class teaching and managing your students. During your instructional time, you'll engage in many of these professional activities:

- Instructing your whole class directly
- Instructing small groups of students directly
- Presenting PowerPoint or other audio-visual instructional presentations
- Helping inattentive or distracted students remain on task
- Guiding students' written responses to direct instruction
- Working with individual students who require extra tutoring
- Monitoring students who are using classroom learning centers, especially computer centers
- Grading papers along with your students, for instant feedback
- Sending ill or injured students to the nurse

- Sending responsible students on important errands to the main office or other classrooms
- Acting as mediator for formal classroom debates and informal classroom discussions
- Acting as timekeeper, critic, and grader during students' oral presentations to the class

Don't try to be a superhero, but instead realize that most jobs, including teaching, can never truly be completed. There's always more to do, no matter how superhuman your efforts. Therefore, work hard, but don't endanger your health or your peace of mind. Keep your nose to the grindstone, but remember that noses are designed for smelling flowers, too.

In subsequent chapters, you'll learn how to do the seemingly impossible task of budgeting your limited, valuable time so that you can effectively accomplish your professional duties and still have time left over to enjoy your life.

Discipline

One of the most important tools you'll ever retrieve from your classroom-management toolkit is the skill of effective, compassionate discipline. The great Tibetan-American Buddhist monk Geshe Kelsang Gyatso says in his book *How to Solve Our Human Problems*: "Discipline is like a great earth that supports and nurtures the crops..." In other words, if you never discipline your students, if you never give them the terra firma of solid values and firm moral precepts they're secretly yearning for, they'll never develop into good, honest, responsible citizens.

But maybe you're a kind-hearted soul, and you believe that children should be free to dance in the sun, leap with joy, and follow their natural instincts. Well, there's some truth to that—kids should have the freedom to play, explore, and test some of the limits of their environment. But there's a time and place for everything, and you and your students must have enough training and discipline to know what to do, what not to do, when to do certain things, and when not to do certain things. You can teach as beautifully as you please, but if most of the class is yakking and gossiping, your efforts are wasted.

Do you need more convincing that discipline is crucial to effectively manage your classroom? Then refer to the writings of the respected American businesswoman and counselor Phyllis York, as she discusses heartbreaking cases of rebellious, pathetic youngsters who wind up in juvenile court because of the unwillingness of parents and teachers to impose discipline. York concludes that what's needed is "a tough but loving solution for our tragic contemporary problem." That "tough love" solution includes consistently pointing out students' misbehavior when it interferes with the good order of the classroom, correcting the misbehavior, and modeling courteous behavior yourself as much as possible.

E-QUESTION

Should I try to intimidate my students by telling them I'm the world's meanest teacher?
Bad idea. You're assuming—erroneously—you'll get cooperation if you make such statements. But many students, far from being intimidated, will decide to test you by being super disruptive. Don't invite trouble; instead, structure your class so that if trouble comes, you'll employ firm, effective discipline.

In Chapter 11, you'll learn how disciplining is actually a form of love—because people who don't care about kids never bother to discipline them. But if you genuinely care, you'll correct misbehavior, for the kids' sake.

Relationship Building

Another important tool in your classroom-management toolkit is the skill of building good relationships. After all, without other people to interact with, your own sense of self-worth and self-identity tend to diminish. American psychologist William Braxton Irvine puts it best in his book *On Desire: Why We Want What We Want*: "You might acquire an expansive wristwatch, only to realize that without other people to meet, you don't need to know what time it is."

Simply put, you need people—young people whom you can teach, parents who will support your efforts, colleagues who will help you in a crunch, administrators who will go to bat for you with unruly parents, a superintendent who supports your staff, a school board that understands and rewards your staff's dedication, and a community that rallies behind your staff when necessary. You get help from other people by being helpful to others yourself. Building professional relationships is like building bridges to carry you safely across turbulent waters.

FACT

If you're wondering what kind of relationship teachers share with the general public, a 2002 British Broadcasting Corporation (BBC) poll found that the British public rated teaching as the third most highly respected profession in Britain. Regarding teachers' relationships with students, a 2005 *Time* magazine poll found that 81 percent of American teens declared they "got along well" with their teachers!

Always begin your relationship-building efforts with your students. They're the ones you interact with more than any other individual or group. Address them formally but pleasantly to maintain cordial yet professional relationships. Also, limit physical contact only to that which is necessary and appropriate to head off any misunderstandings. Conduct any student-teacher conferences with courtesy, and without raised voices or snide remarks. And try to model good manners and considerate behavior for your students at all times—even when you're boiling mad, and even when you're dealing out discipline. Show your students you want to have good relationships with them by praising them constantly, inquiring after their friends and families, and remembering birthdays and important details in their lives.

And as far as all other groups are concerned—parents, administrators, teachers' associations, etc.—just use the common sense you've acquired over a lifetime in learning how to deal with people. Consider how you want to be treated, then treat others that way. Do you want a child to scream at you? Then don't scream at a child (unless your gut instinct tells you there's no choice—if the kid is about to play in traffic, for example). Do you want parents personally insulting you? Then don't personally insult parents; find ways to communicate with them. Building relationships is about earning trust, helping others, and manifesting courtesy, kindness, dependability, and honesty. In subsequent chapters, you'll learn how building relationships actually means building a solid foundation for a good career and a fulfilling life.

Job Protection

Your students really need you. They need your training, education, experience, compassion, and dedication in order to become well-educated citizens. And yet, if you, as a classroom teacher, continually make thoughtless, unnecessary mistakes, then your students will lose out because you'll lose your teaching position. Remember what the great American educator Henry Brooks Adams once said: "A teacher affects eternity; he can never tell where his influence stops." You'll never be able to affect eternity if you're cashing unemployment checks, so protect your teaching job by maintaining the highest professional standards and by delivering the highest-quality instruction possible.

Teachers' average annual salaries vary from state to state. For example, Alabama's average is $40,347, while the District of Columbia's average is $61,195—a $20,848 difference. If you think your state might be dragging its feet in terms of teachers' salaries, and if you want more pay equity nationwide, think seriously about supporting the legislative efforts of your local teachers' association.

Job-protection also involves supporting your local teachers' association because sometimes, misunderstandings arise and administrators think you've blundered when you're convinced you really haven't. Teachers' associations have been straightening out misunderstandings and protecting the rights of public school teachers since the founding of the National Education Association (NEA) in 1857 and the American Federation of Teachers

(AFT) in 1916. Both of these national labor organizations have local chapters in virtually every school district in America, and can often help you protect your job when you and your principal can't see eye to eye.

Don't think of job protection merely as paycheck protection, to the exclusion of every other consideration. Sure, you want to protect your livelihood, but if you're certain you've seriously messed up, you'll often have no choice but to wave good-bye to your students.

On the other hand, if you can improve or if no insurmountable problems exist or if your principal has simply made an error in judgment, then stand up and hold on to your job so that you can continue to affect eternity. In subsequent chapters, you'll learn how standing up for your rights means standing up for the rights of all teachers as well as students and administrators.

CHAPTER 2

Get Organized

You've seen that your personal classroom-management toolkit contains five critical domains: Academic instruction, time management, discipline, relationship building, and job protection. You've gotten an overview of each domain, gaining familiarity with each one. Now, you need to master each domain if you're to become the best teacher and classroom manager you can be. Begin by learning the time-management secrets that veteran teachers use so you can make the most of every instructional day.

Create a Daily Schedule

You'll need to create a daily schedule, a written plan where you arrange blocks of time to squeeze in the myriad tasks you and your students must accomplish each day. You'll actually need two schedules: (1) one for your own use, to arrange personal adjuvant instructional time for such tasks as lesson planning, meeting with parents, grading papers, etc.; and (2) a second schedule for your actual instructional time, showing the times when you teach certain subjects, break times, etc. This schedule should be shared with students and parents.

FACT

Many interesting types of schedules exist. For example, a *timetable* shows preplanned activities and the designated times for those activities. A *rota* is a linked set of timetables. And a *tickler file*, invented by businessman David Allen, holds twelve monthly folders and thirty-one daily folders, all containing tasks to be completed timely.

Create your adjuvant instructional schedule first, and keep it in your lesson-plan book, on your classroom desk. As you create your schedule, don't forget to write a starting time that's one-half hour earlier than the start of the instructional day. Most schools do have such an "early arrival" provision as one of your specific job duties.

For example, assuming an instructional starting time of 8:00 A.M.—typical for many schools—begin your schedule at 7:30 A.M. Also, assuming a typical ending time of 3:00 P.M., schedule an additional half-hour for yourself after the kids leave. True, none of this extra work time is compensated, and that may seem unfair; but working somewhat late is normal for any professional job such as teaching, and you'll bless yourself for scheduling extra time each morning and each afternoon to clean up, plan, and prepare. Take a look at Table 2-1 on the following page for an example of what your adjuvant instructional schedule might look like.

TABLE 2-1 DAILY ADJUVANT INSTRUCTIONAL SCHEDULE

TIME BLOCK	ACTIVITIES
1. 7:30 A.M.–7:45 A.M.	**Yard-Duty Supervision Activities**
	a. Perform any scheduled morning yard duty.
	b. Otherwise, go immediately to item number 2 below.
2. 7:30 A.M.–7:35 A.M.	**Classroom Preparation Activities**
	a. Write any necessary information on whiteboards.
	b. Write homework assignments on whiteboards.
	c. Straighten students' desks, learning-center desks.
	d. Stock tissues, paper towels, students' supplies.
	e. Put out any necessary textbooks, pencils, etc.
	f. Complete any incidental cleaning.
3. 7:35 A.M.–7:40 A.M.	**Materials and Equipment Preparation Activities**
	a. Collect mail, bulletins, information from mailbox.
	b. Copy work papers, information papers, etc.
	c. Laminate charts, posters, work displays, etc.
	d. Cut paper for academic lessons, art, etc.
	e. Set up any necessary audio-visual equipment, etc.
4. 7:40 A.M.–7:45 A.M.	**Teacher/Parent/Student Communication Activities**
	a. Answer student/parent notes, voicemails, e-mails.
	b. File, update papers in students' dossiers.
	c. Answer notes, e-mails from administrators.
	d. Answer notes, e-mails from teachers, other staff.
	e. Complete any school or district paperwork.
5. 7:45 A.M.–8:00 A.M.	**Morning Lesson-Planning Activities**
	a. Thoroughly review lesson plans for the day.
	b. Make any necessary changes to the day's plans.
	c. Review lesson plans for upcoming days, weeks.
	d. Make any necessary changes to upcoming plans.
	e. Ask for any necessary lesson input from colleagues.

TIME BLOCK	ACTIVITIES
6. 8:00 A.M.–3:00 P.M.	**Instructional Time: See Daily Instructional Schedule.**
7. 3:00 P.M.–3:15 P.M.	**Yard Duty Activities**
	a. Perform any scheduled morning yard duty.
	b. Otherwise, go immediately to item number 8 below.
8. 3:00 P.M.–3:05 P.M.	**Hall or Area Monitoring Activities**
	a. Help students leave school in an orderly manner.
	b. Resolve student disputes, issue necessary citations.
	c. Erase old information from whiteboards.
	d. Collect and store textbooks, supplies, equipment.
	e. Pick up classroom trash, do incidental cleaning.
9. 3:05 P.M.–3:10 P.M.	**Teacher/Parent/Student Communication Activities**
	a. Answer student/parent notes, voicemails, e-mails.
	b. File, update papers in students' dossiers.
	c. Answer notes, e-mails from administrators.
	d. Answer notes, e-mails from teachers, other staff.
	e. Begin or finish any school or district paperwork.
10. 3:10 P.M.–3:30 P.M.	**Afternoon Lesson-Planning Activities**
	a. Plan and briefly pencil in abbreviated objectives, standards, anticipatory set, teaching strategies, guided practice (pages and exercise numbers), closure strategies, and independent practice (homework) for each lesson for the following day in plan book.

Remember, change anything in Table 2-1 that doesn't meet your specific needs, times, or procedures—it's all exemplary, not mandatory. After you've created your adjuvant instructional schedule, it's time to write your daily instructional schedule—the times and activities that you and your students will adhere to during the instructional day.

Your daily instructional schedule will probably vary from those of your teacher-colleagues who work in other districts, owing to widely differing starting times, lunch periods, recess periods, ending times, and grade levels taught. Also, different states may have different requirements as to the number of instructional minutes teachers must devote to particular academic subjects. Keep all this in mind as you devise a schedule that's right for you. Then, keep your schedule in your lesson-plan book, along with your adjuvant schedule. Look at Table 2-2 for an example of what your daily instructional schedule might look like.

TABLE 2-2 DAILY INSTRUCTIONAL SCHEDULE

TIME BLOCK	ACTIVITIES
7:55 A.M.–8:00 A.M.	**Morning Greeting Activities**
8:00 A.M.–8:05 A.M.	Morning Housekeeping Activities
8:05 A.M.–9:30 A.M.	Mathematics: Directed Instruction
9:30 A.M.–9:55 A.M.	Mathematics: Guided Practice Activities
9:55 A.M.–10:00 A.M.	Mathematics: Class Work Correction, Collection
10:00 A.M.–10:30 A.M.	Language Arts/Reading: Directed Instruction
10:30 A.M.–10:55 A.M.	Language Arts/Reading: Guided Practice Activities
10:55 A.M.–11:00 A.M.	Language Arts/Reading: Class Work Correction, Collection
11:00 A.M.–11:30 A.M.	English/Language Arts: Directed Instruction
11:30 A.M.–11:55 A.M.	English/Language Arts: Guided Practice Activities
11:55 A.M.–12:00 P.M.	English/Language Arts: Class Work Correction, Collection
12:00 P.M.–12:30 P.M.	**Lunch, Recess**
12:30 P.M.–1:00 P.M.	Science: Directed Instruction
1:00 P.M.–1:25 P.M.	Science: Guided Practice Activities
1:25 P.M.–1:30 P.M.	Science: Class Work Correction, Collection
1:30 P.M.–2:00 P.M.	Social Studies: Directed Instruction
2:00 P.M.–2:25 P.M.	Social Studies: Guided Practice Activities
2:25 P.M.–2:30 P.M.	Social Studies: Class Work Correction, Collection
2:30 P.M.–2:45 P.M.	Art/Music/P.E.: Directed Instruction
2:45 P.M.–2:55 P.M.	Art/Music/P.E.: Guided Practice Activities
2:55 P.M.–3:00 P.M.	Art/Music/P.E.: Class Work Correction, Collection
3:00 P.M.	**Dismissal**
3:00 P.M.–3:05 P.M.	Hall or Area Monitoring Activities

After you've created your daily instructional schedule, make two copies for every student—one for the student and another for her parents—and distribute them no later than the first day of instruction. Also, don't forget to make an oversized chart of your instructional schedule, then laminate and post it in a prominent place in the classroom. That way, students, administrators, teaching colleagues, and visitors (parents, school-board members, the superintendent) will be able to see at a glance what you're doing and when you're doing it.

Get an Organizer or Palm Pilot

Your daily schedules are invaluable organizing tools, but you'll need more if you want to excel as a teacher and get anything accomplished. Remember, you've got friends and family, too, and you'll have to organize those areas of your life as well if you expect to be happy and productive. Therefore, you'll need to add one of these two important tools to your classroom-management toolkit: (1) a paper-based personal organizer; or (2) an electronic personal organizer, also called a personal digital assistant (PDA).

ALERT!

Keep in mind the number of instructional minutes your state legislature may have mandated for core subjects. For instance, in California, 200 minutes must be devoted every ten school days for physical education in grades one through eight. Ask your administrator or access your state's website for more information. Use the keywords "instructional minutes" to conduct searches.

A paper-based personal organizer is any kind of bound ledger or loose-leaf notebook, with pages containing consecutive calendar dates and blank lines for use in organizing the tasks you need to accomplish daily, weekly, monthly, or yearly. These organizers can be purchased at office-supply stores and may feature at-a-glance calendars, pages for telephone numbers, lists of zip codes, and more.

However, the most important part of the organizer consists of pages where you write your essential to-do items. These pages are organized in pairs and represent several calendar days. The top of each page displays the current month and year, followed by day sections underneath, which are further divided into line-by-line hours, A.M. to P.M. Each page actually consists primarily of blank lines, where you pencil in what you must get done. Little monthly calendars representing the entire year generally appear at the bottom of both pages. Don't try to work as a teacher without using a personal organizer.

But if you're the kind of person who isn't afraid to embrace new technologies, consider getting a personal digital assistant (PDA), sometimes called a palm pilot. A PDA is a tiny computer with a compact view screen and data-entry mechanism, all of which fits in the palm of your hand. The PDA can accomplish many wonderful chores, including keeping a record of your daily tasks and schedules; surfing the Internet; handling your e-mail traffic; word processing; doubling as a cell phone; and other magical functions. Some PDAs use a tiny keyboard and stylus for data entry, while others use simple touch screens and a touchpad.

Using manufacturer-supplied software, you can also connect your PDA to a computer and rapidly access information, keeping your PDA's data current.

One of the latest PDAs is the versatile BlackBerry, produced by Canadian PDA manufacturer Research in Motion (RIM). The BlackBerry can access the Internet through wireless networks and can surf the web and retrieve your e-mail. With over 8 million current subscribers, the BlackBerry is proving increasingly popular.

If you think you're ready to take the leap into the twenty-first century and buy a PDA, a few of the more popular models are the BlackBerry, by Research in Motion (RIM); the iPAQ, by Hewlett-Packard; the N Series, by Acer; the Sidekick, by T-Mobile; and the Wizard, by Sharp. You may never go back to paper-based personal organizers again.

Grade Papers the Smart Way

In 2002, the United States Supreme Court ruled unanimously in the case of *Owasso Independent School District v. Falvo* that students may grade other students' papers, and may even announce scores to the class. Such "trading-and-grading" does not violate the provisions of the Family Educational Rights and Privacy Act (FERPA), passed by the United States Congress in 1974 to protect the confidentiality of students' records. So the smart thing for a teacher to do is let students grade each others' papers as often as possible!

Are you leery of this advice? Then try the alternative. Take home every paper that your students complete and see if you can grade them all as you sit bleary eyed in front of the TV, beginning with the 6:00 P.M. news and ending with Jay Leno. Most mere mortals can't do it. Little things like eating, sleeping, and participating in the lives of your loved ones keep getting in the way of grading all those wonderful papers.

Give yourself permission to let your students help grade each other's papers. With a little guidance from you, they can generally do a marvelous job, time after time. True, they won't always be perfect, but then neither will you, because perfection isn't of this world. All you have to do is skim and rapidly double check what your students have already graded, and all those papers will have been graded twice! Of course, the only times you don't want your students grading papers is when it comes to essays, reports, complex projects, and other work that requires your subjective evaluation. But for work-a-day tests, exercise sheets, and the like, if the U.S. Supreme Court says trading-and-grading is okay, then it's okay.

Finally, remember that when students trade-and-grade, they get something valuable in return: instant feedback. Instead of waiting days or weeks for you to struggle to finish grading their work, they can see how they've done within minutes. This kind of instant feedback is treasured by high-performing students and helps low-performing students see immediately where they need to improve.

Trade-and-Grade Basics

Once you've made the decision to let students trade-and-grade, follow some commonsense procedures for best results. First, require students to bring red or other colored pens from home, storing such pens in their book bags or desks. Or, if you prefer, pass out red pens or pencils to your kids every time you need them to grade. Don't forget to collect all these grading materials afterward.

Next, require your students to trade with their nearest seat mates. Do not let students get up and trade with their best buddies. You'll get to know your students quite well, and if there's any question in your mind as to whether two kids have sought each other out because they'll grade each other's work too "creatively," have those students immediately retrade with other students.

Circulate about the classroom with an answer key or your teacher's-edition textbook for the exercises your students have completed. Then, you can read the answers in one of two ways: (1) as a straight run-through, saying, "Number one, A. Number two, D," and so forth if you're pressed for time; or (2) in a more measured manner, where you ask questions and use the time as an opportunity to reteach your earlier lesson. The first approach has the virtue of being a great time saver. However, it may also leave some kids wondering, "Huh? Why'd I get *that* one wrong?" without receiving an explanation. Over time, such feelings can lead to frustration and impaired academic performance, as students struggle to figure out what went wrong and why they got certain problems incorrect.

Interestingly, the U.S. Supreme Court declined to rule on the question of whether students' graded papers are protected under FERPA after a teacher has collected the papers and recorded them in a grade book. To be on the safe side, once you've collected and recorded papers, keep them strictly confidential thereafter.

You may wish to try the second approach, where you select students to reread the questions, and select other students to read the correct answers.

During these exchanges, you are constantly reiterating concepts, answering questions, and reteaching. Time may not always permit such an exercise, but you might be surprised to find that once your students learn your routines, a lot can be accomplished in five minutes or less. This approach can prove extremely valuable to kids, especially the underperformers who no longer have to scratch their heads in bewilderment, but will understand why they missed certain problems. Try using this approach to grading if you feel it's right for you.

There are many ways for students to mark problems, but try this: Have your students mark each correct problem with a small letter "c" next to each correct problem and a small "x" next to each incorrect problem. You'll find that this is the easiest set of marks to see and comprehend. However, if some other set of marks seems better suited to your needs, use those. You might, for instance, have kids only mark incorrect problems, or use checkmarks for incorrect problems. Always use an individualized system that's best for you.

E-QUESTION

Does it matter if I use red pens for grading? Or must I use some other color?
Use the color you prefer. Professors at Princeton University in New Jersey have determined that red, the traditional "teacher" color, increases respiration and heart rates—maybe not the best thing for your kids. Green, on the other hand, conjures images of calming, soothing, natural greenery.

Actually, you'll quickly discover that kids have no problem marking incorrect problems with a nice, juicy red "x." You'll generally find that kids are honest graders. After the trade-and-grade session is finished and you've answered any remaining questions, tell the kids to draw a small circle near the top of the paper. Then, they should write a grade fraction within the circle, with the denominator or bottom number representing the total number of problems possible and the numerator or top number representing the number of problems marked correct. For example, on a paper with twenty problems, if a student got nineteen correct the grader writes 19/20 in the circle. Remind students to mark neatly and never write extraneous comments or draw pictures on someone else's paper. Assign a monitor to collect all papers and promise your students you'll double check, record, and file the papers as soon as possible. Keep your promise, and finish by the end of the workday, if possible.

Congratulations! You're now grading papers the smart way and getting ten times more work done.

Basic Forms No Teacher Should Be Without

Preprinted forms constitute a powerful tool in your classroom-management toolkit. The fast pace of most classrooms makes writing every message by hand impractical. In fact, certain disciplining situations—for example, two students fighting—require such a quick response that sitting down to write a note or letter in the middle of the crisis can often prove virtually impossible. Forms save valuable time, which allows you to swiftly help students in need or restore order to an unruly classroom or transmit vital information to parents or administrators.

Agendas

One of the most basic forms that many schools and school districts have adopted is the agenda, also known as a student planner. Agendas are plan books that are ordered by schools or districts, printed with particulars such as a school's name, behavioral rules, dress codes, and bell schedules as well as useful information such as mathematics charts, scientific tables, etc. An agenda is almost identical to your teacher's lesson-plan book, except that students use their agendas for recording assignments, and you use the agenda for communicating with parents on a regular basis. If your school doesn't use agendas, you'll need to think seriously about creating your own classroom agendas for your students. Here's what the agenda looks like:

- Pages are presented in pairs, with the name of the current month and year printed across the top.
- As with your plan book, the agenda displays a week's worth of specific dates down the left side, with the first row beginning at Monday and the last row ending at Friday.

- Core academic subjects appear in columns across the top, from left to right.
- The columns and rows intersect in large white squares, where students can write homework assignments and any other planning notations. But even more importantly, you can write messages to parents in these squares, or in white space at the bottom of each page.

Yes, you might use assorted scraps of paper to write messages to parents, but it's unprofessional. With agendas, you have a neat, written record of parental communications—proof, should you need it later, that parents have received notification of problems.

Of course, no form is foolproof, and there's no guarantee a student might not rip your messages out of his agenda. That's why you need to be sure to always make a copy of any message you place in a student's agenda.

If your school assigns certain penalties for a certain number of violations, note the ordinal number of the violation. For example, if school rules mandate an agenda warning for a student's first tardy of the quarter or semester, you might write, "1st T. Bruce Wayne was tardy to 2nd Per. Please speak to him. Thanks." Don't forget to sign your entry—some parents get offended if you've forgotten your signature.

After you've returned the student's agenda, immediately take a few seconds to file the copy in the student's dossier or classroom file, which you keep along with all your students' dossiers in a lockable two-drawer file cabinet beside your desk. These are reference folders to use if students try to scratch out or rip out agenda notations or if parents try to claim that you never notified them of problems. Get in the habit of instantly filing agenda notes in dossiers; otherwise, they'll get misplaced or lost and you may have no proof that you ever notified the student or his parents of anything. Use agendas and agenda notes consistently.

Hall Pass

Another essential form to keep on hand is your school's hall pass. Hall passes generally come in tear-off packs and are used when students want to leave the classroom for bathroom breaks, etc. Remember, keeping watch over your students is a sacred responsibility, so never let kids leave your classroom without a signed hall pass. Fill in all the information requested on the hall pass, and if there are no lines to notate the student's departure and return times, write the information there anyway. Remind each student to return in a timely manner and to hand the hall pass back to you immediately upon returning. Then, instantly file every hall pass in the students' dossiers.

Hall passes can constitute an important record, because if graffiti or vandalism is discovered in a restroom, the hall pass might help establish who was in a restroom at a particular time. Hall passes can also be shown to a student's parents during a parent conference as evidence of a large number of out-of-class trips. Keep a good stock of hall passes and replenish them early and often.

Memorandum Forms

Also keep a good supply of memorandum forms on hand. You make these yourself, to send messages to teaching colleagues, administrators, and other staff. Here are the simple steps in creating memorandum forms on your computer:

1. Use a word-processing program such as Microsoft Word.
2. Use the rulers along the top and side of your document to create four equally sized memorandum forms on one sheet of paper, all containing the same information. In other words, you'll divide the sheet into equal fourths.
3. For each form, center and type the title "Memorandum."
4. Next, align left and type "From:" followed by your name and classroom number.
5. Then type "To:" followed by a blank line.
6. Type "Date:" followed by a blank line.
7. Finally, type "Subject:" followed by a blank line.
8. Print the form and make 200 copies, sufficient to last the school year.
9. Cut the forms into equal fourths and staple them so that each form has two sheets.

Keep these memorandum forms on your desk with your other essential forms. Always be sure to make a copy of completed forms for your files.

Detention Slips

Unfortunately, you'll also need to keep a good supply of detention slips on your desk, if your school uses such forms as part of an in-school detention process. Detention is a discipline tool for students who chronically misbehave. The student is assigned a certain number of minutes that she must serve after school, usually in your classroom, although procedures vary. Detention forms are a necessary evil because some misbehaving students simply don't respond to warnings, counseling, agenda notes, or phone calls. Fill out a detention slip for a student whenever warranted. Mark the date of the detention at least one day subsequent to the day you fill it out and staple the student's copy in her agenda so that parents have time to read it and make any necessary arrangements. Then, as always, file your copy in the student's dossier.

Suspension Forms

Finally, you'll have to keep suspension forms on your desk for the most serious disciplinary problems. Suspension forms should be used only in two cases: (1) when all other disciplinary steps have produced virtually no improvement in a student's chronically disruptive behavior; or (2) when a student suddenly engages in an egregiously defiant or disruptive incident of misbehavior, such as fighting in class or cursing at you. Quickly fill out the suspension form, give the office copy to a trusted student, and have that student escort the offender to the front office.

ALERT!

If there's any question whatsoever of a safety issue for a student you've told to escort a suspended student to the office, excuse the escort and instead telephone the front office so an administrator can pick up the student along with the suspension form.

Keep all of these basic forms handy and in good supply and you'll seldom have to worry about your class grinding to a halt while you try to resolve the pesky classroom-management problems that inevitably arise in any classroom.

Hygiene and Health

Considering the runny noses, grubby hands, sneezing, and coughing that you're exposed to each day, you'll need to zealously safeguard your health if you expect to be present for your students on a regular basis. Just follow the simple, commonsense rules that your parents taught you:

- Eat sensible portions of a nutritious, well-balanced diet.
- Consider taking appropriate daily multivitamin supplements.
- Keep yourself clean, including bathing and shampooing daily, using personal hygiene products, and brushing, flossing, and using dental rinse after every meal.
- Consistently follow your doctor's instructions, including taking prescribed medications, and make sure to schedule regular physical examinations.
- Exercise regularly and sensibly, after first consulting your doctor.
- Get your recommended eight hours of sleep every night.

There's an old saying: "If you miss school, you miss out." Don't rob your kids of your excellent instruction. Take care of your precious health; your classroom truly won't be the same without you.

Go to Sleep!

The December 23, 2007 issue of *Parade* reported that up to 70 million Americans are sleep deprived, negatively impacting their health and perhaps decreasing their life spans. Also, the January 31, 2008 edition of the *Health-Day Reporter* revealed that sleep deprivation is one of the worst health-care crises in America, even contributing to an increased incidence of Type 2 diabetes among many American workers. The simple message is: If you expect to serve your students, you'd better get some sleep. Follow as many of these simple steps as you're comfortable with to help ensure you get sufficient rest:

- Maintain a climate-controlled, pleasingly dark, quiet, comfortable bedroom.
- Cut back on the alcohol. Excessive alcohol can easily disrupt sleep patterns.
- Decrease caffeine, which can stay in your body for nearly twenty-four hours.
- Enjoy some quiet, soothing music before bedtime.
- Meditate quietly, and empty your mind of worrisome problems before bedtime.

Get a good night's sleep and you'll be ready to tackle each instructional day refreshed, recharged, revitalized, and ready for the exciting daily challenges of being a classroom teacher.

CHAPTER 3

Preplanning

Before your students arrive for the first day of instruction, you need to do some preplanning. Preplanning means getting your classroom ready to receive students. You've got to meet teaching colleagues, pick up sets of textbooks, set up your computer grading program, schedule library time if possible, organize your classroom, prepare lessons, and do the thousand and one other things that teachers do to get ready. In this chapter, you'll learn how to prepare quickly and efficiently so when your students walk through your door they'll think you've been teaching for years—even if it happens to be your first day.

Become Familiar with Your School Facility

Familiarize yourself with your school before the kids arrive by doing a walk-about. Walkabout is an Australian aboriginal term, meaning a long trek over unfamiliar terrain, done to honor one's ancestors. Your journey is a similar endeavor, done to prepare yourself for your students and honor the professionalism and dedication of all the teachers who have gone before you. Budget a bit of time for this task, as it might take upward of half an hour or more.

You've got many excellent reasons for conducting a walkabout, but perhaps the best one is safety. If your school schedules a fire drill during the first month of school, will you know where your line-up area is, as well as the quickest way to get your kids there? Or, if there's a school lockdown and you're required to retrieve your kids early from lunch, do you know where the cafeteria is? If you're followed by a stranger on campus after hours, do you know the quickest way to the front office? Safety's a big consideration when it comes to learning the ins and outs of your school. Also, you simply need to know where to go each day in order to do your job.

FACT

Some public school sites have amenities that might surprise you. For example, the Yadavindra Public School in Punjab State, India, boasts horse stables, tennis courts, badminton courts, and cricket fields. Closer to home, Beverly Hills High School in Beverly Hills, California, has its own functioning oil well, which provides some $300,000 in annual oil revenues to the school.

Take at least one day, if not more, before the kids come streaming through the front gates to learn where everything is. You may be pleasantly surprised to discover a well-tended student garden or a large volleyball area complete with nets or a second copy room with numerous additional copy machines. But you'll never know unless you start walking. And don't forget to ask your teaching colleagues and principal any questions you might have about your school site.

Organize Your Classroom for Maximum Efficiency

There's an important preplanning tool that you'll want to retrieve from your classroom-management toolkit—the skill of effectively organizing your beautiful little realm, otherwise known as your classroom. After all, you're the one who'll be teaching, grading papers, and lesson planning in your classroom for six to eight hours a day (or more), so organize your room so that it's comfortable for you, as well as for your students.

Furniture

To create a classroom where you can enjoy teaching and students can enjoy learning, start with your desk. Some teachers like to put it right up front so they can directly monitor every student face to face. The advantage of this arrangement is that all eyes must ostensibly be on you, and if they're not, you'll notice instantly. Many teachers insist that this desk arrangement is the best because it increases student attention and decreases student talking and horseplaying. However, many other teachers put their desk in the rear or on the side based on the theory that if you discreetly monitor students while they're working, they never know whether you're watching or not. Thus, they'll think to themselves, "I'd better behave." Consider the question of desk position carefully and decide what's best for you.

Be cautious about trying to move heavy furniture, like a classroom desk, by yourself. Such exertions can cause a painful lower-back injury if you don't have the training, strength, experience, or equipment to move heavy items properly. By all means, let the custodian or other trained personnel do it.

Also, you'll need to order a couple of two-drawer file cabinets from the office or purchase them yourself. You'll use one file cabinet to keep student dossiers, those information folders that you maintain for every student. You'll use the other file cabinet for miscellaneous forms and papers.

As for your desktop, keep several large trays to hold your students' collected work until it can be graded, recorded, and filed—and don't let the work pile up. Grade it promptly or you'll find it rising high enough to topple over and bury you.

Also keep several trays on your desktop that are well stocked with frequently requested student supplies, such as paper, black or blue pens, sharpened pencils, erasers, rulers, tape, safety pins, paper clips, etc. Close to your desk, keep one classroom computer for record keeping such as attendance taking, recording grades, planning lessons, e-mailing, Internet research, etc.

Make sure to set aside an area somewhere in the classroom for student portfolios—a set of file folders, one for each student, arranged alphabetically by students' last names, to hold graded and recorded work. Students, parents, and administrators can use these portfolios to view students' work. In fact, some schools require teachers to maintain portfolios as official documents, which are then sent to the next grade level. Your students will also enjoy looking through their own portfolios, when time permits.

You can access numerous websites that will provide you with tables and charts for grading, such as Forms and Testing, Mrs. Perkins, First Grade, www.mrsperkins.com/testing.htm.

If possible, not far from your desk you should find a wheeled, lockable, upright cupboard. If you don't see this invaluable piece of furniture, courteously request it from your principal. Keep it stocked with district-supplied materials such as construction paper, oak tag, crayons, colored pencils, scissors, tape, staples, paper clips, etc.

Learning Centers

Your classroom should also have a few engaging learning centers, consisting of a table and some chairs where students can engage in self-directed educational enrichment, using the supplemental books, audio-visual equipment, or other materials you've provided. One of the most popular learning centers is a Reading Center, also called a Classroom Library. Roll out a nice rug, throw down some sofa pillows and beanbag chairs, move in a bookcase crammed with grade-appropriate books, and your Reading Center will become an instant hit. Here are a few more ideas for great learning centers:

- **A Listening Center** with a CD player and several grade-appropriate story CDs
- **A Writing Center** with paper, dictionaries, thesauri, and laminated pictures to jog creativity
- **A Research Center** with paper, encyclopedias, almanacs, and other reference books
- **An Art Center** with construction paper, crayons, glue, and other art supplies
- **A Computer Center,** where students can access FunBrain and other appropriate websites

Another great instructional space is a large Classroom Meeting Area, where you and your students can sit on the carpet or gather in chairs and resolve problems or discuss topics of interest when necessary. Say that a frightening event occurs at your school, such as an incident involving violence—use your meeting area to discuss the situation and help calm your students. If the class is having trouble resolving a moral issue, use your meeting area to discuss it. You may not have a lot of space or time, but if you have a bit of both, use your meeting area to help students resolve problems in a responsible manner.

Bulletin Boards

Your classroom bulletin boards are important, too, because they serve three purposes: (1) they provide lively and appropriate decoration for your room; (2) they provide timely information your students need; and (3) they provide a showcase for your students' magnificent schoolwork. Limit the decoration to posters and charts that inform and motivate. Limit the information to up-to-date postings, including large charts displaying your classroom rules, and all applicable state standards for your grade level. Finally, keep the schoolwork current, changing the kids' papers at least once a month.

A particular type of bulletin board called a Word Wall is a wonderful classroom display that helps kids get excited about learning words. There are different types of Word Walls, but a popular one employs sentence strips for posting useful vocabulary words. During writing assignments, when a student asks how to spell a word, write the word on a sentence strip, then have the student look up the word in a dictionary and write the definition neatly on the sentence strip. Post enough of these strips on the Word Wall and you'll have an impressive student-created writing resource. The students can use the Word Wall as they write, and visitors will admire the amount of work required to create such a beautiful and practical display.

E-QUESTION

Will I need to spend hundreds of dollars stocking my own supplies? Try ordering supplies from the front office first. Most schools have a form or an e-mail procedure for getting supplies. With luck, you should be able to obtain what you and your students need, as long as you don't request too much too quickly.

Finally, here is a checklist of details to make your classroom nearly perfect:

❏ Make copies of your college degrees, your state teaching credential, and any academic awards you've earned—whiting-out details you don't want the kids to know—and display these materials near your desk. The kids will enjoy seeing the evidence of your accomplishments and may be inspired to accomplish something themselves.

❏ Use curtains to partially cover any of your classroom windows that face a hallway. Position the curtains so they're about halfway up, so that administrators can see into your classroom as they walk by.

❏ Place as many labels and signs around the classroom as necessary. Label everything for younger kids, including signs that say "Pencil Sharpener," "Sink," "Cubbies," "Coat Hooks," and so on. For older kids, learning-center signs are usually sufficient.

❏ Make sure the American flag is placed near the front of the room for the daily flag salute. Keep a poster with the text of the Pledge of Allegiance near the flag.

❏ Consider the soothing power of houseplants placed around the classroom. They purify the air and add natural beauty to the room environment.

Organize your room before your students arrive and your classroom management will be far more effective than if you wait until the last possible second. As special-education teachers John Beattie and LuAnn Jordan note in their book *Making Inclusion Work: Effective Practices for All Teachers*: "Efficient classroom organization reflects a mature, 'together' teacher, and these qualities are highly attractive, no matter how long (or how little) you have been teaching." Be wise, and organize.

Make Sure Your Classroom Equipment Works

You'll also want to make sure your computers and audio-visual equipment are in good working order before your students arrive for the first day of instruction. You won't gain anything by procrastinating, except possibly the humiliation of loading an important video into a totally nonfunctioning VCR or trying to display a transparency on a burned-out overhead projector. What follows is a discussion regarding some of the most important pieces of instructional equipment in your room and how each device functions. This information will help you ensure that everything's in working order before your little saints come marching in.

The Multimedia Cart

If you can arrange it, ask your principal to provide you with a multimedia cart—a wheeled, portable trolley, about four feet high, well stocked with modern audio-visual equipment. Perhaps not every school will have multimedia carts for every teacher, but talk to your teaching colleagues so that you can at least share whatever multimedia carts are available. Or, work with the computer-lab teacher to assemble at least one multimedia cart for your own use.

The top tier of your multimedia cart should feature a color television, properly fastened by the custodian or the computer-lab technician. You'll find your TV invaluable for playing educational videocassettes on the VCR, which sits on the cart's second tier, hooked up and ready to use. Get the computer-lab technician to help you with proper wiring or read the VCR's user manual. If your school provides a DVD player, that's even better, because the picture quality, sound quality, and ease of use are far superior to VCRs.

The bottom tier of your multimedia cart contains a standard desktop computer. Use your computer in conjunction with a focus box, a piece of technology that lets your computer display documents and animated presentations directly to your TV. If you're looking for a "magic lantern" that can get kids to sit up and pay attention, the computer/focus-box combination is your answer.

You'll also need a second wheeled cart, if you can get it, to hold your overhead projector—called overhead for short. An overhead is an optical device for showing enlarged images on a white screen. The overhead consists of a light source housed in a metal box with a fresnel lens placed over the light source. A vertical rod extends above the lens, holding an adjustable mirror arrangement that magnifies and projects images. You write or print out text or images onto a transparency, a piece of clear plastic, then place the transparency on the lens, and suddenly you've got something that can really capture kids' attention.

But check your overhead before you use it, or your brilliant visual presentation can turn out to be a resounding dud. Flip the power switch and make sure the interior halogen lamp or arc lamp isn't burned out. If it is, contact your librarian or the custodian to get the bulb replaced or to get a new overhead projector. Also, properly position your white screen and overhead projector ahead of time so that you won't have to spend class time doing it. Finally, experiment with the adjustable mirror lens so you can focus transparencies quickly, because while focusing isn't super difficult, it does require a bit of practice.

Other Supplies

If you intend to augment any of your lessons with music, you've got to have a portable stereo somewhere in the room. They generally come with two speakers, a radio, a tape player, and a CD player. Some newer ones feature a plug-in support for MP3 players such as the iPod.

Finally, here's a list of other miscellaneous equipment that you might want to round up:

- An electric pencil sharpener
- An electric stapler
- A plier stapler to staple packets of up to twenty pages
- A stopwatch for timing oral presentations, etc.
- An electric fan in case your air-conditioning system breaks down
- A desk clock in case it's not convenient for you to keep checking the wall clock
- A cell phone in case you need to make calls during an emergency
- A small digital voice recorder, or small notebook for making notes to yourself regarding errands, ideas, etc.

Remember, when it comes to preplanning, the effort and time you spend gathering, checking, and familiarizing yourself with your classroom equipment will pay off in improved student attention spans and better schoolwork from your excited, motivated learners.

Stock Adequate Supplies

You'd better stock adequate classroom supplies for your kids before the first instructional day. You'll have to re-stock periodically throughout the school year, of course, but give yourself some breathing room initially by gathering plenty of materials beforehand.

However, note that supplies can be notoriously hard to procure at some schools. You might gasp in disbelief at the appearance of your supply room, which may have a steel door that looks more like a bank vault than the entrance to a room full of pencils and paper. But that's how some schools treat their supply rooms—as vaults full of costly treasures.

The trick is to be reasonable and persistent, courteously; reasonable in the quantities you order and persistent in not giving up until you get some significant part of your order filled. After all, you are the professional responsible for educating our future leaders; those supplies belong to you so you can teach and to your kids so they can learn. You're just asking for the supplies you need to do your job.

Here's a checklist of some basic supplies you'll want to retrieve from the supply room or put on order or even purchase yourself if you simply can't get them any other way:

For yourself:
- ❏ A tape dispenser and two rolls of tape, plus four rolls of duct tape for various emergencies
- ❏ A stapler and four boxes of staples, plus four staple removers
- ❏ Four pairs of adult scissors and a dozen glue sticks for creating bulletin-board displays, etc.
- ❏ Four dozen blue or black pens for writing and four dozen red or green pens for correcting
- ❏ Four dozen pencils, four plastic rulers, and four metal straight edges
- ❏ Four boxes of jumbo and four boxes of small paper clips, plus four boxes of paper clamps
- ❏ A three-hole punch
- ❏ Twelve notepads and a dozen sticky-note pads
- ❏ Twelve spiral notebooks for writing ideas for lesson plans, etc.
- ❏ Twelve black whiteboard markers and four whiteboard erasers
- ❏ 100 manila folders
- ❏ 100 hanging folders
- ❏ 100 transparencies

For your students:
- ❏ Four dozen pencils—all of which you'll sharpen before the kids arrive
- ❏ A class set (thirty-two) of kid scissors
- ❏ A class set of rulers
- ❏ Four reams of writing paper, appropriately ruled for your grade level
- ❏ Four packs of 9" × 12" and 18" × 24" multicolored construction paper for projects

❑ Four dozen pink or white erasers
❑ Twelve dozen multicolored crayons
❑ Four dozen glue bottles
❑ 100 inexpensive three-prong report folders
❑ Twelve dozen boxes of tissue

You can augment these basic supplies with anything else you think you'll need, such as white note cards, rubber bands, rubber cement, your own classroom paper cutter, colored markers, colored pencils, gold stars, plastic paper sleeves, whiteboard cleaner, happy-face stickers, three-ring binders, colored yarn, scalloped bulletin-board edgings—anything appropriate. Just don't bankrupt yourself—always order materials from your school first, and only dig into your own pockets if there's no other choice.

Emergency Supplies

As you're stocking supplies, don't forget to get a good amount of disaster supplies for your classroom. In preparing for disasters, assume that you and your students might not be able to leave your classroom for a while. You'll want to visit the school nurse and ask her which disaster supplies you should stock in case the unthinkable occurs, such as tornados, hurricanes, earthquakes, security lockdowns, etc. Keep enough of these supplies so you can use some of them for the everyday "emergencies" that your kids will experience, such as cuts, scraped knees, etc.

It is vital to remember that many pathogens and dangerous diseases are blood-borne, meaning they can be transmitted from one person to another by means of contact with human blood. Don't allow other people's blood to contact any part of your body, either externally or through bodily orifices, or through any cuts or abrasions.

A necessary emergency item is adhesive bandages. You can always send a student to the nurse in the case of an apparent injury, but in many cases a bandage may be all that's needed. Certainly, let the nurse double check a student after you've issued a band-aid, but often the nurse will return the student with a note saying that your band-aid fix was adequate.

Don't forget basic sundries like gauze, facial tissues, and paper towels. These versatile materials are good for a multitude of cleaning tasks as well as when your kids have colds, allergies, minor cuts and scrapes, abrasions, etc.

If your school hasn't created an emergency kit for every teacher, you'll need to assemble one yourself. Get a clear plastic container with a snap-on lid (and don't get one so large or bulky that your students can't lift or carry it). Ask your school nurse for supplies and suggestions for the emergency kit's contents. Your emergency kit should contain the following basic supplies:

- ❏ Twelve dozen adhesive band-aids of assorted sizes, from small to extra large
- ❏ Larger elastic bandages and clips to hold bandages in place, gauze, scissors, surgical tape
- ❏ Disposable rubber gloves, gauze, paper towels, and infectious-waste bags
- ❏ Antiseptic wipes, rubbing alcohol, and disposable protective face masks
- ❏ Cold packs and antiseptic creams for burns, abrasions, etc.
- ❏ Feminine sanitary napkins
- ❏ Smelling salts, to revive unconscious persons
- ❏ A first-aid manual or first-aid reference card
- ❏ A rechargeable flashlight or flashlight with fresh batteries

If you and your students truly can't leave the classroom for a significant length of time because of outside obstructions or the nature of students' injuries, make provisions for a private lavatory for yourself and your students. In addition to toilet paper, keep a supply of rope, some inexpensive bed sheets, nails, and a hammer, and use these items to curtain off a corner of your classroom. Inside place a five-gallon plastic bucket, lined with one or two heavy-duty trash bags. When students are finished relieving themselves, tie off these bags securely and place them as far as possible from your students.

No one can prepare for every eventuality, but a little preplanning and a lot of stocking can carry you and your students a long way, during daily instructional time and emergencies.

Have Enough Papers

Copy enough of the papers you'll need for your first day of instruction and beyond so that you don't have to rush down to the copy room every morning, frantically copying papers while your blood pressure shoots through the roof. Print sufficient copies for all students of the following essential documents:

- Introduction letter, detailing your certifications, degrees, accomplishments, and goals
- Classroom rules
- Daily instructional schedule and bell schedule
- Any documents your school has asked you to distribute
- Academic worksheets sufficient to last the first week or longer

Research Your Students' Cumulative Files

Schools maintain a cumulative file, also known as a cum (pronounced "kyoom"), for every student in the school. A cumulative file is a comprehensive record containing a student photograph, contact information, health data, grades, teachers' comments, and other personal information about a student. Parents, teachers, and authorized educational personnel may access the cumulative files, but otherwise these records are confidential. Cumulative files are generally kept in a series of file cabinets in the main office.

Peruse the cumulative files for each of your students before the first instructional day to determine if any of your students have special medical needs, emotional or behavioral issues, or academic issues. If you diligently study the cumulative records, you'll be better prepared to address the needs of each student before instruction begins.

Plan Your Lessons

Modern school districts have given teachers a planning period, also called a preparation period, a block of time you use to plan lessons and get ready for your students. Type your planning period in your daily schedule only if you prefer to meet parents and students during that time. But you might want to consider meeting parents after school and using your planning time for planning.

Your planning period may seem like free time, but remember, there's rarely such a thing as free time for teachers. Your planning period is a time to get your work done, so use the time wisely. The list below shows just a few of the productive activities you can engage in during your preparation period:

- Organize and beautify your classroom, which may include nominal cleaning
- Post and upgrade bulletin boards
- Grade papers such as essays, reports, homework, etc.
- Record grades
- Briefly confer with a student regarding an egregious academic or behavioral problem
- Copy worksheets, tests, or other informational papers for your students
- Laminate charts and posters for your classroom walls
- Restock necessary forms and supplies
- Plan lessons as far into the future as possible

Planning periods last about an hour, depending on the school district. You'll find that even an hour is not enough to accomplish all the tasks you'll set for yourself as a busy, conscientious teacher.

CHAPTER 4

Every Little Detail Counts

Now that your preplanning is complete, you're nearly ready to greet your students and begin teaching. However, a few details still need your attention. You've got to consider the issues of dressing professionally, meeting your colleagues, organizing tasks for your teachers' aides, checking messages, getting your principal to evaluate your classroom, and doing your own final white-glove walk-through of your room. These details are just as critical as everything else you've done so far, so continue to be diligent and professional as you make your final preparations.

Dress Professionally

One of the most important tools of classroom management is dressing professionally so students don't ridicule or disrespect you.

There are the two schools of thought on how teachers should dress: Some teachers will strongly advise you to dress casually in jeans and sneakers, to better connect with your young pupils, who generally don't wear suits, neckties, pantsuits, or pumps. However, other teachers will just as strongly advocate suit jackets, pressed trousers, and neckties for male teachers and suits and pantyhose for female teachers, citing society's expectation that all professionals will dress formally.

If you decide to go casual, don't wear ragged jeans, rubber flip-flops, midriff-baring T-shirts, backward baseball caps, and the like, because you'll find that neither students nor parents will respect you. Instead, choose business casual. The business-casual look for men generally consists of tasteful polo shirts, pleated slacks, and comfortable yet presentable shoes. For women, business casual is generally quite similar to that of men, except that tasteful, below-the-knee shorts or tailored skirts are often substituted for full-length slacks.

If you choose the standard business attire model, you don't necessarily have to wear the latest or most expensive suits. For men, a suit jacket, button-down dress shirt, tasteful necktie, slacks, and presentable shoes are widely accepted. For women, a suit jacket, blouse or knit top, tasteful skirt, pantyhose, and presentable pumps or flats are acceptable. Bear in mind that even standard business attire has to be sturdy and durable when you're around kids, so don't wear anything too costly, delicate, or hard to clean.

FACT

"Suit" is a word that has descended from the French word *suivre,* which means "follow." In other words, all the pieces of a suit follow each other—the pants, jacket, and vest are all cut from the same bolt of fabric.

Like it or not, society judges you by your appearance. Dress unprofessionally and you'll probably be treated unprofessionally. Dress professionally—whether business casual or standard business attire—and you're more likely to be treated with dignity and respect, by your students and everyone else you come into contact with.

Meet Your Next-Door "Buddy" Teachers

Go over and meet and greet your next-door "buddy" teachers as soon as possible before the first day of instruction, because they can save your life. When school starts, if you discover that you've got a kid who's impervious to warnings, counseling, or disciplinary action because he's been misbehaving so long he's not really motivated to change, you might have to send him temporarily to a buddy teacher. Write a brief note for your buddy, then hand the note to a responsible student, along with some schoolwork or a book for the troublemaker, and ask your helper to escort the student next door.

You're under no obligation whatsoever to accept misbehaving students from buddy teachers. In fact, your district's collective-bargaining agreement may contain provisions regarding average numbers of students permissible per classroom. But you should strongly consider assisting your buddies whenever possible because, "What goes around comes around."

Don't limit your definition of buddy teachers to those who are physically next door. Get to know as many of your fellow teachers as you can so that your buddies can include virtually every teacher in the school, if possible. That way, you can rotate your buddies, making sure not to send too many students to the same teacher in the same month or school year.

Do little courteous favors for your buddy teachers whenever possible. Remind them that they're welcome to send "guests" to your classroom whenever they have a problem with a disruptive student. Don't be afraid to make this kind of offer, and don't secretly fear that your buddy's problem will become your problem. You'll be amazed to see that much of the time, when a disruptive student has been removed from familiar surroundings and has lost her usual audience she becomes docile and quiet. And on those occasions when a student continues her shenanigans after she's been sent to your room, send her back with a note that she was noncooperative; you'll depend on your buddy to handle the matter from there. Likewise, if one of your students is returned from a buddy with a note about noncooperation, you'll need to call the parent later or even consider suspending the student and sending her to the office immediately.

Becoming buddies with your teaching colleagues will involve a bit more than just walking next door, chatting for two minutes, and leaving. While you should never loiter in another teacher's classroom and waste her limited preparation time, you also shouldn't consistently ignore a teacher then send her a stream of misbehaving students whenever it suits you. Eat lunch with the other teachers sometimes, inquire after their health, ask about their families, and just be a friend. It's human nature to unconsciously ignore people who ignore you and help people who help you. In order to have a buddy be a buddy, and you'll have help when you need it the most.

Organize Tasks for Your Teacher's Aide

You may be lucky enough to get a teacher's aide, a person to assist you with the many classroom-management tasks you'll face each day as a teacher. A teacher's aide can be a paid employee of the district, a parent volunteer, or a student. Regardless of who the person is, you'll want to treat him courteously and professionally and have appropriate work ready for him when he arrives each day. The worst thing you can do is tell him, "Oh, I've got nothing for you today. Would you like to sit and read?" You're wasting your aide's valuable time—and yours, too—because there are always a multitude of jobs that need to be done.

The trick is to get organized before your aide even walks through the door. First, set aside a part of the room where your aide can work without interruption. Make certain your students know that the aide's area belongs to him primarily and shouldn't be intruded upon when the aide is present. A single chair at the end of one of your learning-center tables should suffice. Or, you can ask the custodian to bring in a desk and chair exclusively for the aide's use if there's room and the custodian is willing.

Next, introduce your teacher's aide to your class at the earliest opportunity. Make clear to your students that an adult aide should be treated with the same respect as any other adult staff member and that student aides should be treated courteously, as with all peers. Have your aide make a few introductory remarks to the class if he wishes. Help everyone understand that an aide is a kind of honorary coteacher and a student aide is an honorary member of your class.

Then, if the district's policy is that your aide does secretarial work primarily, have work ready for him. That means you have to stack papers, write instructions where necessary, put different tasks in different folders, and generally make things as easy as possible for your aide. For instance, much of his time might be spent grading papers. Separate stacks of papers by assignment and by period number if you're teaching secondary school. Have answer keys copied and ready, placing a different answer key in each folder if necessary. Provide correcting pens for marking and a pocket calculator for figuring grade percentages. Write some brief instructions for or briefly tell him what you want done.

If you need your aide to copy papers, and if your aide is a responsible adult, organize your copy masters, or originals, into folders and tell him how many copies you need for each master. Provide trays for him to put the copies into upon his return.

Recall that most schools don't permit students to operate copy machines or even hang around in the same room with copy machines because of possible damage to the machines. If your aide is a student, you'll probably have to do all copying yourself, unless your school is unusually tolerant. Learn your school's policy and adhere to it.

Another secretarial task your aide can perform is filing papers in students' portfolios. Filing can become quite time consuming, yet it must be done because when parents visit they'll want to see their child's work. The folders must also be available for each individual student's perusal, of course. If you don't have an aide, you'll have to file papers yourself and that means working at a rapid pace to complete the job. But if you're lucky enough to have an aide, consider asking him to file the previous day's papers first thing when he arrives.

If your school permits adult aides to work with students, set up a table and some chairs for that purpose—a semicircular table and five chairs constitutes an excellent arrangement. Provide daily written instructions, student work, and textbooks or other books. Make sure the aide has appropriate answer keys to grade written work, if feasible. Aides can also walk around the classroom helping students who require extra tutoring.

A teacher's aide can be a marvelous human resource and an invaluable part of your daily instructional program. Treat your aide with respect, utilize his talents, and your classroom management will become more efficient and professional.

Check Your School's Message Boards

Nearly every school has one or more whiteboards or corkboards, usually located in the staff room or near the mailboxes, where staff and administrators leave general-interest messages for the entire staff. There's often no official requirement that you check these boards on a daily basis, but if you don't, you'll miss out on a lot of important information.

There's bound to be a general message board with personal announcements about new babies born to staff as well as kids who've graduated, teachers' illnesses, upcoming parties, and more. You'll also see professional announcements about upcoming seminars, staff members who are out ill that day, scheduled conferences, and so on. If you don't check this board, you'll probably commit blunders like showing up for meetings that have been canceled because you didn't read the board.

There's also bound to be a message board maintained by your local teachers' association, full of news about the association's insurance benefits as well as teachers' rights, upcoming seminars, important legislative developments, etc. If you don't glance at this information occasionally, you might be inadvertently giving up your rights or missing an opportunity to grow professionally without even realizing it. Read this board as often as time permits.

You should also see a board with legally required postings about your federal and state employee rights, information about wages and benefits, sexual-harassment information, etc. Take time to study this board, copying down phone numbers and e-mail addresses if necessary.

In your daily rush to get to class and get ready for your students, take a minute to read your school's information boards and catch up on the latest news. There's nothing worse than missing the principal's latest impromptu meeting because you never read the board or missing an important association meeting about the latest increase in district salaries. Read the boards!

Ask Your Principal to Evaluate Your Classroom

Once you've done just about everything you can think of to prepare yourself and your classroom for your students' arrival, do the unthinkable—invite your principal in for a last walk-through and critical evaluation.

True, most people don't relish criticism, but a fresh pair of eyes can often be extremely helpful. For example, your principal may notice that you've positioned the white screen for your overhead projector in such a way that half the class won't be able to see it. It has nothing to do with incompetence—it's just that with all the things you're doing, you didn't happen to notice. It's better to correct the problem immediately, before the kids arrive, than to wait until they're complaining that they can't see the screen.

E-QUESTION

Should I tell off my insensitive principal?
If you work as a teacher, you've given up any right you may have had to yell insults at a principal. That's insubordination, and it will get you fired. However, your principal has no right to treat you cruelly. If the situation is egregious, speak to your school's association representative.

Sometimes, teachers are leery to consult their principals about much of anything because—believe it or not—a small minority prove to be mean, petty, vindictive, and untrustworthy people. The last thing you want is to have one of these individuals walking around your classroom with a cold, critical eye. However, the vast majority of principals are helpful, open minded, and fair, and even if yours isn't, you still have to work with her, so find out what she likes and doesn't like.

And don't forget to be open minded yourself, because, as the old saying goes, "Even a fool can teach you something." If your principal says that the arrangement of your classroom desks is blocking an exit, listen—she just might be right. Of course, you are the person who will be teaching in that classroom, but the principal's opinion matters, too. See if you can accommodate her. Move a few chairs, make a few changes; and if the principal gushes with praise for the way you've organized things, so much the better.

Your Final Classroom Walk-Through

It's been said that you must be your own harshest critic in life if you expect to put forth your best efforts and really impress people. So it is with teachers. You'll now have to make a final white-glove walk-through of your classroom.

One of the final things you'll want to do is critique the arrangement of your students' classroom desks. Most modern classrooms use rectangular two-student tables, about two feet wide by four feet long, finished with a wood-grain plastic laminate top. However, older one-student desks can still be found, with thick plastic desktops fastened to a metal frame, usually with a metal wire frame under the seat for storing books.

The easiest and most traditional desk arrangement is to organize four rows of four tables each, each table abutted end to end, with two chairs per table, accommodating a total of thirty-two students—enough for any reasonably sized class. All four rows should extend across the long dimension of the classroom, facing the front of the classroom where the instructional whiteboard (and the teacher's desk, in many rooms) is generally located. Learning-center tables and chairs, plus the classroom library, can be ranked along the left and right sides of the classroom, facing the walls. This traditional arrangement focuses student attention on you and places as many students as possible as close to you as possible.

However, other classroom desk arrangements are possible. Many teachers favor arrangements where students sit in cooperative groups, tables abutted in clusters of four or six, facing one another. These arrangements can enhance lesson discussions among students and simplify cooperative assignments.

ALERT!

Make sure you have at least one lockable drawer or cabinet where you can store your personal effects and confidential information. Many people will be in your room when you are not there; don't assume that anything in your desk—or classroom, for that matter—is private.

Whichever arrangement you've chosen, ask yourself, "Is this really right for me?" Will you be comfortable teaching within this arrangement year after year? If not, now is the time to change it, before your students arrive. Most modern tables and chairs are reasonably lightweight, so if you think you can move them yourself and you feel a change is required, effect that change immediately. Otherwise, do not hesitate to ask the custodian to come in and move the tables for you.

Here, then, is a final checklist of a number of other white-glove items you'll want to double check before school begins:

❑ Are all the students' desktops fairly clean? If not, get some rags or paper towels and a bit of cleanser or soapy water and give the desks a quick wipe-down.

❑ Have you switched on all your equipment one last time to check if everything's in working order? Do so and quickly replace faulty equipment.

❑ Have your wastebaskets been emptied and have all your filled trashbags been taken out? Ask the custodian to please attend to this.

❑ Have you asked the custodian to remove and replace any rickety, unsafe furniture? Ask him to do this before the first day.

❑ Have you rounded up all your required textbooks? Speak to the principal or a responsible colleague about this one.

❑ Have you copied all the work papers and information papers your students will need, at least for the first day? It's not too late to visit those copy machines one last time.

❑ Do you have sufficient pencils, writing paper, and other supplies for your students and yourself? Do a final inventory.

❑ Have you identified and corrected all safety hazards—that is, wires that kids can trip over, junk left in the aisles, etc.? Tidy up all such loose ends.

❑ Are all necessary signs, posters, charts, and labels in place? You've still got time to write and even laminate a few more, if necessary.

Finally, one of the most important items you've got to attend to before the first instructional day is yourself. If you've really done all you can humanly do, then go home and get a hot meal and a good night's sleep. You won't be any good to your students if you're shuffling around with your eyes half closed. Relax, spend time with your loved ones, and congratulate yourself on all the magnificent preplanning you've managed to do. Your hard work will pay off throughout the entire academic year because when you're prepared, you're confident; and when you're confident, you generally deliver the highest-quality instruction possible.

CHAPTER 5

Class Begins

This is the day you've been preparing for—your students stream into your classroom freshly scrubbed, bright eyed, and (you certainly hope) eager to learn anything and everything you can teach them. Class begins! Now you need to focus on some of the strategies detailed in this chapter, the methodologies that separate really great teachers from merely adequate ones.

Public Speaking

Remember that teachers are public speakers. If you're not comfortable speaking in public, you've got to remedy this situation immediately. Teaching is all about standing before groups of people and communicating information to them clearly and effectively. You can't teach if you're paralyzed by fear or you're so shy that you can barely be heard even in the front row. To be a good teacher and a good public speaker, you must speak with a certain amount of power, self-assurance, and confidence.

None of this means that you have to have a booming baritone voice or that you need to overpower your audience with bullying and arrogance. Nothing of the sort! You just have to inspire trust in your students. They have to feel that you're knowledgeable, prepared, organized, and professional. They have to feel that you're a leader and that you know where to take them and the best way to take them there. You'll never inspire trust if you don't trust yourself. Speak up clearly, as if you know what you're talking about (because you really do).

Remember, in any classroom, large or small, some students must sit in the last row or at least in a part of the room that's somewhat far from you— perhaps ten feet away or more. If they can't hear you properly, they'll fidget, talk, draw pictures, and generally zone out, so make an effort to project your voice.

There's a huge difference between projecting and screaming. Projecting means "turning up the volume," but constant screaming invites chorditis, a medical condition where your vocal cords become so inflamed you temporarily lose your voice. Teachers who can't talk are like fish that can't swim— dead in the water. Speak up, but never thoughtlessly abuse your voice.

Try to relax as much as possible when you teach, because extreme nervousness can increase your heart rate, elevate your blood pressure, and cause your voice to "flutter" in a potentially embarrassing manner. Making eye contact with each student momentarily as you teach can help you focus your thoughts. Scan the room from left to right then back again continually, and even smile courteously as you make eye contact. You'll be surprised to see that many students will smile back, and this can often help you relax.

Also remember, you're a role model for your students, and you must use correct English at all times unless you're making a funny point and your kids know it. For example, if a kid asks a male teacher to grow a beard, the teacher might reply jokingly, "It ain't gonna happen, bub!" But except for such witticisms, stand as a shining beacon of correct English grammar.

Establish and Reinforce Your Rules

It's a good idea to have a stapled two-page introductory document ready to pass out to your students on the first day of school. The first page of the document will consist of a letter, greeting the parents and introducing yourself. Include some information about your education, teaching experience, and a bit about required supplies, daily routines, and your goals for the academic year. Don't write a full resume—you're not applying for a job—you're just letting parents know a little bit about you so they'll have confidence in you as a classroom teacher. Don't forget to sign your letter.

The second page of the document is, in some ways, even more important than the first page because it will contain your classroom rules. Many teachers feel that very broad, general rules are sufficient to run a classroom efficiently. For example, many of your teaching colleagues may recommend that you give a set of simple rules such as, "1. Be polite. 2. Be prompt. 3. Be productive."

Simplicity has its place, but remember what the great physicist and mathematician Albert Einstein once said: "Simplify as much as possible, but no further." Simple rules are good for kids, but if they're as simplistic as the examples above, kids may not know exactly what to expect in certain situations. For example, are kids allowed to navigate the classroom—to get up and walk around—any time they please or do they have to ask your permission first? What's your tardy policy? What's your rule if a student consistently fails to do his homework?

Therefore, you might want to consider a letter of rules that is as simple as possible, but no simpler. Think of your classroom rules as a kind of Constitution for you and your kids to adhere to, setting forth specific rules that enable all of you to work together in a professional manner. Perhaps an extremely simplified model might seem more kid friendly, but such a model may also tend to cause unnecessary confusion and arguments. You'll have to decide what's best for you. The following is an example of a somewhat more detailed rules letter:

1. **General:** Students will respect all peers, visitors, and school personnel, obey all rules, and work diligently, in and out of class. Noncompliance will result in disciplining, such as conferences, loss of privileges, detentions, suspensions, etc.
2. **Manners:** Students will address peers, visitors, and school personnel respectfully, and should use courteous phrases such as, "Please," "Thank you," "You're welcome," etc., liberally. Students should call me, "Mrs. Jones," or, "Ma'am." Students will not use profanity for any reason. Students' behavior will reflect courtesy and propriety at all times.
3. **Student-Teacher Discussions:** Students wishing to discuss personal behavioral or academic issues with the teacher will do so in private, and in a respectful manner. At no time will a student disrupt instructional time with public disrespect and defiance.
4. **Navigating the Classroom:** Students wishing to leave their seats and navigate the classroom to sharpen pencils, etc., will raise their hands first and secure permission, in every instance, unless otherwise instructed. Students will navigate safely at all times by walking—not running—in a courteous, considerate manner.
5. **Absences:** Students returning from absences will immediately give me a note of explanation from a parent or parents may briefly stop in.
6. **Tardiness:** Students will be seated prior to the ringing of the tardy bell. Tardy pupils will immediately give me a note of explanation from a parent or parents may briefly stop in.
7. **Homework:** Generally, I assign homework every school day except Friday, and on some Fridays, as well. Students will complete all assignments and give them to me the next school morning. Students with

missing or incomplete homework will immediately give me a note of explanation from a parent or parents may briefly stop in.

8. **Parent Communications:** Students will immediately return to me all written parent communications given to them on the next school morning after receipt, signed by a parent.

9. **Parent Conferences:** Conferences with parents may be held during my daily planning period or before or after school, by prior appointment only. Call the secretary and schedule an appointment, giving a requested date and time. Please confer with me often, and after receiving any written communication from me. Parent conferences are not held during passing periods or during instructional time.

10. **Record:** Students' infractions will be recorded in writing, and discipline will follow.

11. **Breaks:** Students must get my permission to leave class during instructional hours for water, the restroom, or any other reason. Students given leave will use a hall pass and return speedily. Students with medical conditions requiring frequent restroom trips must give me a note of explanation from parents.

12. **Schoolwork:** Students' schoolwork will be completed per my instructions and given to me immediately when due. I will determine all schoolwork grades. Criteria include neatness, organization, and content.

13. **Grade Reports:** I will determine all grades based on work received and my professional observations and judgment. I will not alter recorded grades without a legitimate reason to do so, such as a proven numerical miscalculation.

14. **Special Privileges:** Special privileges such as field trips are for those students who show continued good behavior and work habits. I will determine who receives special privileges.

15. **Parent Visits:** Parents are cordially invited to visit and observe in my class during instructional hours, after first checking in at the main office. During visits, parents must sit and observe unobtrusively.

Certainly, many of the words in the rules letter above are probably too difficult for really young kids to understand; so, go ahead and modify the letter or just explain the gist of each rule or do both. Or, you can stick with these rules, "1. Be polite. 2. Be prompt. 3. Be productive." The choice is yours.

Sign your rules letter and make sure the letter has a tear-off portion at the bottom for the students to return to you, signed by themselves and by their parents. The tear-off can look something like this:

We have carefully read and discussed Mrs. Jones's introductory letter and the attached classroom-rules letter. We will abide by all terms, and we understand that every item is a material term, without exception.

Student's Name, Printed: _____

Student's Signature: _____

1st Parent's Name, Printed:_____

*Parent's Signature:*_____

2nd Parent's name, Printed:_____

*Parent's Signature:*_____

The words, "material term," mean that every provision of your rules letter is equally important and no provision is meant to be ignored by parents or students. Have your students promptly return their signed tear-offs. File the tear-offs in the students' dossiers for those times when a parent claims he was never informed about your rules. Produce the tear-off at parent conferences to remind the parent that he was fully informed beforehand. The tear-off can also be shown to the parents of misbehaving children, as a reminder to everyone that they agreed to follow the rules and aren't honoring their agreement.

Establish your rules early, make them as specific as you're comfortable with, and get the kids and their parents to sign the tear-off. That's how you begin the school year like a seasoned professional—a teacher deserving of deference and respect.

Model Good Manners and Common Courtesy

If you demand courtesy from your students, don't you owe them exactly the same thing? Shouldn't a classroom be a place of mutual respect between a teacher and her students? Then be sure to model basic good manners for your students.

One of the most important tenets of good etiquette is addressing people properly and respectfully. If you had lived in the nineteenth century and had a chance to meet President Abraham Lincoln, would you have grabbed his hand and blurted, "Hey there, Abe, how's it shakin'?" Of course not; it wouldn't have been appropriate. Instead, you would have said, "Good morning, Mr. President. I'm very pleased to meet you," or something to that effect. Then why not practice these same courtesies with students? Why not address them with a similar level of respect? Why not call them "Miss" and "Mr." along with their surnames?

While students might feel nervous on the first day, this nervousness will quickly disappear if you make them feel safe, welcome, and engaged. Remember, you set the tone for your class.

Some of your fellow teachers will strenuously object to such a formal convention. They'll urge you to call your students by their first names because it's a venerable American tradition. Also, they'll maintain that using first names establishes a warm bond of friendship between you and your young charges. These are strong arguments, and you'll have to balance such reasoning against the advice you'll get from other colleagues, who will warn you against the dangers of over familiarity with your students.

All teachers ought to maintain a certain amount of professional distance from the children who've been entrusted to them. How much distance? That's up to you. Some teachers hug their students every day; other teachers scrupulously avoid any physical contact whatsoever for fear that such behavior might be completely misinterpreted. The latter group of teachers may well advise you that strictly formal working relationships are best, especially for male teachers. These teachers will counsel against using first names and instead will suggest using courteous phrases such as, "Thank you, Miss Smith," "That's right, Mr. Jones," and "Would you pass these out, Miss Doe?" when speaking to students.

But of course, good manners involve more than just using courteous forms of address. You should also get in the habit of phrasing your orders as polite requests. The truth is, as a teacher you're a little bit like a military commander, in the sense that you issue direct orders and your students are honor-bound to obey those orders. However, because your subordinates are children and not soldiers, do what smart commanders throughout history have always done—pretend that your orders are requests. Try not to say things such as, "Jennifer, get yourself over here *now!*" Such barked commands can easily cause Jennifer to lose face among her peers; and at that point, she may feel constrained by her own pride to stubbornly defy you in an effort to regain some dignity.

FACT

Remember what the great American philosopher Ralph Waldo Emerson once said about manners: "[T]here is always time enough for courtesy." Or recall the words of the English author and noblewoman Lady Mary Wortley Montagu, in one of her famous eighteenth-century letters: "Civility costs nothing and buys everything."

Instead, try saying, "Miss Lee, would you come up to my desk for a moment, please?" Such camouflaged orders can often produce the desired result. If your polite request is unsuccessful, then you'll need to be a bit firmer. "Miss Lee, I need you to come to my desk for a moment, please." In the end, direct, undisguised commands sometimes have their place—"Jennifer, get yourself over here *now!*"—but you may want to use them as a last resort rather than a first resort. After all, it's hard for kids or parents to fault you if you're always elegantly courteous. Use good manners to legitimately gain the respect and cooperation of your students.

Praise Students Constantly

In his bestselling book, *How Full Is Your Bucket?*, American businessman and author Tom Rath writes that based on a Gallup Organization survey of 4 million workers in over 10,000 companies worldwide, employees crave one type of remuneration more than any other: Praise. Rath also notes that according to the United States Department of Labor, the primary reason that good employees quit their jobs is lack of appreciation by management. In other words, millions of adults yearn so deeply for praise they'll change jobs if necessary, in the hope that they might get some professional recognition in a new setting.

ALERT!

Control your urge to buy mass quantities of stickers, candy, etc., as rewards for students who exhibit proper behavior. You don't necessarily have to believe the experts, who say that motivation should always be from the heart, but you do need to safeguard your precious money and not bankrupt yourself purchasing too many expensive goodies.

And just like adults, kids need praise, too. The liberal use of praise in the classroom can often achieve seemingly magical results, including the following:

- Getting kids to work harder and more efficiently
- Helping kids to interact more positively with their peers
- Raising kids' innate self-esteem
- Convincing kids to remain more loyal to your academic program and to you
- Enabling kids to achieve better academic grades and citizenship grades

You can find 1,000 opportunities to praise kids during the instructional day, if you just keep an open mind. Negative reprimands are sometimes required, but focus as much as possible on all the positive things you can say and do for your students.

- When you praise, let it come from your heart so you sound sincere. Say something brief and compassionate, such as, "That's absolutely right, Juan; excellent work."
- Any time and every time a student says something correct, no matter how small, praise her: "That's the correct answer, Tasha. You are so smart!"
- Praise students for trying, even if they give an incorrect answer. Say, "Not quite, Ricky. But you'll get it next time." You're trying to encourage all your students to take a chance and raise their hands. If the really shy ones fear condemnation, they'll remain silent all year. Don't say, "Mike, do you *ever* pay attention? My cat could've given a better answer than that!" Mike might clam up for the next nine months after such a cutting remark. Instead, try, "Mike, take a look at your notes again" or, "Mike, remember when we discussed linking verbs?" Encourage your students to keep trying.
- Briefly praise every student at least once each day. You'll have to be creative and really stretch it for some students, saying things like, "Ann, you can be so wonderfully polite and respectful—I'm a bit surprised at your behavior today." Find something to praise, especially where the challenging students are concerned. Say, "Lisa, I'm really pleased with the way you walked into the class today—you were so quiet and courteous." See if Lisa doesn't grin from ear to ear.

You never need to praise misbehavior or utter compliments you don't believe, but you do need to seek out positive behavior and reinforce it.

Finally, think of how much you crave praise. Aren't you hoping for a bit of positive reinforcement from your principal a few times each year? Admit it; you're just waiting to hear, "That was a *wonderful* lesson!" from an administrator or a colleague. And of course, the best praise of all comes from a straight-talking little kid: "I usually hate long division, but you're the first person to explain it so I can understand it!" Just as you enjoy praise, other human beings enjoy it, too. Go ahead and praise your students as much as you like. Praise is exactly like good manners—it costs you nothing and brings you everything.

Learn Your Students' Names in Five Days

If you really want students to listen, then one of your most important tools is your willingness to learn students' names quickly—so that you don't keep saying, "Hey, you! Please quit talking to what's-his-name!" How would you respond if a student constantly referred to you as, "Hey, teacher?" The following are techniques that veteran educators use to learn students' names rapidly, perhaps in as little as five days or less. Use any or all of these and check them off as you go:

❑ Get your name roster from the front office or an administrator at least one day before school starts. Then, the night before, say each name aloud three times and write each name three times.

❑ On the first day of school, continue memorizing each student's name. Students will believe that you're really interested in them if they see you're at least attempting to learn their names.

❑ As you continue to take attendance during the first week, say each student's full name aloud and look at each student for a moment, to connect faces with names.

❑ Expect that some students will ask to be called by nicknames. Try to respect such requests, and make brief notations on your roster. Then, practice with the nicknames.

❑ Don't hesitate to ask students their names repeatedly until you've memorized them all. Apologize to kids who seem upset, and explain that you're just trying to learn each name quickly.

❑ Create a seating chart with every student's name carefully recorded before the first day of instruction. Use this seating chart to refer to students by name. Glance down at it any time you get stuck.

The main thing to remember is to say each student's name as much as possible during this first crucial week—and don't forget to look at each student as you speak a name, constantly reinforcing a face-name connection in your mind. But don't overdo it. You don't have to say, "Thanks, Alvin. I appreciate it, Alvin. That was well done, Alvin." Now you sound a little crazy. "Thanks, Alvin," will suffice.

Then, as soon as you can, try to say every student's name, pointing to each child and forcing your memory to recall each moniker. If you get stuck on any one kid, glance down at your seating chart. By the end of the week, if you've worked diligently, you should be able to point to each child and say each name with some degree of accuracy and confidence. Good luck.

The French Emperor Napoleon Bonaparte had a foolproof method for learning names. Whenever Napoleon would make a new acquaintance, he'd jot down the person's name, study it briefly and intently, then toss the paper. Reportedly, using this method, Napoleon could memorize any name. Don't hesitate to use this method if all else fails.

Get Library Cards for Your Students

As a college-educated professional, you already know that a person becomes truly educated by doing two critical things: (1) working hard in school, gleaning everything she can from her teachers; and (2) reading books constantly. You already know that if a person doesn't read voraciously on her own time, she probably won't be as well rounded and highly educated as she might be. Therefore, you know how important it is for your students to read, read, read. The easiest way for kids to get their hands on books is to go to their public library and check out books for free. But that won't happen until the kids first get library cards. Your job is to encourage kids to do just that.

Some libraries will allow you, as a teacher, to take a pack of library-card applications and distribute them to your students. Many libraries, however, have strict rules requiring parents and guardians to accompany their kids to the library to fill out the applications there, prior to any library cards being issued.

If your neighborhood library has such regulations, write a form letter to parents encouraging them to visit the library and fill out card applications for each of their children as soon as possible. Mention in your letter that the application process will probably require parents to show a state driver's license or a state photo ID at the library. Children will also need to be present for cards to be issued.

E-QUESTION

I teach preschool. Should I encourage three-year-olds to get library cards and read?
Why not? Writers and educators Diana Hughes and Rhona Stainthorp report in *Learning from Children Who Read at an Early Age* that historically, many children have acquired reading skills at a tender age—including American novelist Truman Capote, who was reading before age five.

Help your kids develop the habit of reading for fun and enlightenment by helping them get library cards. You might just be creating an entire group of lifelong readers, thinkers, philosophers, and fully contributing American citizens.

CHAPTER 6

The Everyday Routines

You've implemented sound teaching practices and your students are responding nicely—working hard, behaving courteously, and getting good grades. To keep your class humming along, use the classroom-management tools in this chapter to reinforce your everyday routines. Your kids will become so used to your schedule and practices that they may well be able to help guide a substitute teacher through the entire instructional day if you're absent. At that point, you can take pride in the fact that you're managing your classroom like a pro.

Get Kids to Participate in Lessons

Some of your students will be so outgoing and extroverted you'll sometimes have trouble getting them to stop talking. They're bursting with ideas, opinions, pronouncements, and free advice. Then there are the kids in the middle, who are a remarkable blend of silence and eloquence, reticence and courage, wariness and boldness. Finally, you have the students who are so introverted that if you don't call their names and practically force them to speak, you'll almost never hear their voices. For all of your students, participation in classroom lessons and discussions is crucial for their academic success. Make sure that all students join in your lessons so they can get the maximum benefit from your teaching.

An excellent way to get a shy kid to participate in a lesson is to ask the child to lead a mini-lesson, as if she were a bona fide teacher. You shouldn't feel nervous about such an idea because you're not expecting a child to lead your class in a complicated lesson for a full instructional day; you're just asking the student to try to conquer her shyness by doing a few minutes of teaching. Your shy kids are probably afraid of public speaking because they automatically assume they'll be ridiculed as soon as they open their mouths. Here's where you, as the teacher, can help.

FACT

The fear of public speaking, afflicting kids and adults alike, is called *glossophobia,* from the Greek words *glossa,* meaning "tongue," and *phobos*, meaning "fear." Fear of public speaking is believed to be the single most common phobia, affecting almost three-fourths of the population.

First, begin your lesson normally by distributing materials, stating the lesson objectives, relating the lesson content to the students' lives, etc. Then, once the lesson has begun, introduce a subtask a student can lead the class in for a few minutes, under your guidance.

For example, during a lesson on adjectives, you'll define an adjective as a word that modifies a noun. However, you'll generally spend time reviewing the topic of nouns first as a lead in to the somewhat more complicated concept of adjectives. Under the whiteboard heading "Adjectives," you can write the subhead "Nouns" on the instructional whiteboard. Underneath, write "What is a noun? A noun is," followed by a long blank line or sufficient white space to complete the definition of a noun.

At this point, explain that one of the students will come up and provide the already learned definition of a noun; in other words, a student will briefly lead the lesson. Draw three wide columns on the board, labeling them "People," "Places," and "Things." Explain that students will be coming to the board to write words naming people, places, and things in the proper columns—under the supervision of your temporary student teacher, who will keep this review portion of the lesson running smoothly.

Next, deliver a mini-speech telling students they are supposed to treat each other fairly and that you won't tolerate any ridiculing, verbal abuse, or insults. Explain that the consequences will be severe for such misbehavior. Remind students that if they can't encourage each other, they should remain silent. Then request a volunteer.

Unless there's a safety issue involved, don't use the full weight of your authority to force a student to perform an academic task that seems to terrify him. If he's genuinely fearful, just skip it; he may have unpleasant memories associated with that particular exercise. Discuss the matter with his parents to discover possible solutions.

But here's what you won't tell all your brave volunteers: You're not actually looking for volunteers; you've already decided to draft someone—the shyest kid in the class. Among the raised hands, there he sits, possibly with his hands folded, slumped a bit in his seat, hoping he'll never be noticed. You smile, and gently explain that you need him to come up for a minute. Once you've skillfully gotten him out of his seat, tell him that he will lead the class, selecting a volunteer to write a noun definition and selecting other volunteers to write five nouns in each column. Encourage him with a few well-chosen words of praise and a parting smile. Then move to the side or the back of the classroom, nodding to offer additional encouragement.

Of course, if you note any real resistance on the student's part, or the onset of trembling or tears, immediately excuse the student from the task and quickly pick one of your more-than-willing extroverts. But remind the shy student you hope to have him lead the class during another lesson. Keep planting those seeds until he resigns himself to the inevitability that he is going to lead the class one day soon. With a bit of luck, he may eventually begin to look forward to the idea.

This tack is not without risk, as your shy kids may prove noncooperative—paralyzed by fear. But the potential rewards are well worth the risk. Helping your shy kids face their fears in this way may constitute the first step toward helping them conquer such fears. Otherwise, their continuing lack of participation may jeopardize their grades and hold them back forever. Take a chance—the heart of a lion may be beating within that gentle lamb.

The Necessity of Homework

In his 1949 book *Principles and Methods of Guidance for Teachers,* American educator Leonard M. Miller states the generally accepted wisdom regarding the dreaded subject of homework: "We seem to be pretty much agreed that homework is necessary and our only plea seems to be for reasonable assignments and distribution of the work. . . ." You'll probably agree that as the year progresses daily homework—also called home learning—is vitally necessary for several important reasons.

First, given the sheer volume of academic work that must be completed during the year, time constraints will force you to assign some work to be completed at home. If every day had thirty hours and if you could spend fifteen of them with your students, you could probably complete everything in class; but since there are only twenty-four hours in a day, homework becomes an indispensable fact of academic life.

Second, homework provides reinforcement for subjects taught by providing students with additional exercises and additional practice at home. Without this extra practice, your students may not learn a concept as thoroughly as you might like. Like sports, if a young basketball player practices fifty free throws from the line, he may learn quite a bit about hitting his shots. But if he stays behind after practice and shoots fifty more free throws, he'll learn considerably more about ball control, and he'll almost certainly shoot better than kids who merely complete a standard amount of practice.

Third, homework can introduce new concepts to students so they'll feel more comfortable discussing the new concepts during subsequent lessons. Such advance preparation can also help students comprehend material better and assuage fears about the material so kids will perform better on subsequent assignments and tests.

Fourth, daily homework completion helps students become more self-directed so they can learn how to study, research, and compile information on their own. Homework helps students learn to appreciate, and perhaps even enjoy, intellectual challenges and problem solving.

Fifth, homework gives moms and dads a chance to keep track of the material their kids are learning and assist them in any way they feel is necessary or desirable. Parents can reinforce what you're teaching and even add their own personal knowledge to the mix.

Don't forget that as with any professional, you'll have to depend on your "clients"—your students—to do some requisite work at home. For example, a doctor will examine a patient and write out a prescription for medication. Would you expect the doctor to then drive home with the patient and spoon feed him the medication every four hours? Of course not; the patient will have to do some of the work at home.

As the noted American educator Marilee Sprenger observes in her book *Learning and Memory: The Brain in Action,* people understand and retain new material only if the information is repeated; a single exposure is seldom sufficient. Homework enhances this process because it provides students with abundant supplemental enrichment.

Some of your colleagues may complain that homework is merely busywork that doesn't really teach anything. The decision is yours, but remember, most districts, administrators, students, and parents expect you to assign homework to reinforce your lessons.

Of course, where homework is concerned, you never want to unfairly overload your kids; but you don't want to just blow off the benefits of homework, either. As with all things in life, keep a balance. Calculate the amount of time students will probably need to complete each assignment and hand out work accordingly.

This is particularly important for secondary teachers, who comprise an entire slate of six or seven classroom teachers, all giving homework. Keep a balance; keep the homework load neither poor nor extravagant, but just enough to accomplish its purpose.

How to Handle Restroom and Water Breaks

If you teach kindergarten, life can often be somewhat easier for you than for other teachers when it comes to restroom breaks. That's because many kindergarten classrooms have two little bathrooms, one for girls and one for boys, right there in the back of the room. You can keep an eye on your wee students and if they take too long, you can send other students to knock on the door and ascertain if there's a problem.

But for those of you who teach first grade and up, you'll have to devise a game plan to handle the constant requests you'll get from kids wanting to visit the restroom.

E-QUESTION

Regarding my legal responsibility to keep my kids safe, what does *in loco parentis* mean?
In loco parentis is Latin; it's a legal term meaning "in place of parents." The law lets you curb a student's misbehavior, just like a parent; but it also legally requires you to act in the student's best interests, just like a parent.

First, you'll recall that you have a sacred, legal responsibility to keep your students secure and accounted for to the best of your professional ability. Parents trust you, as a highly trained professional educator, to watch over their children and keep them safe. Therefore, you can't blithely send students traipsing around the school by themselves. The possibility of accidents and injuries is ever present, even for the most careful and responsible students.

Also, some students may misbehave while on a restroom break, perhaps even committing acts of graffiti or vandalism in some cases. After all, it's not only your trustworthy students who will ask to go to the restroom. The temptation to act out may be too hard to resist for some of your more immature students, and they may succumb to the impulse to do something inappropriate.

Moreover, you can't escape the reality that some students continually ask to go to the restroom for the purposes of disturbing other classrooms, roaming the hallways aimlessly, evading their responsibility to do school-work, missing important classroom instruction, and generally wasting time.

On the other hand, there's another extremely important issue that you've got to face: Human beings frequently have to *go*. The call of nature can't be resisted for long, either by responsible students or by your not-so-responsible students. If you arbitrarily issue a blanket, "No!" to every restroom request, you can cause a lot of discomfort, such that many students won't be able to concentrate on anything else you say or do. After all, how would you like it if you really had to relieve yourself and some authority figure told you, "Nope, Miss Smith, you can't go to the bathroom, and that's final."

Therefore, you might want to think about handling the restroom-break dilemma in this way:

- Remember your classroom rules? Have your kids occasionally review the rule about breaks: Students may only leave with permission, and must return promptly. Students with medical problems requiring frequent restroom trips must bring a parental note.
- When a student asks to go to the restroom, you courteously and immediately ask, "Can it wait?" In other words, does the request reflect a pressing emergency? Often, you'll be surprised to hear a kid answer, "Yes, it can wait." Problem solved.

- If the child says it can't wait then you should tell her she may leave the classroom, use the restroom, and return promptly. Remind the student that excessive time spent outside the room (more than five minutes or so) can result in disciplining.
- Provide a sign-out list for all students allowed to leave. On each line record the date, the student's first and last name, departure time, and return time. Then, have the student sign at the end of the line. With practice, all this information can be recorded in mere seconds.
- Fill out a hall pass as discussed earlier, with the same information as the sign-out list. With practice, this information can also be recorded in seconds. Avoid large, hard hall passes, as no information can be recorded on them and they can be used for hitting, etc.
- Remember, only one student at a time in the hallway from your class. Send more than one student out only if extenuating circumstances and time constraints truly require it, in your professional opinion.
- If a student takes too long to return, inquire as to the reason for the delay; and if the student's response seems unsatisfactory, either threaten to impose discipline the next time the infraction occurs or call the parent that afternoon to immediately discuss the problem.
- Promptly record the returning time on the list and on the hall pass, then immediately file the hall pass in the student's dossier.

An issue closely related to the eternal restroom-break saga is the granting of water breaks. But this little matter will prove a somewhat easier nut to crack. Almost every modern classroom has a sink with a working faucet as well as a drinking fountain. Just make sure your kids ask your permission before jumping out of their seats for a drink.

However, if you work in an older classroom and you have to let your kids leave to find a drinking fountain, follow all the steps detailed above for granting restroom breaks. Ask, "Can it wait?" and then complete the sign-out sheet and hall pass for the student. In this way, you're still fulfilling your responsibility to safeguard your students while not arbitrarily or unreasonably denying water, a basic human necessity.

How to Send Kids to the Nurse

Just as some kids attempt to use excessive restroom breaks as an excuse to ditch class, some kids also attempt to use excessive trips to the school nurse for the same reason. An identical thorny issue arises here as with restroom breaks: Do you let a kid go to the nurse even when you strongly suspect he's just trying to get out of working? After all, kids should be in class learning, not lollygagging in the nurse's office.

FACT

True, many headaches, or *cephalagia,* are commonplace ailments, treatable by kids or their parents (not by you!) using over-the-counter medications. But some headaches may indicate the presence of meningitis—a brain-inflammation—or extremely high blood pressure. You might want to let a medical professional take a look at a kid who says he has a headache.

And yet, if a kid says he has a headache, can you trust that your medical training is good enough that you'll know for sure that the kid is faking? If not, then you might consider letting the kid go to the nurse because—just as people sometimes desperately need to visit the restroom—people also become genuinely sick and injured from time to time.

You can resolve this issue in much the same manner that you resolved the restroom- and water-break dilemmas. First, ask yourself a common-sense question: Is the student in obvious distress? Then go ahead and send her down. Here, you'll doubtless want to skip the step where you ask, "Can it wait?" because in all likelihood neither you nor the student is medically qualified to properly answer that question. If the kid seems as if she's suffering, send her. Use the sign-out sheet and hall passes, as with restroom trips. But if the emergency seems immediate, you might skip the sign-out sheet and even skip the hall pass, if necessary. Have another student escort the ailing student to the nurse. Yes, this will be one of those rare times when you let more than one student leave the classroom at the same time.

If you're unsure whether a student is faking or not, err on the side of caution and send her to the nurse's office. Remember, you are not a medically trained professional. No teacher wants a student to leave class and miss instruction unnecessarily; but no teacher should needlessly endanger a student's precious health, either. If in doubt, consider sending the child to the nurse. The nurse may be a bit annoyed, and you can apologize later, but where there's smoke there's often a fire.

What Recess Is Really For

Ask many kids what their favorite academic subject is, and their answer will be, "Recess!" Recess breaks are the student versions of adult coffee breaks— a chance for students to do two critically important things:

1. Romp and play and get some much-needed physical exercise
2. Relax for a while before returning to the process of learning

Generally, recess takes place outdoors, but you'll want to be sure to follow your school's inclement-weather policy and supervise your kids in your classroom during rainy days, etc., if that's what your school requires.

Many psychologists, teachers, and other professionals who work with kids will tell you that recess is critical to a child's social development. For example, the distinguished law professor John E. B. Myers, a veteran prosecutor of child-abuse cases, says in his book *Myers on Evidence in Child, Domestic, and Elder Abuse Cases*: "Teachers know children have a limited attention span for schoolwork, and that recess is essential for learning." In other words, recess helps kids learn.

And don't forget about all the talk regarding childhood obesity that's been streaming from the news media for the past few years. The Centers for Disease Control and Prevention (CDC), a division of the United States Department of Health and Human Services, has said the number of obese children in this country has tripled since 1980. In full agreement, Dr. Stewart Trost, Professor of Kinesiology at Kansas State University, says on the "Cartoon Network Rescuing Recess" website, available at *www.cartoonrecessweek.com /experts_say.html*: "Kids who have recess display an improved ability to stay on task. . . . Movement is essential to the physical and social development of all children."

ALERT!

When it comes to recess, make sure to use the right word in the right country. In America, every kid knows what recess means, but if you use the word in other English-speaking countries, they won't have a clue what you're talking about. It's playtime or playlunch in Britain, and morning tea in New Zealand and Australia.

Recess helps kids learn. Remember that the next time a parent or even a fellow teacher tries to tell you that recess is a waste of time. Consider the issue of recess this way: Recess is beneficial to the mind, body, and soul.

What Is Cooperative Learning?

Often, you'll want your students to complete class work individually, because the annual standardized tests that every state administers require individual—not group—performance. However, you'll also want your students to work in groups from time to time, because students need to cultivate teamwork skills if they expect to eventually function cooperatively in the adult world as businesspersons, teachers, scientists, lawyers, engineers, etc.

Cooperative learning can be quite simple, with pairs or small groups encouraging each other's educational growth by asking intelligent questions about the assignment at hand in order to elicit intelligent answers. In this way, students can be nudged in a nonthreatening manner to think efficiently, creatively, and supportively—just like real team players in the adult world.

On the other hand, cooperative learning can be somewhat more complex, with certain team members being assigned specific duties such as completing certain portions of a research report by a due date. Some team members can even be responsible for organizational duties such as coordinating meetings and reminding other team members of deadlines.

Regardless of the degree of difficulty, a cooperative-learning assignment should be taught by you and completed by students in accordance with the following general guidelines:

- Help students understand that they need each other and should complete their assignment in an atmosphere of reassurance, support, and collegiality.
- Students should understand that team members rely on each other and therefore, each member absolutely must complete his share of the work, on time and in full.
- Students need to be present when the team reasonably requests it, whether to furnish new input or to assist in completing requisite tasks.
- Each team member should utilize his strengths and give freely of his unique, personal skills—whether academic, artistic, or managerial—for the good of the team.
- The team should engage in ongoing assessments of the consistency and quality of the work being produced, constantly keeping an eye on the end result.

Cooperative learning is a wonderful tool for teaching kids how to get along with each other and how to work interdependently with each other to produce high-quality work. Such skills will prove invaluable later in any professional work setting.

Bilingual Education

Bilingual education is a process where limited English speakers or non-English speakers are taught in English and in a home language, generally

Spanish in the United States, although many other languages such as Vietnamese, Chinese, Korean, French, Arabic, etc., are also utilized. The idea is to help immigrants and others make a smooth transition toward English fluency and comprehension. In transitional bilingual education, students are taught in their own language for a few years then moved into mainstream English-only classes. In multilanguage bilingual education, non-English speakers attend classes with English speakers in order to gain assistance and encouragement from peers.

The challenge with bilingual education is that often your English learners are temporarily pulled from your mainstream English classroom on a daily or weekly basis to attend a primary-language class. Such primary-language instruction is arguably not only beneficial but even requisite for English learners; and yet the academic instruction that your English learners consistently miss can eventually constitute a serious problem.

E-QUESTION

What is an LEP?
An LEP is a limited-English-proficient student. LEP is a term created by the United States Department of Education to identify students who are learning the English language. A somewhat more modern and widely accepted abbreviation is an ELL, or English-language learner.

If you don't want your English learners to suffer needlessly, you should consider developing a tutoring schedule where you can briefly work with your English learners after school to make certain they are not falling hopelessly behind. Also, make sure to provide your school's bilingual instructor with as many classroom assignments as she requests, along with a good supply of supplemental materials, if feasible. Finally, assign extra homework on a regular basis where necessary to make up for any deficit in your English learners' classroom-instruction time.

In the end, you'll find that most kids are incredibly eager to learn new languages. As educational psychologists Mildred R. Donoghue, Ruane B. Hill, Allen E. Koenig, and Henry Clay Lindgren have noted in their book *Educational Psychology in the Classroom: Educational Psychology Today*:

"It is a psychological fact that young children learn new languages easily and idiomatically." Ideally, you'll be pleased with the remarkable progress of your English learners as they move from limited proficiency to a high degree of English fluency.

Individualized Education Programs

An individualized education program, also called an individualized education plan or an IEP, is both a document and a personalized instructional program created for disabled students under the Individuals with Disabilities Education Act (IDEA), which was passed by the United States Congress in 1975. The IEP for each disabled student has as its goal the provision of a free and appropriate public education (FAPE), a right that was arbitrarily and unfairly denied to disabled students in the past. The IEP is designed to provide an educational environment that is as nonrestrictive and accessible for disabled students as possible.

Each disabled student is carefully evaluated and his IEP is then fitted to his specific educational requirements. The evaluation must take into account the student's current academic proficiency; desired annual goals; means of assessment of progress toward those goals; procedures, materials, and personnel to assist the child in meeting educational goals; necessary modifications to programs and methodologies; and any other relevant information such as behavioral histories, in some cases.

Your challenge regarding IEPs is to make absolutely certain you don't perpetuate the exclusionary and discriminatory practices of the past. Just as parents doubtless have high expectations for their disabled children, you also should fully expect that your disabled students will progress as far and as fast as they possibly can, despite any limitations imposed by their disabilities. You should follow the IEP's requirements and help your disabled students adequately prepare for their future.

That future may include college, as with many of your students. Educator and author Leanna Landsmann, in her nationally syndicated column *A-Plus Advice for Parents* (November 2007), quotes Dr. Arlyn Roffman of Lesley University, Cambridge, Massachusetts, on the subject of disabled kids making it to college: "Doors get closed when students with disabilities are underestimated and prematurely guided into taking non-college track courses. . . . Only 20 percent of students with learning disabilities enroll and many of those never graduate. We need to change these numbers."

Make sure you help your disabled kids advance as far as possible. Adhere each day to their IEPs, try to instill a sense of confidence, try to eliminate feelings of helplessness, and assist with goal setting. In this way, you'll encourage your disabled students to turn their focus away from their disabilities and focus on their magnificent individual abilities, which every child possesses in abundance.

CHAPTER 7

Do What the Pros Do

New teachers often have a great deal of formal college education, and even a wealth of social skills. But in general, only the veteran teachers have the experience that brands them in the eyes of students and colleagues as pros—teachers who know what to teach and exactly how to teach it. If you want to become a pro, you don't necessarily have to spend decades learning what the pros have learned; instead, just copy their secrets and their methodologies. This chapter will show you how.

Maintain Student Portfolios

You need to keep students' schoolwork neatly filed and readily accessible in your classroom for a number of extremely important reasons.

First, if you allow yourself to develop the habit of letting schoolwork languish in heaps around the classroom, you'll find it impossible to organize these materials in the future. Second, students love to retrieve their file folders and look at their papers. Third, many parents constantly ask to inspect their children's schoolwork to assess academic progress. Fourth, fellow teachers will appreciate having samples to refer to if any of your students are transferred into their classes. And fifth, teachers use the portfolios to assess academic progress as students matriculate to higher grades.

Creating student portfolios is simple. Ask your school to provide you with at least three plastic milk crates, the kind that hold hanging file folders. Or go to an office-supply store and buy the crates yourself, if necessary. Next, ask your school for three boxes of fifty hanging file folders, or purchase them yourself. Then, before the first day of instruction, get class roll sheets listing all of your students. Label one folder for each student, using plastic folder tabs, and alphabetize the folders; you'll be ready to file your students' schoolwork as soon as it's generated.

FACT

Student portfolios are mirrors of career portfolios, which are collections of documents that highlight educational and professional achievements. Career portfolios are used by savvy adults to attain professional positions, gain coveted promotions, or win much-deserved raises.

Certainly, filing papers in student portfolios is a time-consuming, never-ending task, but the rewards are well worth it, because when a parent shows up for a conference or open house demanding to know why Johnny received a D+ in Science, you can quickly pull out Johnny's portfolio and announce triumphantly, "Johnny will now sit with you and explain all of the grades you'll see in his portfolio." Meanwhile, you'll give every appearance of being a well-prepared, well-organized pro. By the same token, when the mother of Joey, an A student, comes to open house to check on Joey's progress, you can hand his portfolio to his mother and say cheerily, "Joey would love to show you his work." Once again, you will look like a super-competent, well-organized pro. Keep your students' portfolios current and organized, and your portfolios will keep you looking like a pro all year long and throughout your teaching career.

Identify Possible Problems and Special Needs

Pro teachers are attuned to their students' needs, dislikes, preferences, and personal problems. You don't have to adopt every student and take her home with you, but you do have to pay reasonable attention to each student's particular needs.

Pay particular attention to any physical problems that may manifest themselves. True, you're not a doctor, nurse, or any other type of trained medical professional, but you do have abundant common sense and you're in a unique position to observe your children every day. For instance, you're always keeping an eye out for kids who seem to be squinting when they look at the whiteboard—a possible indication of vision problems. Send any such students to the nurse with hall passes and explanatory notes briefly touching on your concerns. Ask the nurse if these children can be tested for visual acuity. Also, try to seat such students as close to the instructional whiteboard as possible.

Listen carefully to kids who complain about ongoing physical problems that they say interfere with their learning. For example, if you've moved a kid to the back row because he's constantly talking with his front-row buddies and he later complains he can't see the whiteboard clearly, you may have to modify your seating chart again and move him closer.

You're also constantly keeping an ear open for students who seem to have trouble hearing you properly. Possible indicators of hearing problems include students who tend to turn their heads to one side to hear instructions better from a favored ear and students who sit or stand near you yet do not seem to hear or respond when you repeatedly speak their names or give instructions. Such problems might result from simple inattentiveness or daydreaming, but if the problems persist, send any such students to the nurse for observation and possible testing. Again, you're not a medical professional, but if you have legitimate concerns get a professional to either allay your concerns or confirm them. Thereafter, the professional may either recommend treatment or consult further with other professionals.

And no matter how hard you work, never let yourself become so exhausted and out of breath that you can't pay attention to kids who appear to have trouble breathing properly. Respiratory distress may indicate the presence of asthma, a chronic disease that causes a child's lungs to tighten, making breathing extremely difficult. According to an article by Dr. C. Lilly in the April 2005 issue of the *Journal of Allergy and Clinical Immunology,* 25 percent of city-dwelling children worldwide exhibit asthma symptoms. Triggers for asthma may include lung infections, air pollution, stress, cigarette smoke, etc. Treatment may include the introduction of medication into the lungs using an inhaler, a portable spray device. If you suspect that a child may be suffering from asthma, talk to the parents and school nurse to get help for the child.

Problems of a different nature may affect certain children who, in your professional judgment, seem to be exhibiting noticeable, ongoing changes for the worse in their outlook, behavior, and academic performance. Find time to discreetly and courteously discuss your concerns with each one of these students, but be mindful of the hypersensitivity of many of your young charges. Calmly voice your concerns saying things like, "I'm worried that your grades in most subjects have gone down in the last two weeks. Are you having any problems?" If you can encourage a child to mention a problem, even in general terms, you might then be able to discuss the problem with the child's parents; and if you believe it's necessary to involve your school's counselor, nurse, or principal, then you can make the call.

Suspicions of Sexual Abuse

A specific crisis that a child may be facing is child sexual molestation, also called child sexual abuse, where she experiences unwished-for, degrading, and emotionally harmful sex talk, embracing, touching, kissing, or intercourse, forced upon her by an adult or another child.

When it comes to child sexual abuse, bear in mind that despite any self-serving claims an abuser may make, the American Psychiatric Association (APA) declared in a statement issued during its 1999 APA Council of Representatives convention that no child ever has the capacity to give legitimate, informed consent to any sexual activity with adults—period.

Child sexual abuse has been found to cause lifelong psychological problems in the vast majority of young victims who were studied for a 2000 report titled "Early Sexual Abuse and Lifetime Psychopathology: A Co-Twin Control Study," by Dr. Stephen H. Dinwiddie of the Chicago Medical School. The report went on to say that child sexual abuse can cause psychological problems as diverse as inability to concentrate, insomnia, depression, stress disorders, complex neuroses, and more. Physical problems can include infections, lacerations, sexually transmitted diseases, and much more. If you suspect child sexual abuse, you are ethically required—as well as legally required, in many states—to report your suspicions to your school nurse immediately.

Mood Disorders

Another problem affecting some kids is depression, a bleak state of mind characterized by listlessness, hopelessness, and deep sadness. Depression can arise in kids as a result of environmental factors such as pervasive community violence or even general dreary weather conditions. Also, problems at home such as intense marital difficulties between a child's parents can trigger the onset of the blues.

Even worse, the ongoing psychiatric disorder known as clinical depression debilitates and saddens some children to such a degree that they are no longer able to competently function in school, nor work productively with students or teachers.

Learning Disabilities

Some students may be experiencing learning disabilities, which are physiological problems that can interfere with a student's speech, hearing, or information-processing skills, and therefore his overall ability to learn. Learning disabilities may stem from malfunctions in a child's central nervous system, including the brain.

The learning disability occurring most frequently among young students is a reading disability, where children have difficulty decoding and comprehending grade-level-appropriate words and passages, especially at the level of correlating letters and letter combinations to the basic sounds that are represented.

Writing disabilities, also called dysgraphia by some doctors, are also quite common. Children with writing disorders may have difficulty with composition, grammar, spelling, and penmanship.

FACT

Learning disabilities are classified by official codes called the International Statistical Classification of Diseases and Related Health Problems, 10th Revision, issued by the United Nations' World Health Organization. For example, the reading disability developmental dyslexia is coded ICD-10 F81.0. Childhood autism is coded ICD-10 F84.0. Unspecified disorders are coded ICD-10 F89.

Students can also suffer from mathematics disabilities, also called dyscalculia, where students experience trouble understanding mathematical tasks such as memorization of math-facts tables, telling time, counting money, the use of place value, etc.

If you suspect that a student may be suffering from a learning disability, ask the school nurse what the procedure is for identifying and assisting such students. Either an on-site school psychologist or another trained professional will evaluate the student based on an assessment of classroom performance as well as special academic testing, intelligence testing, and assessments of skills and aptitude. Specific testing instruments include the Woodcock-Johnson Test and the Stanford Achievement Test.

If a learning disability is identified, recommended classroom modifications to help the student may include intensive instruction to master particular skills prior to accessing more difficult skills; scripted instruction; instant feedback to correct errors; specialized use of computers and word-processing programs; trained teacher's aides; and possible assignment to a special-education classroom for all or part of the instructional day.

The main thing is to help your students resolve some of their problems and special needs by referring students to other professionals who can help. In general, you actually see your students for more waking hours on a daily basis than their own parents. If parents come home at 7:00 P.M., 8:00 P.M., or 9:00 P.M.—as many do—you may be in a better position to spot incipient problems than parents are. Take an interest, ask questions where appropriate, and take action when needed. That's what pros do.

Take Online Classes for Professional Growth

Many states impose a legal requirement on teachers to pursue professional growth or the accumulation of additional information and training subsequent to graduation and employment by completing a certain number of hours in college classes, district seminars (also called in-services), teachers' association seminars, or private for-profit conferences.

Make certain that you work closely with your district to determine if a particular course, whether online or traditional, satisfies your state and district requirements for professional-growth hours. Never launch into a course without first finding out if it qualifies for your purposes.

Nowadays, professional growth can easily be completed over the Internet. This is done via online learning, also called electronic learning or e-learning. According to a 2007 article by The Sloan Consortium, an e-learning advocacy group, nearly 4 million students were studying via the Internet as of 2006, and almost 20 percent of all college students were taking Internet courses, with those numbers expected to increase. You can surf this educational wave into the future by signing up at most institutions of higher education to take online courses.

Numerous ingenious teaching techniques are utilized in e-learning courses. For instance, some courses are taught through the use of screencasts, where prerecorded computer data, including visual and audio elements, can be played on your computer just like a movie using a DVD or the information can be streamed to your computer over the Internet.

Also, text chat or synchronous conferencing technologies are also utilized to allow students and course instructors to confer with each other over the Internet. Using synchronous conferencing, you don't have to sit in a real-world classroom; instead, you log on at convenient times and dates and in convenient places—as long as you've got a computer and Internet access—and get busy querying the instructor and studying your coursework. The instructor posts her lectures and assignments and you and the other students complete the assignments and chat online with the instructor and with each other. E-learning helps you eliminate problems associated with cross-town commuting, campus security, and baby sitters so you can concentrate on fulfilling your professional-growth requirements instead.

Prepare Your Class for Substitute Teachers

Though you love being a teacher, sometimes you're going to have to be absent. Either you'll catch the latest flu bug or a pressing emergency will come up that you'll need to take care of or your car may break down. In such instances, you'll need to get a substitute teacher, commonly called a sub, for your class.

Before a sub ever sets foot in a pro-teacher's classroom, the pro has already done everything necessary to ensure that when he returns from his absence his students will have completed their assignments, behaved in an honorable manner toward one another, and treated the sub with courtesy and respect. If you wait until the last possible moment to prepare your students and your classroom for possible sub days, you could be in for some unpleasant surprises when you return from your absence: indignant notes from the sub, assignments left uncompleted, and a classroom that looks like a hurricane hit it.

One of the first things you must do is prepare a substitute-teacher's notebook, for use by any sub who may be assigned to your class. The sub notebook should be a sturdy three-ring binder, clearly labeled and easily accessible from your desk, containing the following materials:

1. Copy of your school's bell schedule, including lunch schedules
2. Updated copy of your classroom seating chart
3. Updated copy of your roll sheet
4. Copy of your daily instructional schedule
5. Copy of your classroom rules
6. List of your most helpful and responsible students
7. List of all classroom textbooks used and where they are shelved
8. Simple map of the school facility and grounds, including emergency-exit routes
9. List of the names, room numbers, and extensions of your closest fellow teachers
10. List of the names and extensions of your school's administrative personnel
11. List of the names, room numbers, and extensions of the nurse, counselor, etc.
12. At least three broad, flexible lesson plans that can be used throughout the year
13. Hole-punched spiral notebook so the sub may leave you informative notes

Don't keep your sub notebook under lock and key where no sub will ever be able to find it; on the other hand, don't just leave it lying around for any kid to peruse. Keep it with your teacher's-edition books and other materials on your desk, and train your students never to touch your materials without your permission, whether you're present or not.

Use every available opportunity to remind your students about proper classroom behavior when guests—and that includes subs—are present. For example, when student monitors come in delivering messages, remind the class that all guests must be honored. Then, model ultracourteous behavior by graciously thanking the monitor and asking his last name. Once you have the name, thank the monitor again, addressing him as "Mr. Tanaka" in exactly the same way you address your own students. Or, when your students report to you that a sub is teaching in a neighboring classroom, casually remark, "Well, who remembers how we should treat a sub when teachers are absent?" Work with your kids to constantly remind them that if you do take an absence day, the class is duty bound to behave properly, bringing honor to themselves and to you.

Don't be afraid to teach and model the important concept of honor for your children. Impress on your children that honor is defined as one's heartfelt love of what is good, just, and right. Remind your students that honor involves good manners, courteous behavior, and constantly treating others as you wish to be treated.

If you know beforehand that you'll be absent on a certain day, any photocopying and preplanning you can do will doubtless be much appreciated by the sub assigned to your class. Leave sufficient materials and specific lesson plans covering the topics your students are currently studying in addition to the all-purpose generic plans in your sub notebook.

However, if your absence day comes as a bit of a surprise to you, your sub notebook will save your life. The notebook's emergency lesson plans and invaluable classroom management information will help ensure that everything runs smoothly while you're gone.

Solutions When Textbooks Run Short

What can you do when textbooks are in such shamefully short supply? After all, a 2002 national teacher survey, conducted jointly by the National Education Association and the Association of American Publishers, found that 34 percent of teachers note a marked increase in scholastic failure when sufficient textbooks are not provided for every student.

The ideal solution is for schools, districts, counties, states, and the federal government to spend enough money so that every student has at least two copies of required textbooks—one copy assigned for classroom use and one copy assigned for home use. However, since this ideal seems unlikely to be achieved in many districts, you'll probably have to come up with your own solutions if you're short on textbooks.

E-QUESTION

When it comes to photocopying books, what is *fair use*?
Under United States copyright law, fair use is a legal doctrine whereby teachers may photocopy and use copyrighted materials such as textbooks for educational purposes without securing permissions from writers and publishers. But if you're in doubt, consult your principal beforehand.

The simple, immediate, low-tech solution is to have students double up on textbooks. Usually, you'll be given enough books to distribute one book to every two students for daily classroom use only, not for home use. It's not fair, and it's not a perfect solution, but kids are pretty adaptable, and they're often surprisingly willing to share textbooks when asked to do so.

Another rough-and-ready solution is to spend each morning photocopying sufficient copies of the textbook pages your kids will need for each day's lesson. Again, this is far from a perfect solution and you'll have to hustle to complete this task in addition to all your other work, but it's worth it if your kids can have their own materials.

Moreover, if you're willing to make a Herculean one-time-only effort, you can create your own classroom binders, one for each student, containing photocopies of all the textbook pages they'll need for the current academic year. The beauty of this solution is that these three-ring binders can be used repeatedly for several years before they show signs of significant wear and tear.

A somewhat more high-tech solution is to use a presentation program, such as Microsoft PowerPoint or Apple Keynote, to deliver information to all your students at once. Fortunately, your classroom is probably equipped with a desktop computer and a television—most modern classrooms are; therefore, use presentation software to create slideshow presentations on your computer, then display the work on your TV. True, if you want to display large blocks of textbook information you'll have to retype it using your presentation software, but this might just be the high-tech solution you need to resolve a potentially disastrous shortage of classroom textbooks.

Spending Your Own Money on Supplies

Teachers are an incredibly generous bunch. As teacher and educational researcher Mark Overmeyer succinctly observes in his book *When Writing Workshop Isn't Working*: "The generosity of teachers never ceases to amaze me." And veteran teacher Brian Crosby, in his book *The $100,000 Teacher*, notes how teachers' innate generosity often leads them to purchase supplies for their classrooms using their own hard-earned money: "In fact, it is estimated that the average teacher spends $400 annually from his own wallet, while many others spend upward of $1,000," says Overmeyer. Therefore, knowing how incredibly generous you and most other teachers are, the crucial question you need to ask yourself is, "Should I subsidize my school district by spending my own money on classroom supplies?"

FACT

During each academic year, states spend widely differing amounts of money per pupil. During the 1999–2000 year, for example, per-pupil expenditures ranged from $10,337 per pupil in New Jersey to $4,378 per pupil in the state of Utah. The top three states in terms of per-pupil expenditures were New Jersey at $10,337; New York at $9,846; and Connecticut at $9,753.

The short answer really should be, "Heck, no!" School districts throughout the United States collect revenues, measured in hundreds of billions of dollars annually. And while you certainly must take into account these districts' equally large expenditures, the fact remains that funding for public education is substantial. For example, according to a 2002 article, "U.S. Education Spending: 1999–2000" by statistician Frank Johnson of the U.S. Department of Education, nearly $400 billion in revenues were collected for the 1999–2000 academic year by U.S. school districts in grades kindergarten through twelfth. Revenues ranged from an astounding $45 billion for the state of California down to a merely breathtaking $750 million in the state of North Dakota.

With all this money floating around, surely some of it should be expended by districts to purchase the classroom supplies your students require. It should not be necessary for you to chip in your own funds to buy basic materials such as paper, pencils, books, etc.

And yet, you've got to face the reality that sooner or later, you'll find yourself purchasing materials out of pocket—it's either that or let your children's learning suffer. Why do school districts often seem to come up short? There's no single definitive answer. Miscalculations, excessive optimism concerning anticipated revenues, and even isolated incidents of reported fraud all enter into the equation; but the bottom line is that sometimes, if your kids need it, you'll have to buy it. Don't forget to take full advantage of the small stipends offered in many states that give you a bit of cash each year to spend on classroom supplies and equipment. Also, ask your accountant about using Form 2106, "Employee Business Expenses," to deduct certain job-related purchases from your federal income-tax return.

In the end, only you can decide if spending your own funds is ethical or necessary. Discuss the matter with other teachers, friends, and loved ones to come up with the answer that best suits your finances and your individual values.

How to Survive as a Floater

A floater is a teacher who doesn't have her own classroom, but moves from room to room in a school. Teachers sometimes wind up working as floaters because the number of students at a school necessitates a certain number of teachers, yet there just aren't enough classrooms in the school to accommodate every teacher.

If you're assigned as a floater, it's vital that you beg, borrow, or barter the largest wheeled book cart you can find. Without a cart, you won't float; you'll sink. The cart is for transporting your teaching materials and personal items—never let it out of your sight and never let any child or adult touch it or rummage through it or borrow it for any reason. You'll have to decide if you want to keep your wallet, purse, or keys on your cart or if you want to hand-carry the stuff around with you. If you choose the cart, keep your wallet, purse, or keys securely stowed under lock and key where no one can see or access them. At a minimum, your cart should also contain the following essential materials, kept constantly restocked:

- Three-ring binder containing important information on assignments, room numbers, roll sheets, etc.
- Two sturdy clipboards with ruled paper for general note taking, etc.
- One dozen black whiteboard markers and two whiteboard erasers
- Five reams (packages of 500 sheets) of grade-level-appropriate writing paper
- Twelve dozen sharpened pencils with eraser tips
- Sufficient textbooks for students to double up if enough individual copies aren't available
- Class set (about 32) of rulers
- Class set of scissors
- Class set of glue sticks
- Umbrella, raincoat, poncho, gloves, muffler, ear-muffs, knit cap, for inclement weather
- Sunscreen, sunglasses, broad-brimmed hat or baseball cap for hot, sunny weather
- Five bottles of water, plus nutritious packaged energy snacks

Of course, you could add many items to this list: a laptop computer with extension cord (keep it locked up!), stickers, calculators, an overhead projector—the possibilities are almost endless. In the end, just remember that many pro teachers have survived the floating experience until they received their own classrooms, and you can survive it, too—because you're a pro. Keep a cheerful outlook as you visit students and soldier on like the pro teacher you are.

CHAPTER 8

Master Teacher Information

Beyond the pro teacher, there is the Master Teacher—
a professional designation created by the American Board for Certification of Teacher Excellence
(ABCTE). The ABCTE is a nonprofit organization
established in 2001 dedicated to "increasing the supply of highly qualified teachers essential for achieving student success." To that end, the ABCTE has
developed the Master Teacher Program leading to a
special certification as a Master Teacher. You might
not attain this formal certification, but you can still
become a master teacher in your own right.

Grow Eyes in the Back of Your Head

Only the most skilled teacher can turn from his class, begin writing information on the instructional whiteboard, and then, as a student begins whispering and snickering, comment without ever turning around, "Suzette, you're supposed to be taking notes. Let's get to work, please." You remember such a teacher from your own schooldays, right? When you asked how she could have possibly known who was talking she replied, "I've got eyes in the back of my head." But how did she really do it? And how can you do the same thing?

It all boils down to your sense of hearing. If you can significantly improve your listening skills, you can amaze your students with your uncanny ability to identify yakkers even with your back turned. Then you can redirect the culprits to the lesson at hand so they can fully benefit from your instruction.

ALERT!

If you use the eyes-in-the-back-of-your-head technique and misidentify a talker, you risk some embarrassment. Initially, try rephrasing a remonstration as a simple question: "Emma, are you talking instead of taking notes?" If Emma protests her innocence, say, "Well, it certainly sounds like you. Please make sure you're working." Usually, the talking will cease at that point.

Here's a suggestion for improving your hearing. A psychiatrist, Dr. Alexander Stevens of the Oregon Health & Science University in Portland, Oregon, has reported in the October 3, 2007 issue of *The Journal of Neuroscience* that many blind people hear better than sighted people because they've trained themselves to rely heavily on aural cues. The blind co-opt an area of the brain called the *medial occipital,* normally used for seeing, and use it for significantly enhanced hearing instead. How this is done is not fully understood, but in his experiments Dr. Stevens learned that when sighted people want to concentrate on outside stimuli, they use their medial occipital to focus their eyes; but when the blind need to concentrate on outside stimuli, they use the same region of the brain to "focus" their ears.

Simply put, when your back is to the class for any reason, concentrate intently on sounds rather than sights. Over time—although you might not be able to substantially rewire your brain as many blind people have done— you may nonetheless greatly increase your listening skills. In this way, you may be able to pick out the individual voices of each of your students and correctly identify a kid even if your head is down or your back is turned. Your students may be sufficiently awed by a few demonstrations of your invisible second set of eyes to never dare throwing crumpled paper or starting to talk while your back is temporarily turned.

Start a Reading Rewards Program

A master teacher is often one of the first people to encourage her school to start a reading rewards program, such as the Accelerated Reader program developed by Renaissance Learning, Inc. or the Reading Counts program developed by the Scholastic Corporation or other such software systems developed by Broderbund, Davidson & Associates, Edmark, The Learning Company, and others. A reading rewards program can help students become avid readers by assigning a certain number of points to particular books; those points are then awarded to students who successfully read the books and pass computer quizzes keyed to the books. The points can ultimately count not only toward a student's grade in reading, but also toward the reward of incentives such as trophies, certificates, etc.

However, a possible drawback to a reading rewards program is its high initial cost. If you want such a program for your school, you'll need to work with your teaching colleagues to convince your administration to purchase it because the cost for the sophisticated software that runs the computer quizzes may be considered somewhat high.

If your school successfully obtains and installs the software, it can prove a boon to many kids who might otherwise turn out to be reluctant, unenthusiastic readers. You and your colleagues can begin the reading rewards program by getting printouts of all of the book titles included in the program you've purchased. Each teacher can arrange the printouts in a three-ring binder and label the binder so students can find and use it in the classroom.

Students can then make tentative decisions on the books they might like to read after referencing the binder. If you've got any of the titles in your own classroom library, create a check-out procedure for your kids and let them take the books home.

Of course, your classroom library may be sparse or nonexistent due to limited materials and funds, especially if you're a new teacher. That's why, regardless of the size of your classroom collection, you should try to schedule frequent trips to your school library—at least once a week if possible. Once in the library, your kids can fan out and look for books that your librarian has identified as belonging to your school's reading rewards program, usually by placing a color-coded sticker on the book's spine. The kids can use the library's three-ring binders to confirm that a particular title is part of the program. The library will generally have multiple binders that cross-reference the books not just by title, but also by author and subject.

Creating your classroom library might be easier than you think. Many public libraries sell used books, videos, CDs, and DVDs for a fraction of their original cost. Softcover books might sell for twenty-five cents, hardcovers for fifty cents, and videos, CDs, and DVDs for $1. Visit your local public library soon to load up on grade-appropriate books.

Time in the library can be spent checking-out books and, ultimately, for sustained silent reading. If students finish their program-related books in the library or have finished beforehand and they're ready to take a computer quiz, they can complete the quizzes in the library if one or more computer terminals are available.

To take a quiz, students generally use a previously issued username and password. The username and password are necessary so that once a student passes a quiz he is correctly credited with the points for that book. In this way, a record can be kept of all the points students are earning under the rewards program, and trophies or other incentives can be rewarded later, possibly in a ceremony at the end of each semester, trimester, or quarter.

The quizzes themselves are not too difficult, as long as the student has read diligently and with good comprehension. For example, for the 1922 novel *Babbitt* by Upton Sinclair, one of the screens displayed during the quiz might ask questions such as the following:

Which statement accurately reflects one of Babbitt's typical views?
A. He valued books more than money.
B. He resisted any form of corruption.
C. He cherished the gift of music.
D. He respected "bigness" in anything.

The student then clicks on the correct answer, which is letter C, then moves on to the next screen until finished. Afterward the student's score is displayed, at which point you might want to ask the student to make a hard-copy printout of his score, which you'll collect.

If you wish, keep a progress chart in your classroom, noting which students have read which books and how many points each student has earned to date. Use a simple graph or gold stars, etc., to indicate every student's progress.

E-QUESTION

Are rewards really required in a reading rewards program?
No. However, incentives such as trophies have become traditional in many schools, and kids seem to love them. Such incentives seem to motivate even reluctant readers to get with the program and read. You, your colleagues, and your principal will decide if rewards will constitute part of your program.

Reading rewards programs can be fun and can help students read like crazy and pass quizzes like crazy in hopes of getting a reward. Sure, motivation should be intrinsic as much as possible, but a little extrinsic motivation such as a trophy or certificate isn't such a bad deal, either. You and your colleagues will decide if a reading rewards program is right for your school.

Wield Humor Like a Professional Comedian

Master teachers know that a little well-chosen humor in the classroom can enliven just about any lesson and can create a wonderful bond of joy between you and your students. Humor also helps kids stay alert and attentive because humor chases away sleepiness and boredom. But if you've never worked as a stand-up comic, where and how do you begin to wield humor like a professional comedian?

You can use humor by using the various time-tested techniques of professional comedians. But there's something you must remember, first: Maintain your dignity. That may sound a bit silly in a discussion about humor, but it's a crucial point to keep in mind. Because, although humor can be useful and fun, you're a teacher, not a comic, and there's a certain line you must never cross. Use your common sense—no wild pratfalls, no profane or bigoted humor, no obscene gestures, no dangerous stunts, no words or actions that are inappropriate for children. There are certain things you'd never want your own children to hear from a teacher, not even as a joke; therefore, make certain you never say those things to your students.

Also, adhere to the number-one rule of professional comedians: Never snicker and guffaw at your own jokes. You'll quickly find that most students don't respect teachers who laugh at their own jokes. You'll also find that kids are a tough crowd. Adults may frequently titter politely at lame jokes because it's the courteous thing to do, but kids will remain stone silent when confronted with those same duds. If your joke isn't funny, your students won't laugh; if it's funny, they'll laugh freely and heartily. If they laugh, you can smile and laugh a bit also; otherwise, just move on and note in your mental joke book never to use that particular gag again.

If you use humor properly, you can bond with your students in a unique, heartfelt way. Include humor whenever it's appropriate and useful to do so, and whenever your educational goals will be advanced. Your kids may thank you for it and you just might become an amusing and effective teacher, unique among your teaching colleagues.

Use Acting Techniques to Dramatize Lessons

Teachers love to read stories and novels to their students. But do you remember how some of your teachers used to read in a droning monotone that never changed, never rose or fell, never changed in volume? Your teachers didn't have a clue about acting techniques or what makes lessons dramatic, powerful, and theatrical while reading or teaching. Their voices never changed, their eyes never widened, their arms never moved, except to turn the pages of a book or write something on the board.

Use some simple acting techniques to enliven your lessons. You know that whether your lessons are exciting or boring your students must pay attention and learn the material, and you can even tell your kids that, if necessary. But why be boring when you can be colorful? Why drone when you can speak up? Why lull your audience to sleep when you can challenge their comfortable assumptions?

The job of a teacher mirrors the job of an actor and vice versa. Teachers and actors must fire the individual and collective imagination of their audiences. Teachers and actors must place strong emphasis on ideas that are of great significance. And teachers and actors must make a permanent lasting impression on their listeners.

And yet, be careful to marshal your energy—it's got to last the entire instructional day and you don't have unlimited amounts of it. As William Shakespeare wrote in his immortal masterpiece *Hamlet,* "[F]or in the very whirlwind of your passion, you must acquire and beget a temperance that may give it smoothness." In other words, passion is good, but so are judgment, perspective, and balance. Don't bore your kids with somnolent mumbling, but don't scare them to death with unbridled screaming, either. Keep them interested and excited with well-chosen words and actions. This will make you a rare breed—an actor-teacher, something only master teachers can aspire to become.

One of the most important questions you need to ask yourself as an actor-teacher is, "Who is my character?" That is, who are you playing?

Ideally, most of the time your answer should be, "Myself." Play yourself; don't try to be someone you're not. If you're naturally soft spoken, don't try to shout to the rafters; but by the same token, surely you can speak up a bit and strengthen your voice so your kids can hear you in the last row. If you're naturally boisterous, revel in your power; yet also learn to temper your passion a bit so that a kid in your front row doesn't whisper, "Please, you're scaring me to death."

When you're reading to your kids you must assume the traits of the characters whose parts you're acting out. When you're reading the words of Ebenezer Scrooge in *A Christmas Carol* by Charles Dickens, remember that your heart was torn in two when you were a boy because your father never loved you and abandoned you to a miserable boarding school, year after year, Christmas after Christmas. If you're reading the part of young Jonas in *The Giver* by Lois Lowry, remember that you've been blatantly lied to since birth by a futuristic community that cares absolutely nothing about love or truth. If you're reading the words of Bottom the weaver in Shakespeare's *A Midsummer Night's Dream*, remember that even though you're poor and uneducated, you've got enough raw courage to try and win the acting competition sponsored by Duke Theseus of Athens—where, if you win, you'll gain not only money, but real respect.

If you want to become a master teacher, then don't be afraid to at least try to use some acting techniques in your lessons. As Professor Cathy Sargent Mester notes in her book *Acting Lessons for Teachers,* "It is the skilled use of one's tools that separates the master from the apprentice. . . . [A]ctors and teachers share many of the same tools. . . ." These tools are voice, gestures, and the love of your material. In your quest to become a master teacher, try to use the tools of an actor-teacher.

Motivate Tired, Bored, and Timid Students

One of the surest ways to motivate tired, bored, and timid students is to relate a particular lesson as directly as possible to the students' own lives. For example, if you're teaching a mathematics lesson on percentages, make a connection between that topic and the frequent 50 percent off types of sales at the local mall. Ask a student who seems to be falling over with sleepiness if he's ever gone to a video-game store during one of these sales and seen a $55 video game marked down 50 percent. If he has he'll answer, "Yes!" enthusiastically, and he'll offer a bit of explanation. If he hasn't, ask if he's ever seen a percentage-discount sale at any store he's visited; he'll probably think of one. Then ask him to come to the board and write as he gives some details of the sale and as you explain how to calculate a percentage discount.

Or, during a social studies lesson when you're discussing the broad topic of the current homelessness problem in the United States, list a typical family's monthly expenses on the whiteboard and get real input from your shy and sleepy students. Ask them to make an intelligent estimate of their family's monthly expenses for food, rent, clothing, electricity, water, trash pickup, natural gas, gasoline, car repairs, and so forth. Then watch their hands shoot up when you ask how much everyone spends at the mall each month during shopping trips and how much everyone's personal cell-phone bills are. Pointedly ask your sluggish kids what might happen to a family if a mom were to break her leg skiing and be unable to work for six months or what might happen if a dad got divorced and saw his annual income decrease by 60 percent. Woozy kids may perk up when required to confront such questions.

You should approach every day as a new opportunity to grow and achieve your goals. Above all, try to have fun. Teaching should not be drudgery, but should be full of exciting opportunities for sharing and growth.

Also, make sure your class discussions regarding academic issues you're currently studying are as fascinating as you can make them. For instance, if you're studying slavery in social studies, define slavery as being forced to work, sometimes brutally, without pay. Then digress for a few minutes and ask a half-asleep student how he feels about working in school without being paid for it. Ask a shrinking-violet student how she feels about such an arrangement. Ask, "Should students be paid for good grades?" Refer to

USA Today reporter Greg Toppo's January 28, 2008 article "Good Grades Pay Off—Literally," where he explains that kids in many school districts are being paid when they perform well on tests. See if your somnolent kids can sleep through *that* lively discussion.

Motivating bored kids is all about helping them wake up. Nothing wakes up kids better than animated, interesting class discussions and well-prepared lessons that bear directly on their lives. Try to make your lessons as relevant and as fascinating as you can.

Enliven Your Lessons with Cross-Curricular Techniques

Cross-curricular teaching, also called interdisciplinary teaching, refers to a master teacher's attempts to enliven lessons by lifting a particular concept from its narrow academic field and relating it to other academic fields. When you use cross-curricular teaching, you can turn on a light bulb in a kid's head because she just might envision the broad application and usefulness of a concept across more than one discipline.

Varying instruction is essential to effective teaching at all levels. Write lessons to appeal to different learning styles. This does not mean you must appeal to all learning styles every day. It simply means that by mixing things up a little bit, student attention will be less likely to waver.

You might, for instance, take advantage of the fact that many spelling books group words in a particular unit into themes—say, orchestral instruments or courtroom procedures or geographical features. And say that the theme of this week's words is the parts of an automobile's internal-combustion engine. You'll see words such as "combustion," "carburetor," "piston," and "cylinder." Latch on to that last spelling word, "cylinder." Ask the kids, "Remember when we studied geometric shapes in math? Well, look at our spelling word 'cylinder.' Who remembers from math what a cylinder is?"

Step back as hands shoot up enthusiastically. Accept the kids' remembered definitions (a tube, a soup can, a pipe, etc.) then explain, "Cylinders have real-world uses. The cylinders inside a car's engine hold the pistons, which move up and down to drive the car." Draw a rough picture on the whiteboard. Your only problem from that point will be to limit the discussion to a few minutes when so many students will want to regale you with tales of their prowess as auto mechanics.

Moreover, consider how your literature lessons on Shakespeare's *Romeo and Juliet* can be related to your social studies lessons on slavery. When Juliet's father vows to throw Juliet into the street if she defies his command to marry County Paris, connect Juliet's plight with the concept of slavery. In Juliet's time, children were legally the slaves of their fathers. Are children still legally the slaves of their parents? Your students may yell, *"No!"* Yet look at Section 7120(a) of the California Family Code—a law typical of many state statutes: "A minor may petition the superior court of the county in which the minor resides or is temporarily domiciled for a declaration of emancipation." *Emancipation* is a legal term meaning the freeing of slaves by a master or the freeing of a child by its parents, and renunciation of the right to take the child's earnings. In other words, children's current legal status does hearken back to the days of slavery. You've just related the concept of slavery across two fields, literature and social studies.

Your cross-curricular objective is to help kids make connections in their developing brains by relating concepts from diverse fields into integrated lessons. If you can help your students make countless mental connections across curricular areas, one of your charges just might make the connection that could someday cure cancer or colonize other planets. That's the kind of teaching that separates a master teacher from all others.

Jazz Up Your Lessons with Music

Teacher Lenn Millbower's 2000 book *Training with a Beat* talks about Howard, a kid who "comes alive" every time his teacher uses music to teach lessons—for example, the letters of the alphabet. "He taps his pencils, toes, hands, and anything else he can get a hold on," says his bemused teacher to Howard's astonished mother, who always thought that all Howard cared about was getting in trouble.

There's a bit of Howard in all of us. Human beings have been responding positively to music for countless millennia. Indeed, wind instruments have been excavated from the ruins of the Indus Valley Civilization, a culture that flourished in India 5,000 years ago. Moreover, the fact that composers such as the German genius Ludwig van Beethoven composed immortal symphonies while completely deaf suggests that music is perceived with the mind and soul as much as with the ear.

So why bar music from your classroom? Bring it in so that children will "come alive." Try this: When you're reading your students a particularly sad passage from *Matilda*, the novel by Welsh author Roald Dahl detailing the child abuse Matilda suffers from her cruel parents, use your CD player to play American composer Samuel Barber's haunting *Adagio for Strings*. You might get comments from your students for several days afterward about how memorable your performance was—and you'll owe their high praise not just to your acting prowess, but to the power of music. Or when you're studying the American Civil Rights Movement in social studies, play American rapper Coolio's 1997 masterpiece "C U When U Get There," lamenting the dashed aspirations of minority youth.

Also, when you study the American Civil War and you get to the part about the thousands of African-American soldiers who fought bravely for the Union Army, take a few minutes to play the memorable opening theme music for the movie *Glory,* a 1989 film about black Union soldiers. The theme, brilliantly sung by the Boys Choir of Harlem, seems hyper-charged with courage, dignity, and nobility—as were the soldiers of the 54th Regiment Massachusetts Volunteer Infantry, the heroes who gave their lives for freedom.

Finally, utilize music's calming effects when students take a particularly rigorous test, perhaps in long division in mathematics or on the parts of a cell in science. Nothing drives away anxiety like soothing music— perhaps German composer Johannes Brahms's *Wiegenlied: Guten Abend, Gute Nacht,* or *Brahms's Lullaby.* Master teachers use music to calm students and enhance academic performance.

CHAPTER 9

Using Technology

Remember when you used to drive to the public library and research topics for days and days? And now there's the Internet—billions of documents crammed with nearly all the information on Earth, instantly accessible from your classroom computer. As a teacher, you know that technological advancements are time savers, work savers, and sanity savers—except when they occasionally malfunction, of course. But when they work properly, they make your professional life a joy. Get comfortable with technology and it'll reward you over and over.

Using Computers

Personal desktop computers can be divided into two broad categories: Computers manufactured by Apple, Inc., which are commonly called Macs, and computers manufactured by most other computer companies, which are commonly called PCs. Most schools throughout the U.S. use Macs, because of Apple's wide-ranging program of donating computers to educational institutions.

One of the most fantastic uses for your classroom computer is to figure your students' grades, using lightning-swift grade-calculating software. Various brands of grade-calculating software include eGrader by Skye Publications, GradeLog Deluxe by GradeLog, Inc., Making the Grade by Jay Klein Productions, Engrade Online Gradebook by Engrade, Inc., Grade Machine by Misty City Software, and many others.

FACT

The world's first personal computer was almost certainly the LINC, or Laboratory Instrument Computer. The LINC was created in 1962 by computer scientist Wesley Clark and graduate student Charles Molnar at the Lincoln Laboratory, a part of the Massachusetts Institute of Technology. LINCs were later sold commercially by the Digital Equipment Corporation and Spear, Inc. for $50,000 each.

Once you use grade-calculating software you'll never want to go back to calculating grades by hand. Today, even the least powerful software is millions of light years ahead of the ancient paper grade books. Whether the software is on a CD for installation into your classroom computer or installed from your school's server (a powerful multitasking computer utilized by all the school's terminals or online, accessible over the web via your password), you must have it and you must use it.

Most grade-calculating software asks you to proceed through a setup protocol where you enter your name, your student's names, your preferred grading scales, and other information. Once the setup is complete, you can enter individual assignments and the kids' numeric or alphabetical grades. Then, click "Save Class Data" or a similar command, and pow!—the calculations that used to take long, boring hours are completed in a second. Make sure to do every ethical thing you can think of to get your principal or your department to shell out the money for grade-calculating software, or buy it yourself if absolutely necessary. It is as essential to your classroom management and to maintaining your status as a master teacher as your computer.

ALERT!

If you use an online grade book accessed directly over the web, understand that if your school's server crashes, as it may do occasionally, you won't be able to access your grade book or input new grades from your classroom computer. That's why you may prefer to use software that's installed directly into your computer from your school's server.

Another powerful use for your computer is for in-class word processing; that is, typing and printing professional-looking documents. The types of documents you can create are limited only by your imagination and energy and may include any of the following and more:

- Tests and quizzes
- Information sheets
- Classwork assignments and homework assignments
- Abridged or full-text short stories, poems, novel chapters, etc.
- Reading logs
- Various listings of students
- Various inventories of supplies and equipment
- Form letters for the class as well as personal letters for individual parents, teachers, etc.
- Classroom-management forms

Most word-processing programs even employ a graphical user interface so you can import graphic elements such as clip art, pictures from the Internet, pictures from your computer, etc., into your documents. Some of the most popular word-processing programs include Word by Microsoft, WordPerfect by Corel Corporation, and Google Docs, a free online service offered by Google that not only allows you to generate documents, but to revise them in collaboration with other online coworkers.

Surf the Internet to Instructional Excellence

Yet another magnificent use for your computer is surfing the Internet. The Internet constitutes a planet-spanning network of billions of computers, all sharing information. The Internet is arguably one of the greatest inventions in human history, permitting the near-instantaneous swapping of every conceivable kind of data from e-mail to real-time discussions to document retrieval and beyond. One of the most important components of the Internet is the world wide web (www), a network of linked documents created using HyperText Markup Language (HTML), many of which are easily accessible, colorful, dynamic, and fun. All this global treasure is yours, and for the most part it's free.

If you're planning on e-mailing any professional articles to educational magazines or journals for possible publication, find out beforehand exactly which word-processing program they use. Otherwise, you might e-mail them something they can't easily open, prompting a likely rejection.

Suppose that your current literature unit is world mythology and you're reading the short story "Phaëthon, Son of Apollo" as retold by author Olivia E. Coolidge. You want to create a list of the names and attributes of some of the ancient Greek gods, but darned if you can remember who the heck Hermes or Hades were. You could thumb through several reference books if you happen to have them handy and have the time. Or, you could go immediately to the Internet and procure the information in minutes.

Use E-mail to Communicate with Virtually Everyone

Electronic mail, or e-mail as it is commonly called, is a system that allows you to send and receive near-instantaneous "letters" using your computer. E-mail is the opposite of so-called snail mail, the standard postal delivery of paper-and-envelope mail—still a crucial service yet not preferable when a vital communication needs to be sent and responded to within a few minutes. E-mail can be sent over the Internet or it can be sent to colleagues via an intranet, a local network set up just to handle e-mail traffic within your school or district.

FACT

Many people don't realize that e-mail—perhaps the single most-popular service offered over the Internet—actually dates from 1961, well before the Internet as you know it came online. At that time, scientists at the Massachusetts Institute of Technology (MIT) created the Compatible Time-Sharing System (CTSS), allowing scientists worldwide to swap files and information.

Use e-mail to communicate with fellow teachers and administrators to complete any number of professional tasks, including many of the following:

- Plan lessons across the curriculum with teachers in other subject departments.
- Inquire about the dates, times, locations, and content of upcoming seminars and workshops.
- Ask about the dates, times, and locations of employee get-togethers.
- Compare notes on how well particular students are doing academically in various classes.
- Compare notes on how well particular students are doing behaviorally in various classes.
- Provide a heads-up to administrators regarding incipient problems with certain students.

- Do initial and ongoing planning with colleagues regarding concerts and school programs.
- Do initial and ongoing planning with colleagues regarding off-campus field trips.
- Ask colleagues for assistance with difficult disciplinary issues.
- Ask for assistance and information during emergencies if phones appear to be nonfunctional.

Also, if you are willing, you can include your e-mail address in your introductory letter so parents can contact you with questions and concerns. Your workplace e-mail address is issued to you by your district; memorize it, or keep it written down someplace handy. Regarding your password—you can't access your e-mail without it—memorize that, too, but also keep it written down where no one can find it. Briefly check your e-mail each morning or each afternoon and try to adhere to a policy of answering each e-mail the same day you receive it. True, this is sometimes difficult, but make same-day replies one of your professional goals.

Learn to Love Answering Those Voicemails

Your school may have voicemail, a complex answering-machine system that uses a series of recordings to shunt telephone messages to your classroom. You access the system with a numeric or alphanumeric code, given to you by your school (generally changed once yearly).

As with e-mail, answer voicemails the same day they're received. Most voicemails are from parents, concerning grades, homework, discipline, etc. If you ignore these voicemails, parents will tend to get angry. At that point, they may approach the principal, believing that they gave you a chance to discuss their concerns but you never responded. Make certain to respond.

You can also use your school's voicemail system yourself to leave phone messages for other teachers, administrators, and secretaries if these personnel aren't available when you need them; but follow up with a personal visit if you don't get a quick reply. Get up and walk across campus because, even in this age of instant electronic communication, it's always nice to have some face-to-face communication with folks from time to time.

Theatrical Effects with the Overhead Projector

The overhead projector, also called an overhead, has been around since at least 1945, when it was initially utilized by the military for briefing purposes. Since then, generations of children have had to sit stupefied while educators droned on about difficult-to-read overhead transparencies, handwritten in cryptic chicken scratchings resembling Egyptian hieroglyphics. C'mon—drag that overhead into the twenty-first century; your kids should be loving the overhead, not dreading it.

E-QUESTION

Must I use the overhead projector in my class? Can't I just skip it?
Well, the short answer is yes; however, the somewhat longer answer is, "Yes, you could skip it, but then you'd be wasting an opportunity to bring a bit of excitement to your lessons; a bit of light, color, and variety. Use your overhead!"

Also, give your overhead a name—The Morning Theater or The Magic Theater—and use the name with the kids whenever you roll out the overhead cart. Then, when it's time to start the show, use a bit of drama. Tell the kids, "It's time to activate The Magic Theater!" You'll almost certainly hear oohs and ahhs of approval. Continue the drama by asking for volunteers to turn off the lights and flip the overhead on.

Now's the moment of truth: Will you display boring transparencies or exciting ones? The answer's obvious, but you may be wondering where you're going to get these fabulous transparencies, because you really don't have time to create five or six individual masterpieces.

Well, have you forgotten those thick packets of beautiful full-color transparencies that accompany most textbook sets? Social studies sets will include dozens of transparencies, featuring photographs and illustrations suitable not just for teaching historical concepts, but for teaching concepts in art, music, literature, and other subjects as well. Far from being bored, kids will probably love these overheads because they're genuinely interesting.

Even the preprinted transparencies that only contain text should be quite interesting to your kids because they're clear and easy to read—not like the scribblings some of your teachers used to create when you were a kid.

FACT

Typically, the clear plastic sheets used to create overhead transparencies are made of a plastic called cellulose acetate, which is actually manufactured from wood pulp. Although this may sound like a very green product—plastic from trees—don't forget the huge quantities of acetone and sulfuric acid needed to manufacture this type of plastic.

Furthermore, if you want to create your own gorgeous color transparencies, it's not that difficult. For example, if you're studying a unit on reptiles in science, find some excellent photographs of snakes, crocodiles, iguanas, etc., from back issues of *National Geographic* magazine or an appropriate book.

Next, use one of your school's scanners to scan your pictures. Then, stick a blank transparency into your printer and print! But be careful; if you use the ordinary glossy transparencies that your school provides, the ink will slide right off. Instead, use the transparencies that are specially designed for inkjet printers. Ask the school to buy them or buy them yourself, if necessary.

You can also use powerful yet inexpensive programs such as Print Shop by Brøderbund Software to mix and match photographs, illustrations, text, and other elements and effects to create your very own custom-designed transparencies. Don't worry that the kids will laugh at your efforts—that's exactly what you want! The kids will come to adore your amateurish creations, which is great, as long as your masterpieces are actually teaching the kids something valuable.

And did you realize that numerous products exist to make The Magic Theatre even more magical? Your school can purchase colorful, oversized, see-through calculators that work just like other calculators, except that they're placed on the overhead screen and the operations can be clearly displayed for the class. Or get some see-through word tiles that you can use to teach phonics, spelling, and syntax. Or use all kinds of mathematic manipulatives such as geometric shapes, tangrams, simulated paper money and coins, and clocks.

Here's another idea: Find opportunities to use music in conjunction with your overhead presentations. If you're studying a unit on square dancing for physical education and you want to show transparencies of the various figures the kids will be learning, why not accompany these pictures with appropriate music. Between the music and the transparencies, your kids will find it difficult to accuse you of being boring!

PowerPoint

You'll recall the discussion of Microsoft's PowerPoint presentation software in an earlier chapter. Now, here's a brief tutorial that will help you begin using PowerPoint properly and efficiently.

1. Open PowerPoint and find the standard toolbar at the top edge of the window.
2. The formatting toolbar icons just below the standard toolbar are used for setting up fonts and textual material. You can *italicize* words, underline them, etc.
3. The drawing toolbar icons at the bottom edge of the window help you create geometric shapes, import art from your computer and the Internet, add text elements, etc.
4. The common tasks toolbar just hovers wherever it wants and helps you create new slide presentations, reconfigure existing slide presentations, or use substitute new themes.

5. To create a slide show for PowerPoint 2000 and beyond, find the Elements Gallery at the top and click on "Slide Themes." Then, choose an overall visual theme.
6. Still using the Elements Gallery, click "Slide Layouts." Then, click "Insert New Slide" to begin creating your slides.
7. Using the Elements Gallery once more, click "Title and Content" to assign a title to your slide show and create its content.
8. Choose "Click to Add Title" and follow the prompt to write your title.
9. Choose "Click to Add Text" and follow the prompts to create your slides.

Of course, the program has many other powerful features, but the information above is pretty much all you need to get started creating professional-looking slide presentations for your kids. Become familiar with PowerPoint or some other equally useful presentation software, because your principal and your teaching colleagues will expect you to use it and will be frustrated and disappointed if you don't.

VCRs, DVD Players, and CD Players

Although the imminent demise of the VCR was widely predicted with the advent of DVD players, VCRs have managed to hang on and still have their uses in the classroom, for some excellent reasons. First, school libraries tend to have numerous VCRs available for checkout when you need them, and few or no DVD players because of budget constraints and just generally lagging behind the times. Second, VCRs can record programs from TV stations for later use in the classroom. So, for example, when the National Geographic Channel airs a program on the Namib Desert in Africa and you're currently studying a unit on deserts in science, you can record the entire program (minus commercials) and show it to your class the next day. Third, when you want to show educational videos or edifying movies to your class, school libraries tend to have tons of excellent videos and few or no DVDs.

Use CD players to play appropriate music in accompaniment to overhead-projector presentations or PowerPoint slide presentations. You can also use CD players to play period music that serves to bring a historical period alive you and your class are studying in social studies. Finally, use your CD player to play educational talking books, which are prerecorded novels and nonfiction books read by professional actors or the authors themselves.

To reiterate, none of these technologies are absolutely required in your classroom, but your students, parents, administrators, and teaching colleagues will expect you to utilize them. Don't disappoint them and don't disappoint yourself—embrace technology.

CHAPTER 10

Powerful Time Savers

Pro teachers are always interested in discovering new ways to save time and energy, both of which are constantly in short supply during the instructional workday. As society's demands on the professional performance of teachers continues to increase, your ingenuity must keep pace. Use the powerful time-saving tips and strategies described in this chapter so you and your students can get the maximum amount of work done within the time you're given.

Advanced Forms That Pros Use

You'll recall the basic forms discussed in detail in Chapter 2—forms you should strongly consider using to maintain proper written documentation of your professional actions and communications. For example, you'll recall the discussion of memorandum forms, those small message notes you create on your computer to use in sending written messages to colleagues, administrators, parents, and others. You'll also recall agendas, hall passes, detention slips, and suspensions forms. But there are additional forms you can create and use to save even more time. However, before you use any of the templates in this chapter, remember that whenever you recognize and identify a professional need—one that you feel can be handled through the use of a well-designed form—immediately type that form and print sufficient copies. You'll save tons of time and work for years to come.

In the area of day-to-day classroom maintenance, one of the most useful forms you can create is a supply order form. This is a handy checklist you use to reorder essential classroom supplies, eliminating the need to waste time sending e-mails every time you need a box of staples. If your school doesn't provide you with such a form, create it on your computer. Once the form is created, use it—don't wait until the last second to reorder vital supplies. Instead, keep track of everything and send in your requisitions early, because your school may take weeks to process a request. In fact, if you haven't received your supplies in two weeks, use a memo form to send a gentle reminder to the office. Be courteously persistent; don't let the office forget about you, because you need those supplies.

The supply order form should feature your name, room number, and a short note politely requesting supplies—always be ultra courteous when begging for stuff from the front office. Also type in a blank line for the date of your order, followed by an alphabetized four-column list of the supplies your school stocks—two sets of columns showing items and quantities requested. While you might not know exactly what your particular school carries, the following list should reasonably cover most schools:

SUPPLY ORDER FORM FOR MRS. JANE DOE, ROOM 4, DATED: ___

ITEM	QUANTITY	ITEM	QUANTITY
Band-Aids		Pens, Blue	
CDs, Blank		Pens, Green	
Chalk		Pens, Red	
Chalkboard Erasers		Popsicle Sticks, Art	
Clipboards		Push Pins	
Crayons		Rubber Bands	
Erasers, Pink or White		Rubber Cement	
Glue, White		Ruled Notebook Paper	
Glue Sticks		Rulers	
Graph Paper		Safety Pins	
Highlighters		Scissors, Student	
Index Cards		Scissors, Teacher	
Manila Folders, Legal		Staple Removers	
Manila Folders, Letter		Staplers	
Markers, Fine Point		Staples	
Markers, Overhead Projector		Tacks	
Markers, Permanent		Tape, "Scotch"	
Markers, Whiteboard		Tape Dispensers	
Paper Clips, Large		Tape, Masking	
Paper Clips, Small		Whiteboard Cleaner	
Pencils		Whiteout	
Pencil Sharpeners		Yard Sticks	
Pendaflex-Type Folders		Yarn	
Pens, Black		Other	

Of course, this list is generic. You can fine tune your supply order form, removing items that your school doesn't stock and adding other useful items your school readily provides. Once your form is more or less perfect, consider offering it to your principal for use by the front office and the entire school. Such individual initiative can often earn you valuable accolades from the administration.

ALERT!

Don't order too many supplies at once. Districts are under public pressure not to waste taxpayer funds, and one way administrators control costs is to carefully allocate scarce supplies. In fact, most schools keep their supplies in locked storerooms.

As with your memorandum forms, be sure to make a copy of your supply order form for your records in the event your form gets misplaced. And even when such delays arise, using your supply order form is much quicker and easier than writing requests by hand. Just a few strokes and your requisition is ready to be filled. With luck, you'll find that you work in one of those wonderful schools where your order is filled within a few hours. Another excellent form you can create is the maintenance-work request form. The maintenance-work request form is a check-off sheet that allows you, with a few checkmarks, to inform custodial personnel that your room requires cleaning or a restocking of supplies or specific repairs. Your form should feature your name and room number as well as specifically requested work, as follows:

MAINTENANCE-WORK REQUEST FORM
Mrs. Jane Doe, Room 4
Date of Work-Request: _____

Air conditioning/heating system requires repair.
Notes: _____

_____

Bulletin Boards require repair/replacement.
Notes: _____

_____

Carpets/floors require vacuuming/cleaning.
Notes: _____

_____

Cleaning /chemicals/supplies require restocking.
Notes: _____
_____

Desks require cleaning.
Notes: _____
_____

Desks require repair/replacement.
Notes: _____
_____

Electrical outlets/wiring require repair/replacement.
Notes: _____
_____

Equipment requires repair/replacement.
Notes: _____
_____

Furniture requires repair/replacement.
Notes: _____
_____

Furniture requires repositioning.
Notes: _____
_____

Lightbulbs/light-tubes require replacement.
Notes: _____
_____

Light fixtures require repair/replacement.
Notes: _____
_____

Paper towels require restocking.
Notes: _____
_____

Sinks require cleaning.
Notes: _____
_____

Sinks require repair/replacement.
Notes: _____
_____

Television requires repair/replacement.
Notes: _____
_____

Tissues require restocking.
Notes: _____
_____

Toilet paper requires restocking.
Notes: _____
_____

Toilets require cleaning.
Notes: _____
_____

Toilets require repair/replacement.
Notes: _____
_____

Walls require cleaning/repairs.
Notes: _____
_____

Whiteboards/chalkboards require cleaning/repair.
Notes: _____
_____

Windows require repair/replacement.
Notes: _____
_____

Other: _____
Notes: _____
_____

As always, make a copy for your files. File the copy and have a monitor take the original to the custodian or the main office. Follow up courteously in a week or so if your maintenance-work request hasn't been addressed.

In the area of classroom discipline, one form you'll want to create immediately is a master listing of all the names, room numbers, and telephone extensions of your colleagues. You'll use this list for sending students to classrooms to deliver messages, complete assignments, run errands, and serve classroom suspensions; and you'll need phone numbers to call colleagues when necessary. Many schools provide such a list at the beginning of the year, but many don't. If you don't receive such a list, create it before the students arrive. Once you gather all this information from the office and double check it, type your master list:

MASTER LIST OF TEACHERS

TEACHER	ROOM #	EXT.	TEACHER	ROOM #	EXT.
Abel	1	001	Nelson	14	014
Bean	2	002	Oyemi	15	015
Clark	3	003	Paola	16	016
Doe	4	004	Quang	17	017
Egan	5	005	Rosenberg	18	018
Frazier	6	006	Strong	19	019
Gomez	7	007	Trent	20	020
Hung	8	008	Uvalde	21	021
Inge	9	009	Volta	22	022
Jimenez	10	010	Wheeler	23	023
Kelly	11	011	Xavier	24	024
Logan	12	012	Young	25	025
Matsuma	13	013	Zane	26	026

Again, consider offering this form to your principal. You're hoping to impress your principal with your team spirit by typing this information so your colleagues don't have to. You're actually doing the job to serve your own interests, and it's your choice whether you choose to share the products of your labor. Keep multiple copies of this master list handy on your desk and update it whenever necessary—when teachers leave the school, when there are new hires, room changes, etc. That way, when you need to contact a teaching colleague in a hurry, you don't have to ask your kids, "Does anyone happen to remember Mrs. Zane's extension?" Such questions are time wasters; instead, glance at your master list and dial Mrs. Zane in an instant.

Another form you'll need is a Back-to-School-Night Parents' Sign-In Sheet. Back-to-School Night is an event held on an evening near the start of the school year, where parents meet and confer with their children's teachers, view classrooms, and examine schoolwork. The next day, your principal will probably ask for a sign-in sheet of all parents who visited your room, so if your school doesn't provide such a sheet, create one. Then you don't have to waste time writing a list from memory, asking yourself, "Well, who the heck came last night, anyway?" Your list can be simple, using only two columns and fifty blank lines, as partially shown below:

BACK-TO-SCHOOL-NIGHT PARENTS' SIGN-IN SHEET

PARENT'S NAME, PRINTED		CHILD'S NAME

Another form that will help you manage your classroom smoothly is a tardiness letter, to mail to the parents of students who are chronically tardy. You don't want students continually arriving late because they miss instruction and disrupt everyone else's education. Usually, a short warning note written in a student's agenda is sufficient to serve as notification of a first tardy and end the problem. But for the second tardy onward, you can't continue using instructional time writing additional notes—especially since the first note clearly hasn't done much good. Follow up with a phone call if you like, but make sure to send out your tardiness letter as well, to serve as official written notification that a student will earn a poor grade in citizenship if the situation doesn't immediately improve. If your school hasn't supplied you with a letter-form, write a tardiness letter based on the template below:

Mrs. Jane Doe
Grade Six Teacher
ABC School
123 South Main Street
Los Angeles, CA 90012
(213) 555-5555

Today's Date:
Child's Name:
Date of Child's Tardiness:

Dear Parents:

Thank you for your time, and I hope all is well. At ABC School, we value our working relationship with you, one based on communication, information, and mutual cooperation. Therefore, in order to keep you informed as to your child's behavioral progress, I must send this letter to you, stating that your child has____tardies in my class for the current grading period.

All of the professional educators and administrators at ABC School believe that academic success depends on consistent, punctual classroom attendance. Please discuss with your child the importance of coming to school on time to gain the maximum benefit from my daily instruction.

Thank you again for your time and for your immediate assistance. Please call me at (213) 555-5555 if you would like to speak to me further regarding this important matter. Thanks again.

Sincerely,
Your Name Here

Sign your letter, because a letter without a signature seems unprofessional and insincere. As always, make two copies of the letter. File one copy in a student's dossier just in case her parents later claim they were never informed about their child's tardiness. Then, address an envelope to the student's parents and place the envelope in a larger manila envelope. Use a memorandum form to ask the office personnel to mail the enclosed letter. File a copy of your memo—now you have proof that the letter was delivered to the office. Such proof could become important if you're challenged about notification of tardiness.

Teamwork means that you cultivate the essential skills necessary for getting along reasonably well with your coworkers and for accomplishing cross-curricular lesson planning and other cooperative activities and projects. To be a good team player, you should learn to communicate good ideas, ask relevant questions, and listen empathetically to others.

In the area of classroom discipline, a time-saving form you can create is a classroom suspension form. Use the classroom suspension form when sending a student out due to nonstop goofing and disruption. Use it as a final resort, after you've tried to reason, persuade, and warn; reason with the kid and warn him that he'll have to leave the room if he keeps disrupting your lessons. If you are forced to make a choice between one student losing instructional minutes and the entire class losing those minutes, it's your professional responsibility to side with the class.

Your classroom suspension form is written like your memorandum form and accomplishes three purposes. First, it saves immeasurable amounts of time when you send your student out, allowing you to get your lesson back on track. Second, it lets your buddy teacher know why you're sending the student. And third, it provides the student with an essay assignment to complete while he's being banished.

CLASSROOM SUSPENSION FORM

Jane Doe [*Sign your initials*]
Grade-Six Teacher, Room 4

To: _____ Room: _____
Student Name: _____   Date: _____

Dear Professional Colleague:

Thank you for your time. Please allow this disruptive student to work in an isolated area of your room for fifteen minutes, or longer if the writing assignment below is not timely completed. If you have any problems whatsoever, please return the student to me and I will instantly take further action. Thank you again for your help.

To the Student:

You must write an essay of at least 250 words on the following: Why it is important for you—for your present academic success and for your future success—to listen quietly, follow all classroom rules, and behave appropriately and maturely during lessons and work periods.

These are only a few of the classroom-management forms you can dream up. The more time-saving forms you can create and use the more precious instructional time you'll save, and that's good for you—and perhaps even more importantly, good for your students.

Delegate Responsibility Whenever Appropriate

American educators Ellen Booth Church and Karen Miller remind us of a fundamental educational principle in their book *Learning Through Play: A Practical Guide for Teaching Young Children*: "Autonomy is an important developmental milestone. . . . Don't do for children what they can do for themselves."

You see, as much as parents and teachers hate to admit it, children must eventually grow up and take control of their own lives. When you look at the small faces of your students, it's hard to recall that one day they'll be on their own, attending college, establishing careers, getting married, raising families. Therefore, as their teacher, you've got to teach a bit of self-reliance and autonomy in addition to academic content and behavioral rules. One way to foster self-reliance is to let kids help in class as often as you think it's safe and beneficial for them to do so. Besides, kids of all ages are so eager to help out in class it's a bit cruel to deny them the opportunity to help you.

You can teach autonomy and democracy at the same time by holding classroom elections for specific officers who can perform daily tasks. You'll help students grow in maturity while simultaneously gaining valuable classroom assistance—and any help you can get will always save you time.

Never allow any student to enter any information in your computer. Data entry is your professional responsibility, and mustn't be delegated to children. When entering absence information, academic grades, behavioral grades, etc., such information is confidential, as well as accessible only through the use of passwords, and is to be entered by you alone.

Classroom elections are fun and easy to do. Begin by having your students group their chairs near the whiteboard. Then, write down the available classroom positions along with their corresponding duties. Here are some suggested class officers and duties:

- **President:** Takes daily attendance, then gives the information to the vice president to double check. The president also orally administers the weekly spelling test.
- **Vice President:** Double checks the daily attendance gathered by the president and gives it to you to enter into your computer after you give it a final inspection.

- **Paper Monster:** Kids enjoy substituting the word "Monster" for "Monitor." The Paper Monster staples, folds, and distributes all papers for the duration of her term of office.
- **Door Monster:** Opens the classroom door whenever there is a visitor or a student re-enters. However, instruct him to raise his hand and get your permission before opening the door.
- **Supply Monster:** Stocks writing paper, tissues, erasers, etc., as well as a classroom set of pencils, which she sharpens each morning. She can also stock supplies for you.
- **Office Monster:** Delivers documents to the office and retrieves supplies from the office.

The list of monitors, along with the tasks they can accomplish for you, is limited only by your imagination and classroom-management needs.

Next, select two trustworthy monitors to run the election. Announce that one monitor will call on students to offer nominations. Each nomination must be seconded or agreed to by at least one other student. Then, explain that the other monitor will write three nominated and seconded names next to each office.

E-QUESTION

Is it okay to interrupt teachers' instructional time with phone calls?
Yes, if the calls are necessary at the time. If you call to ask if your colleague watched *American Idol* last night on TV, that's unconscionable. But if you're asking if a student can come over to discuss important matters, that's what telephones are for.

After nominations close, it's voting time. One monitor instructs the students to put their heads down while admonishing, "No peeking!" She announces each nominee for each office, asking for a show of hands for each, while the other monitor tallies results on the whiteboard. When you and the two monitors agree, the tally marks are erased (to spare the losers embarrassment) and the winners announced. Once officers are elected, you'll marvel at how eagerly many officers perform their daily duties, often without being reminded. Hold new elections each month to give as many kids as possible the honor of serving their classmates.

For example, when you administer your weekly spelling test, let your president do it. He'll stand beside you and loudly call the words while you sit and grade papers. Keep half your brain on what your students are doing and half on your grading. After the test ends and your students have traded-and-graded, let the vice president administer the test to the president. All tests are now finished and graded, and you've also graded papers or completed office paperwork at the same time. Other tasks that students can accomplish: Stapling schoolwork to bulletin boards, mixing paints, cleaning desks, arranging books in the classroom library, operating the VCR or DVD player, turning on lights, filing schoolwork in portfolios—the list goes on. Delegate whenever appropriate so that you and your students can concentrate on your main goal—becoming responsible, highly educated citizens.

Harness the Power of Parents, Volunteers, Student Aides, and Teacher's Aides

If you're not harnessing the power of volunteers, you're denying parents and others the joy they experience when they help others. As Dr. Alan Loy McGinnis, family therapist, says in his book *Bringing Out the Best in People*: "There is simply no substitute for the rewards of helping other people. . . ." Surely, it's time to let volunteers into your classroom.

Use caution before allowing parent volunteers to enter your classroom. Meet with these adults beforehand and briefly interview them to see if they possess the knowledge and character to work responsibly with children. If they seem at all questionable, thank them profusely and formulate an excuse for why you won't be able to use them this year.

Send a cheery letter home with all your students at the beginning of the school year, asking parents to please consider donating their time, energy, and intelligence to helping your students. Parents can generally photocopy papers, cut construction paper and oak tag, grade work papers, create bulletin boards, work with small reading groups or math groups per your instructions, and do a million other important and time-saving (for you) tasks.

If your school sends you a student aide, utilize him in the same ways you would utilize a parent volunteer—except, perhaps, for small-group instruction, which is often better left to your adult volunteers. Student aides can also file work papers in student dossiers, grade consumable workbooks using your answer key, glue and staple papers, deliver documents to the office, and so forth.

Teacher's aides aren't strictly volunteers because they're paid by the district; yet the spirit of volunteerism is alive in them, too. Their wages are quite low and there are usually other jobs they could be doing to make more money; they simply enjoy helping kids. Use these aides for secretarial duties, small-group instruction, and most importantly, individual student tutoring.

CHAPTER 11

Discipline: End Problems Before They Begin

In your classroom-management toolkit, the one tool that is more important than any other is discipline. Discipline is the indispensable means by which you educate your magnificent students. By utilizing proper discipline, you can inspire students to soar to new academic heights. By failing to utilize proper discipline, you won't even be able to inspire yourself to get out of bed each morning. Use the strategies in this chapter to end disciplinary problems before they begin.

Establish Your Rules Immediately

You've already learned that you must create and photocopy a list of your classroom rules before your students arrive for the first day of instruction. Then, on that all-important day, you must distribute the rules to every student, with instructions to return the tear-off section, signed and dated, by a particular due date.

But before you move on to academic instruction, take sufficient time to discuss your classroom rules with your students. Don't worry about the kids being bored—they understand that they'll have to sit through "the rule stuff" sometime during the first day; and they'll probably be a bit confused if you fail to discuss what you expect of them regarding behavior and work habits.

On the other hand, don't drone on by reading verbatim from your list. You might be tempted to read your rules word for word because otherwise, you strongly suspect many of the kids will never read the stuff. That may be true, but your rules are so crucial to the smooth functioning of your class that you can't take chances that the kids will zone out. Instead, paraphrase in a clear, conversational manner. Convey the spirit of each regulation by explaining the rationale behind each one. After all, when your kids bring back their signed tear-offs, they're supposed to be affirming that they and their parents have read the material and will abide by it.

The English word "discipline" is actually related to three original Latin words: *disclere,* a verb meaning "to acquire understanding"; *disciplina,* a noun meaning "the imparting of understanding"; and *discipulus,* a noun meaning "a person who acquires understanding." Therefore, discipline can be defined as teaching kids to understand what's expected of them.

What you're trying to do on the first day is to make sure the kids understand the rules. Also, you're setting an overall tone by immediately establishing the importance of your rules and explaining the unpleasant consequences awaiting rule breakers. True, you're not running a prison camp, but you're not running a circus, either. You're running a classroom, where students must be able to learn in a safe, orderly, and reasonably tranquil environment. You don't have to whip the spirit out of your kids, but you do have to ensure that your kids work hard, listen carefully, and gain as much education as possible. None of these laudable goals will be achieved if your kids are dancing on their desks. Establish your classroom rules immediately and stick to them for the entire year. That way you'll have fewer challenges from potential misbehavers, because they'll understand from the beginning that you won't tolerate time-wasting nonsense.

There Can Only Be One Boss

Often, kids will say of a particular teacher, "That teacher is mean!" You might even overhear such a comment made about you. But before you blow your stack, consider what your kids might actually mean by calling you "mean."

If you're constantly screaming at kids for petty reasons, barking at kids instead of conversing with them, crassly favoring certain students over others, or imposing onerous punishments for trifling infractions, then when your kids call you "mean," they're indicating that you're genuinely unreasonable and unfair.

When disciplining your students, don't embrace elitism, a philosophy that presumes some people are inherently superior to other people, and therefore, the feelings of superior people are more important than the feelings of inferior people. Remember that all human beings—all kids—must be afforded as much dignity, equity, and compassion as humanly possible.

However, if you calmly warn students of impending punishments for disruptive behavior, carry through when your warnings are ignored, enforce your rules equitably for all students, and maintain a professional attitude of zero tolerance for unsafe and counter-productive behavior, then when your kids call you "mean" they're indicating, "We can't get away with any of the stuff we'd like to get away with."

In other words, deep down your children understand that there can be only one boss in a classroom, and that's you. Kids need and want guidance (even if they never admit it) because they're learning everything, not just reading, writing, and arithmetic, but also interacting positively with diverse personalities; resolving conflicts; and grappling with ethical dilemmas. They need and want a firm hand to guide them safely through the frightening forest of childhood and adolescence.

Kids want a role model whom they can respect. Be the someone they're looking for. Be their instructional and behavioral leader. Be the boss—not because you're an egomaniac, but because you care deeply about your students' education.

Call Parents Early and Often

Because you care about your kids, you won't keep their parents in the dark about chronic misconduct. Rather, you'll call parents early and often so that you can discuss problems and formulate mutually agreeable plans to correct misbehavior.

If phone calls fail to produce any significant improvement in a student's behavior, you'll want to move on to the next step: scheduling a face-to-face parent conference. You can even ask the principal to hold the conference in her office and mediate. Where phone calls sometimes fail, parent conferences can often succeed.

However, you might protest that with all you have to do as a teacher you simply don't have time to sit down and engage in lengthy telephone calls with parents. While there's a bit of truth to these protests, the bottom line is that you must make phone calls or you are dead as a teacher. Parents will rightly accuse you of never notifying them of their kids' misdeeds, and your principal will rightly accuse you of failing to fulfill one of your most important professional duties—keeping parents informed about their kids' academic and behavioral progress.

Again, you might protest that if you simply write in the students' agendas, and send e-mails letters by snail mail home then you are notifying parents. Again, these protests have some validity, but consider the potential consequences of failing to make even one phone call. A likely scenario is that an irate parent arranges a conference with you and your principal, then during the meeting loudly asks, "If my daughter's behavior is so bad, why didn't you call me?" When you trot out your documentation, showing copies of notes in the student's agenda, letters home, etc., none of that material will be as convincing as a note that you made a phone call on a particular date. When you produce evidence of one or two phone calls, then add that to your other documentation, you'll have a rock-solid case.

E-QUESTION

When a parent verbally berates me do I have to take it?
Never. Nobody—students, administrators, parents—has a right to scream at you, threaten you, or insult you. Parents may not always be able to control their tempers, but they're certainly required by civilized society to try. Terminate conversations that turn ugly and then inform your principal immediately.

Besides, you'll find that you really do want to talk to parents by phone because the phone provides back-and-forth communication that notes, letters, etc., can't. You'll probably be delighted to see the miraculous overnight improvement in the behavior of many of your little rebels once you've chatted by telephone with their parents.

But you might be hesitant to make phone calls because the thought of delivering bad news to parents makes you nervous. What if a parent yells and uses profanity? What if a parent vows to drive down to the school and continue the conversation face to face?

The unfortunate reality is there really are people who think that hysterical screaming and mindless violence are all permitted in a civilized society. There really are parents who think it's okay to berate and threaten teachers. The existence of these characters is undeniable, and you must be watchful for such unacceptable behavior any time you interact with parents.

On the other hand, such infantile parental behavior is rare. Most parents are reasonable, rational, and thoughtful. They want to be informed of their kids' misdeeds on a regular basis so that they can step in and offer guidance and even punishment where necessary. The reality is that most parents work long hours nowadays and are aware of the possibility that their kids may be misbehaving during school hours. These parents deeply appreciate being informed of problems so they can take action. Remember, if you don't tell them they won't know. Don't let fear stop you from working with the wonderful parents of your wonderful students in the ongoing war against classroom disruption.

Also, don't let an unreasonable fear of being unprepared stop you from making calls to parents. You're always fully prepared to speak to parents because (as you'll recall from previous chapters) you've carefully filed written documentation regarding each student's behavior in their student dossiers. Each dossier may include the following materials:

- Notes regarding counseling you've given to a student
- Copies of notes you've written in the student's agenda notifying parents of problems
- Copies of memorandum forms mailed home to notify parents of problems
- Copies of classroom suspension forms showing when you had to send a student out
- Copies of tardy letters mailed home
- Photocopies of typed letters mailed home detailing ongoing, serious behavioral issues
- Printouts of e-mails sent to a student's parents regarding problems
- Dated and timed restroom passes in case frequent classroom exits become an issue
- The signed tear-off from your classroom rules, to be referred to as a behavioral reminder
- Progress reports signed by parents indicating that all grades were read and understood
- Notes regarding phone calls you've had with a parent

You'll probably refer to your documentation during the call, even citing each document individually if challenged to do so by a parent.

Furthermore, there's no reason to feel unprepared regarding the subject of behavioral and academic grades. If a parent suddenly asks you during a call, "Would you tell me my son's grades?" you reply, "I'd be happy to," and start reading the grades from your computer-screen—because you had the foresight to call up the student's grades from your computer grade book before you placed your call.

When you're ready to place your call, you might find that your heart is racing from nervousness. Spend a minute slowing your heart rate by taking several deep breaths until you feel calmer and more relaxed. Your feelings of anxiety are the result of adrenalin rushing through your body—a natural occurrence whenever the body senses that it's about to engage in battle. But try to remind your body that this is a phone call, not a gladiatorial contest.

FACT

The telephone is the greatest communication device ever invented, and most people love it—particularly teens anxious to discuss life's monumental issues with friends. But not everyone adores the phone. In a 1925 issue of *Interstate Druggist,* published by the University of Michigan, the phone was called "the most outstanding destroyer of silence and concentration in modern history."

When you call, always courteously introduce yourself first. Then, even if you suspect that the responder is the parent you're seeking always ask the responder, "May I please speak with the mom or dad of [insert the first and last name of the student at issue]?" Sometimes, the responder will inform you that the parent is at work or that you've dialed a wrong number. In that case, you'll be glad you were cautious and courteous because you could've started blurting out confidential information to someone not entitled to hear it.

One of the most important things you must do when beginning your conversation is to always start with the positive. If you start listing the good stuff about a kid, it'll be much easier on you and on the parent when you skillfully segue into the bad stuff—and of course, the bad stuff constitutes the reason for your call.

Every kid, without exception, has good points. Most misbehavers are just immature, not evil; their disruption is the result of lack of self-control. Go ahead and mention the kid's virtues. Is he always courteous to you (not counting his constant classroom disruption)? Then say so. Does he frequently raise his hand and contribute to your lessons? Does he smile brightly during the day? Even in the case of a student who's defiant and disrespectful, you can still grit your teeth and say, "He has a good heart and he's a decent person." Then, when you've established some rapport, gently begin discussing the kid's problems. Beginning with praise doesn't mean you ignore the kid's faults—after all, that's why you called, to remedy misbehavior—but you must accentuate the positive in order to soften the crushing blow of the negative and lessen the possibility of screaming arguments.

The use of unnecessary, unwarranted rudeness with parents can get you fired. You're a highly trained professional educator, not some person your principal dragged off the street. Losing your temper and screaming is what laymen do, not what teachers do. Stay calm so that with a bit of luck, your students and their parents will stay calm, too.

You'll doubtless find that the majority of parents will welcome a courteous, professional phone manner and will support you throughout the conversation. Some parents, however, will seem to regard your compliments suspiciously, grunting rudely and perhaps even saying something like, "Can we skip all this crud and get to the point?" In that case, maintain your professional cool and console yourself with the knowledge that you've done your best.

When you discuss the kid's problems, don't be rude, don't raise your voice, but do express yourself forthrightly, making it clear that such disruptive behavior will not be tolerated. Although you're courteous, you're also leaving no room for doubt that the kid will be disciplined when necessary and will receive failing marks in citizenship unless you see some drastic and immediate behavioral improvement. You're not browbeating, you're just stating facts. With luck, the parent will get the message and will discuss the problem with their child.

But what about parents who scream and lose their minds during a call? Such calls should be politely and immediately terminated. As the great Chinese philosopher Lao-Tzu wrote in his classic work *The Way of Lao-Tzu*: "A good man does not argue." Or as your mom may have said, "If you argue with a fool that makes two fools." If it's obvious that you're dealing with a fool, politely excuse yourself, then discuss the matter with your principal as soon as possible—even walk to her office that minute, if you're free to do so.

Ask the office for a list of telephone numbers for all your students before the first school day. However, if the office fails to supply this information you'll have to compile a list the hard way—collect the emergency cards students will return to you during the first week and copy every phone number by hand.

Remember at the conclusion of every call to jot a brief note regarding the substance of your discussion. What did you say and what were the parent's replies? What promises did the parent make regarding what she will do to improve her kid's behavior? Did the two of you part amicably or was the parent uncooperative or belligerent? Note the call's date, time, and the phone number used. Then, file the note in the kid's dossier as part of your system of keeping written documentation of your professional actions. That way, when you encounter parents who try to claim they were never notified of their kid's misbehavior you can pull out the dossier and your notes—rock-solid evidence, to be sure.

Keep the Principal Apprised

Suppose you were walking down one of the hallways in your school and a parent suddenly stepped out and punched you squarely in the nose. You'd doubtless hold your throbbing nose and blurt out indignantly, "Why in the world did you do that?"

Well, that's what it's like when your principal is confronted with an angry parent yelling about a problem he's been having with you and the principal has no earthly idea what the parent is talking about. No principal appreciates being sandbagged in this manner. Therefore, as often as necessary, keep your principal apprised of what's going on before the parent goes charging down to the front office.

E-QUESTION

Do I have to inform my principal of every little thing that goes wrong in my class?
No. Use your professional judgment to decide which issues may blow up and which ones will probably blow over. But whenever your inner alarm goes off—whenever you think, "I bet this parent will call my principal over this issue"—contact the boss.

For example, after you've made a parent phone call where the parent was combative and angry, contact your principal as soon as possible because there's a real possibility the parent may dial your principal right after she finishes talking to you. But if you have the foresight to visit the principal immediately—or call or send an e-mail—about the student's misbehavior as well as your efforts to remedy the situation, the principal will be adequately forewarned. When the parent subsequently arrives flinging wild accusations, the principal will probably be able to calm the parent without even requesting your participation. However, if you are summoned after school to meet with the parent and the principal, bring the student's dossier as a record of your ongoing efforts to help the student.

Don't just focus on parent phone calls that go wrong, however; you must seriously consider contacting your principal immediately if any of the following types of situations develop:

- A student receives a classroom suspension for continual disruption during lessons
- You send a student to the office with an official suspension form

- A student directs threats toward you or other students or the entire school
- A student makes vague or specific allegations of emotional, physical, or sexual abuse
- A student is involved in any situation involving tobacco, alcohol, narcotics, or weapons
- Any parent shows up unannounced, and appears noncooperative or threatening
- A student gets into an angry altercation or a physical fight with another student

Keeping your principal apprised is not simply a matter of common sense and common courtesy—it's a matter of survival, for your principal and for you. If your principal is unexpectedly waylaid too many times by too many of your parents, he may conclude the district would be better off without your services. You don't need to live in perpetual fear of being fired by the school board, but if you repeatedly anger your principal by failing to forewarn him of potential problems you might want to start updating your resume.

Be Fair, Firm, Honest, and Consistent

Never abuse your disciplinary powers; instead, be firm, fair, and consistent. Because believe it or not, as a teacher you have a staggering amount of power, given to all professional educators by every state legislature in the land as well as by hard-won local contracts. Depending on which state you live in and what your contract stipulates, you are authorized to invoke most or all of the disciplinary powers listed below:

- Require all students to obey your reasonable, individually generated classroom regulations
- Require students to sign and honor specific behavioral contracts
- Require students to receive counseling from the school psychologist or counselor
- Require students to receive counseling from an assistant principal or the principal herself

- Revoke a student's privilege to participate in field trips, graduation programs, etc.
- Issue after-school detentions to students for chronic classroom misbehavior, tardiness, etc.
- Suspend a student from your class for statutorily enumerated reasons for up to two days
- Decline to readmit a suspended student to your class for the entire period of the suspension
- Entirely remove a student from your class roll, whereupon administrators must reassign him
- With written parental permission, administer corporal punishment (however, avoid this one)

You must not and shall not abuse your powers because those powers were given to you to help youngsters develop into well-educated, responsible, independent citizens, free to embrace life, liberty, and the pursuit of happiness.

FACT

A person's height can affect how he's treated. American author Jerome Barkow observed in his 1995 book *The Adapted Mind*: "Height is associated with power and status and . . . confers an economic, political, and social advantage." That's just one example of how irrelevant considerations can influence your treatment of different students. Make absolutely certain that you treat your students equally.

"Teaching is a sacred calling," notes an article in the 1905 edition of the *CTA Journal*, a magazine published annually by the California Teachers Association teachers' union. "It must not be desecrated by the layman nor profaned by the professional," the article continues. In other words, use discipline as a tool to facilitate teaching, not as a weapon to gratify your ego at the expense of those younger and smaller than yourself. Some teachers in the past were demonstrably guilty of unnecessary cruelty—maybe even teachers in your own experience. You'll never be guilty of such a sin. You'll apply discipline equitably and you won't play favorites because of a student's family connections or other irrelevant considerations.

Certainly, you may differentiate punishments between different students, just as society at large does not impose the death penalty on jaywalkers or impose monetary fines on first-degree murderers. The punishment must fit the offense and the offender, and in your classroom students do not have identical disciplinary histories. You might suspend one student for speaking disrespectfully to you simply because you have patiently tried every other disciplinary technique without success. In the next hour, another student might commit a very similar offense, yet you merely ask for the student's agenda and write down what he has said. You treat the second student differently because he has never given you any problems to date and an agenda note constitutes the beginning of the disciplinary process, while school suspensions come at the end. These kinds of differentiations are permitted; what's never permitted are differentiations based on race or teacher's pet status—or on good old-fashioned bribery.

There are state laws that forbid teachers from accepting valuable gifts from the public. It's one thing to accept a five-dollar necktie at Christmas; it's quite another thing to accept $400 in theme-park tickets from a student. A presumption may now arise in the mind of the student—and in the minds of your other students—that you've just sold a bit of preferential treatment. In other words, you've been bribed.

Always act honestly and fairly and make sure you also give the appearance of acting honestly and fairly. Treat everyone with the same equitable, firm, honest discipline in order to forestall unfounded accusations that you're acting from racist, sexist, or elitist motives.

Apologize and Make Restitution Whenever Appropriate

You're not perfect and you shouldn't pretend to be, especially with kids. You shouldn't try to trick your students into believing you're infallible. Instead, when you make a blunder—and you'll make plenty—learn to apologize and even make restitution when appropriate. Kids will appreciate your honesty and will use you as a role model, someone who exhibits humility after making a mistake.

For example, consider a situation where your students are working on a complicated assignment involving polynomials. One student raises her hand and asks if she may wash her hands at the sink. You're sitting at your desk with four students, giving them intensive tutoring so they can complete the assignment. You blurt, "Sure" to the student with her hand up, then immediately resume explaining polynomials to your tutees. Unnoticed by you, the student takes two full minutes to finish eating a cookie before going to the sink.

As she advances you look up, alarmed—having completely forgotten her earlier request because of your intense tutoring session and the elapse of two minutes. You demand, "Why are you out of your seat? You know you have to raise your hand first!"

She and the kids stare at you in evident disbelief. The girl says nervously, "But I raised my hand and asked. You told me, 'Yes.'" Several other kids murmur in agreement.

Suddenly you remember. "Ohhh," you whisper. Tears trickle down the girl's cheeks and her whole body trembles. This is a moment of truth for you: Do you blame everything on the girl or do the right thing and apologize? The class awaits your next move; they want to see if you're like so many other adults—someone who always has to be right even when you're clearly wrong.

At this point you could disappoint your kids by falling back on an old standby used by many grownups—the nonapology apology. This tactic implies the person you've offended is too sensitive. "C'mon, Linda," you say impatiently, "I'm sorry you're taking this so hard. Go wash your hands." You can hear the collective sigh of disappointment as your class realizes you've failed an important ethical test.

Instead, offer a real apology. You don't have to prostrate yourself on the floor, but you do have to say, "Oops. I'm sorry, Linda. My mistake. I was helping kids and I just forgot. Go ahead." Your class goes back to work, smiling and nodding, secure in the knowledge that they've got a real human being for a teacher, not a hypocritical would-be paragon.

The other important component of apologizing is making restitution where appropriate. Restitution means that you restore a person to "wholeness" you earlier damaged in some way. For example, one day a student who's left his yearbook in the lunchroom asks if he can quickly go back and retrieve it. Without thinking you say, "No, we've got work to do." After class, he runs to the lunchroom and sure enough, the yearbook has been stolen—thanks to your obtuseness. When you learn of this, you call his parents and offer to make restitution; that is, to pay for a new yearbook. The student and his parents are so impressed with your gesture they either allow you to pay half or forgive you altogether. Mission accomplished, as far as showing kids that real adults apologize and make restitution when they're in the wrong.

CHAPTER 12

Problem-Free Classrooms

Managing a classroom really means weeding out as many problems as you can as early as possible, before those problems blossom into monstrosities so huge they can't be eradicated. If you ignore classroom-wrecking issues such as defiance and disruption, you'll soon find yourself in a position where the class manages you instead of the other way around. Kids are intelligent little people, and they'll eat you for breakfast unless you master the techniques presented in this chapter for running reasonably problem-free classrooms.

Minimize or Eliminate Classroom Disruptions and Defiance

Your overall attitude toward classroom disruptions must be, "I won't permit anyone to disrupt the educational process of those students who want to learn." This mantra may seem harsh, but it's the only one that will guide you through your darkest times as a teacher. Ask yourself, "Why do the kids and I come to this classroom every day?"

In a nutshell, you're teaching kids how to survive. In some tribal societies survival training might include hunting skills or learning to distinguish beneficial plants from poisonous ones; but in our modern society, education encompasses reading, writing, mathematics, science, history, geography, law, economics, technological skills, and more. This kind of survival training is essential to the well-being and prosperity of society's individual members. Survival knowledge must be comprehensively and efficiently transmitted from those who have the knowledge to those without it.

That's where you come in. You're in the classroom every day to teach kids how to survive and they're in the classroom to learn survival. You're not there to waste time, suffer abuse, play mind games, or quarrel endlessly. And your students are not there to learn slovenliness, cruelty, and irrationality. You've got limited time to impart your hard-earned wisdom and they've got limited time to acquire it. Therefore, even though you're brimming with affection for your students, you're nevertheless prepared to crack down on all disrespectful nonsense at all times. This isn't a form of heartlessness; it's a form of love.

Above all, never ignore disruptive behavior and hope it'll just vanish. Only a fool would just ignore a glaring problem. You're no fool, and you won't ignore classroom disruptions.

What does this mean in concrete terms? Suppose a student has been talking and giggling for many minutes during your social studies lesson on California's ancient Chumash Indians. Eventually, you have no choice but to waste some of the class's valuable time asking the student to quiet down and pay attention to the lesson because a quiz will follow. The student rudely talks back, protesting that he wasn't talking—which you and your students know is a lie. Don't be intimidated. Interrupt the student by courteously but firmly reminding him, "Yes, you certainly were talking," and inform him that such rudeness will not be not tolerated. For many students, this kind of chastisement is sufficient to modify the misbehavior.

Accentuate the Positive

Strongly consider the power of positive reinforcement before you move on to equally powerful negative consequences. Positive reinforcement is a term formulated by the eminent American psychologist Burrhus Frederic Skinner (or B. F. Skinner). Positive reinforcement means that a person who exhibits a desired behavior should instantly receive a reward for that behavior to induce a repetition. Skinner asserted that positive reinforcement can often solve problems more easily and quickly than punishments if a student is receptive and reasonable and not too firmly entrenched in a years-long pattern of classroom disruption. Skinner recommended that teachers use positive reinforcement in the following manner:

1. Make sure that each concept that is taught is broken into easy-to-understand steps.
2. Progress from the easiest concepts to more difficult concepts.
3. Reteach the concept as many times as necessary until kids get it right.
4. Instantly let kids know what they've done right and what they've done wrong.
5. Instantly give a reward when kids exhibit a desired behavior.

The crassest kind of instant reward would be to throw the kid a piece of candy when he does something right, whereupon the kid would catch it and shove it in his mouth. But since human beings aren't trained seals, a more effective form of positive reinforcement is to praise, praise, praise. You might think that kids find praise phony or embarrassing, but they love it—just as adults love it. You probably don't enjoy being told by your principal, "Jones, your classroom isn't stimulating enough for your students." But you probably love hearing, "Jones, I want you to know how much I appreciate your arriving half an hour early every day. You're really dedicated. Keep up the good work." What a difference! And if you crave this kind of praise, your students will crave it, too.

Consider one of your worst troublemakers: she suddenly raises her hand one day and answers a question correctly. Praise her. "Miss Smith," you say, beaming, "that's the right answer. Excellent work." You don't have to go on for ten minutes, but a few seconds of praise will doubtless persuade her to listen even more carefully and answer a few more questions correctly. Or consider another of your rebels: he raises his hand and informs you that he's just received 100 percent on his history test. Praise him. "That's great, Mr. Lee. Magnificent work."

When Disruptions Persist

However, some of your students just won't conform sufficiently if all you use is positive reinforcement. Sometimes, such students are emotionally immature; and sometimes, they come from challenging home environments where poverty, divorce, or abuse can cause them to develop into combative individuals. If you find that such students are persistently engaging in time-wasting tantrums, you'll have no choice but to warn them of a punishment to follow then impose that punishment if it becomes necessary. Various types of punishments have already been discussed earlier, but they bear repetition here—along with many other ethical penalties you may devise:

- Counsel a disruptive student on the inappropriateness and consequences of disruption.
- Write a note in a disruptive student's agenda informing his parents of the problem.
- Mail a memo home to a disruptor's parents informing them of the problem.
- Send disruptive students to a buddy teacher with a behavioral essay to complete.
- Have disruptors briefly sit in an isolated time-out area to contemplate proper behavior.
- Revoke one or more of a disruptor's special privileges, including recess or a field trip.
- Issue one or more after-school detentions for repeated or egregious disruptions.

- Send disruptors to the school psychologist or counselor for behavioral counseling.
- Send disruptors to the principal or other administrator for behavioral counseling.
- Write a suspension for chronically disruptive, defiant, disrespectful, nonrepentant students.

Never punish a student by sending her to sit out in the hallway. If the student gets disgusted, decides to walk home, and then gets hit by a car, what can you possibly say in your own defense? "I thought she'd stay outside the classroom! I never dreamed she'd leave!" Such unprofessional negligence rightfully constitutes grounds for termination.

Here are some punishments that you will never use as a professional educator:

- Battery, meaning unwanted or offensive touching, beating, and corporal punishment
- Assault, where a student is placed in psychological fear of injury
- Screaming tirades and unprofessional verbal abuse
- Gross personal insults and crass remarks about family, friends, relationships, hygiene, etc.
- "Standards," where mindless statements are written over and over again
- Ejections, where students are forced to loiter outside classrooms, often in inclement weather
- False imprisonment, meaning locking students in closets, etc.
- Torture, such as forcing students to stand upright for long periods, kneeling on sand, etc.
- Incitement, where other students are encouraged to ridicule or attack a particular student

When you punish you do so because positive reinforcement hasn't produced the desired result and because your little rebel might yet modify his misbehavior if penalized properly and because the vast majority of your students deserve to learn in a reasonably quiet, problem-free classroom. You are the moral arbiter in your classroom—make sure you use your disciplinary powers to maintain an atmosphere of intellectual stimulation, camaraderie, support, security, and even a little fun.

Harness the Power of Administrators

Most administrators are hard-working, dedicated professionals. If you need help with a disruptive student and you've tried everything to get the student to cooperate without success, your last resort is your principal.

After you've counseled a student, written in her agenda, sent letters home, made phone calls, had a parent conference, sent the kid to buddy teachers to write behavioral essays, issued detentions, and have even suspended the kid, it's time for her to go see the principal.

You don't ordinarily bow or prostrate yourself before entering your principal's office because she's a human being, not some Empress of the Nile. Nevertheless, your principal deserves your deference because she's earned it. She has probably taught for many years, earned an administrative credential, and may even possess a doctoral degree. Show the proper respect.

Talk to your principal beforehand and let her know what's been happening with a particular student. Of course, you've mentioned this kid's problems to the principal occasionally, but now you'll go into detail and request assistance. Don't beg, don't weep—don't give the appearance of someone unable to control children; such behavior won't endear you with your principal. But do politely ask for assistance, emphasizing that the principal, as an authority figure with broad experience, can make a powerful impression on the student. You'll find that in nearly all instances, after you've made your case in this way, your principal will be happy to help.

Later, when your chronic misbehaver disrupts class and defies your authority, take a few seconds to write a brief note using one of your preprinted memos. As with all memos, write your initials and the date, fill in your principal's name on the "To" line, and your misbehaver's name on the "Subject" line. A quick memo might look something like this:

MEMORANDUM

From: Mrs. Jane Doe, Rm. 4
To: Mrs. Juno, Principal
Date:
Subject: Lucy Hades

---

1. Chronic disruption.
2. Throwing paper, arguing.
3. Discipline produces no change.
4. Please counsel and return.

Fold the memo, staple it, write, "Principal" on the outside, then pick a responsible student to deliver Miss Hades and the note to the principal. Remind your escort that she must return as quickly as possible. Say, "Please take Miss Hades and my note to the principal and come right back. We've got lessons to finish and we need you." You're implying, of course, that you do not need Miss Hades and that she won't get to enjoy the great lessons you're about to teach. Also, remind Miss Hades to bring the note back signed or bring a signed office slip, indicating she received counseling from the principal. Otherwise, she might simply wait in the office for five minutes then rush back and claim, "Okay, I talked to the principal." Retrieve the signed note the moment she returns or ask your escort to return her to the principal's office.

Unfortunately, you'll sometimes find that a few administrators are averse to hard work, and even more averse to interacting with children. Expressly and implicitly, they make it clear to their teaching staffs that they do not want to receive misbehavers at any time, as they are far too busy with more important matters. Such administrators exist, and if you're saddled with one you'll have to be careful about sending them disciplinary problems.

Make sure you've dotted every "i" before dispatching kids to such a principal because he's made clear in staff meetings and in endless memos that he doesn't want to deal with misbehavers. He's used tactics such as instilling guilt in his teachers: "How have you failed this child, discipline-wise?" he has intoned in staff meetings. "What have you failed to do to meet her needs?" Never mind that the kid laughs uproariously whenever the wind blows and hollers to numerous students during lessons and work periods. Your principal wants to know how you have failed.

E-QUESTION

Do principals have to teach for decades before they become administrators?
No. In many states, a credentialed teacher who has taught for three years may pursue a course of study and gain an administrative credential. That's one of the main reasons a few unworthy candidates manage to insinuate themselves into administrative ranks. Luckily, most principals are dedicated professionals.

Don't buy it. Yes, there's a grain of truth in this principal's sermons, but his intentions are tainted and insincere. He's not thinking of what's best for students; he's only trying to make certain he doesn't have to do his job. A part of any principal's job is to counsel misbehaving children and take an active role in their guidance and rehabilitation. He might not like it, but disciplining is one of the reasons he gets paid the big bucks. After you've tried every other disciplinary method available, send the kid to the principal. It's the right thing to do.

Show Mercy Whenever Appropriate

It's okay to be merciful to your students sometimes. In fact, it's often a lot easier to show mercy to a student than to punish her. That's where you sometimes get into trouble as a teacher, by giving your kids chances over and over again. But you just can't help it; you're a teacher, so naturally you're compassionate and merciful toward kids. If you didn't love kids, you never would've become a teacher. And caring about kids the way that you do, it's hard to punish them—and easy to forgive.

And you should forgive; you should show mercy. But only where and when it is appropriate to do so. If a student yells out in class, you admonish him, and he quickly apologizes, you probably don't need to write in his agenda—forgive him. He's human, these mistakes happen. If a student accidentally trips another student then apologizes profusely and you trust his sincerity, you probably don't need to call home—forgive him. Or, if a student glances at another student's paper during a test and you admonish, "Keep your eyes on your own paper" and he instantly buries himself in his work, you probably don't need to issue a detention—forgive him.

After all, have you ever had to be forgiven for a mistake? Of course you have; you wouldn't be a human being otherwise. Therefore, if you need to be forgiven, other people need the same thing, especially kids who make so many silly mistakes because they're learning every day how to live in society and how to become thoughtful human beings. Also, you give chances so that later on your own conscience will be clear. Specifically, if a chronically misbehaving kid or her parents claim you've been unfair, you can point to the documented chances you've given the kid, over and over, such as agenda notes, calls, personal counseling, etc., before you were forced to move on to detentions, suspensions, and meetings with the principal.

The bottom line is you do what is ethically required to make sure no one interferes with your students' education, even if you must send a student out occasionally. On the other hand, if an act of mercy seems warranted in a particular situation for a particular child, then give the kid a chance.

Control Your Class During Fire or Civil-Defense Drills

You must control your class during fire drills, civil-defense drills, and other types of drills for reasons of safety. Most school districts hold regular fire drills not only for safety reasons, but because they are legally required to do so by state statutes. In most districts, teachers have to participate in a fire drill with their class sooner or later. Keep everybody safe.

Fire drills are generally announced ahead of time to minimize panic. Drills usually commence with the sounding of the school's fire-alarm system. Next, students, teachers, administrators, and other staffers quickly form lines and exit their respective rooms and buildings using designated emergency routes. Everyone subsequently assembles in assigned safe areas away from potential danger zones. Sometimes, drills even involve the transportation of students by bus, etc., to areas remote from the school site.

The purpose of fire drills is to ensure that if a real fire occurs, everyone will have practiced sufficiently beforehand to ensure a safe, orderly, rapid evacuation without injury or loss of life. However, if you blithely allow your kids to goof, scream, stumble, horseplay, and fight during a fire drill, you're defeating the drill's purpose because your class' evacuation suddenly becomes disorderly and unsafe. If the unthinkable eventually happens and a fire menaces your school, you'll never forgive yourself if a child is harmed due to your lack of professionalism during drills.

Instead, spend a bit of time before each drill discussing the rules that apply to all drills with your students. In general, students participating in drills should make an effort to pretend that the drill constitutes a real emergency because in a real emergency, students must:

- Keep unnecessary talking to a minimum in order to hear potentially life-saving instructions
- Not panic, shove, or run to eliminate the danger of falling or being trampled
- Walk calmly but quickly to minimize the possibility of danger catching up with the group
- Not engage in horseplay to minimize the danger of accidentally injuring other students
- Stay with the teacher so as not to get separated and wander into potentially unsafe areas
- Keep cell phones turned off in order to hear potentially life-saving instructions
- Obey the instructions of all valid authority figures to minimize the possibility of injury

In addition, there are several things you must make certain to do during fire drills. While you are pretending that the drill is real—just as the kids are—you must be sure to:

- Keep a careful eye out for each of your students so that no one is accidentally left behind
- Permit no horseplaying, screaming, fighting, running, shoving, arguing, or silliness
- Bring your first-aid kit, supplied by the school, filled with bandages and other medical items
- Bring a copy of your roll so you can take attendance at the first opportunity
- Bring a clipboard, paper, and pens so notes may be written and delivered, if necessary
- Bring your cell phone in case you need to make any emergency-related calls
- Bring the American flag, if there's time or opportunity to safely do so

Take fire drills seriously and teach your kids to take them seriously. Afterward, you might even print out some certificates, which are easily created using simple software preloaded on your computer, to reward exemplary fire-drill behavior.

Civil-defense drills, too, are important and must be taken seriously. Civil-defense drills are designed to help kids practice safety procedures that might save their lives during earthquakes, cyclones, hurricanes, etc. When kids hear a siren or other signal, they commence the drill by ducking under their desks, tucking themselves into a fetal position (curling up like an unborn baby), and lacing their fingers together over the backs of their necks.

Again, teach your students to approach these civil-defense drills seriously, as with fire drills. When students are under desks, if they thrash around and act silly they may cut themselves on bits of protruding metal or snag their clothing. Instruct your students to make themselves as comfortable as possible, ignore gum and other detritus under the desks, and behave properly. That way, if a real disaster strikes they'll be mentally prepared to protect their lives.

Discreetly Handle Dress-Code Violations

Don't publicly humiliate your students when they deliberately or inadvertently commit dress-code violations. For example, suppose that one of your boys, Joe Boxer, is "sagging," which is kid slang for exposing a large swath of his underwear by wearing his pants too low on his posterior. You could shout, "Goodness, Mr. Boxer—I see England, I see France, I see someone's underpants!" As the class laughs uproariously, you could then write a note and have Mr. Boxer escorted in shame to the front office to receive punishment in the form of a detention.

Or, you could discreetly take Mr. Boxer aside and courteously ask him to please pull up his pants and tighten his belt before you cite him for a dress-code violation. You'll probably find to your delight that Mr. Boxer will immediately cooperate, and you'll have no further problems from him that day. If you do have problems, then he was fairly warned and has only himself to blame if he has to trek down to the office to get a detention.

ALERT!

Don't verbally abuse your kids by making smarmy, inappropriate remarks about their clothing. Clothing constitutes a very personal realm—a realm that you don't want to venture into. You do have a duty to enforce your school's dress code, but such enforcement must be done professionally. Approach the problem like a highly trained professional educator.

Conversely, suppose one of your girls, Minnie Tea, comes to class wearing a T-shirt that does an extremely poor job of covering several inches of her midriff. You could exclaim, "Heavens, Miss Tea, I never knew before today that you had such a huge navel!" After the class has finished gasping, you could choose to have Miss Tea marched down to the office in disgrace.

Or, you could discreetly take Miss Tea aside and courteously ask her if she happens to have a sweater or a jacket with her. Many times, when you ask this question the answer will be, "Yes." Ask Miss Tea to please put on her sweater or jacket and keep it on for the remainder of the day before you cite her for a dress-code violation. If she has no jacket, warn her that if she again comes to school similarly dressed, you'll send her to the office. You shouldn't have any further problems.

Allow your students to maintain a little dignity when they make dress-code blunders and everyone will be much happier.

Put an End to Fights

Stay vigilant and stamp out fights before they ever have a chance to get started. You do this by making sure your kids understand that you have a strict zero-tolerance policy for any form of violent behavior, bullying, racism, sexism, ethnic discrimination, religious discrimination, or homophobia. If you let your class know that you won't permit such gross misbehavior, and if you keep your word, your kids will know that if they want to treat other people cruelly they'll have to do it some other place and some other time.

When you witness bullying on the schoolyard or in your classroom, immediately step in and inform the offender that his behavior is utterly impermissible. If necessary, walk through all of your disciplinary steps with the student one by one until the bullying comes to an end. Don't let bullying rear its ugly head while you're around.

In your classroom, you have a certain amount of control over what can and cannot be said—and what cannot be said are poisonous, ugly, evil words drenched with ill will and aggression. A classroom isn't a place to learn about hatred; but rather, to learn about intelligence, cooperation, and tolerance.

CHAPTER 13

Legal Issues

As a teacher, you must familiarize yourself with legal issues applicable to the teaching profession. However, you don't have to spend years earning a law degree. Instead, audit a few university law courses, talk to professional colleagues who have legal knowledge, and read as widely as possible. While no book can provide a perfect explication of the entire legal system, you can nevertheless begin your preliminary study of education law by carefully reading the information presented in this chapter.

Spanking

Stay as far away from corporal punishment as possible. This commonsense decision has nothing to do with the eternal debate regarding the morality of spanking. Rather, your decision never to use corporal punishment is based on the simple fact that in twenty-seven of the fifty United States, the practice is illegal. Unless you happen to live in one of the twenty-three states where teachers may legally spank students, forget it. As of the writing of this book, the states allowing teachers to use corporal punishment are listed below:

Alabama	*Mississippi*
Arizona	*Missouri*
Arkansas	*New Mexico*
Colorado	*North Carolina*
Delaware	*Ohio*
Florida	*Oklahoma*
Georgia	*Pennsylvania*
Idaho	*South Carolina*
Indiana	*Tennessee*
Kansas	*Texas*
Kentucky	*Wyoming*
Louisiana	

If you don't see your state on that list, use the various means of disciplining students that have been discussed in previous chapters. Accept the fact that the majority of the people of your state, through their representatives, have decided that corporal punishment is *verboten*. For instance, in California, Section 49000 of the California Education Code, which prohibits corporal punishment, announces emphatically that, "Children of school age are at the most vulnerable and impressionable period of their lives and . . . the safeguards to the integrity and sanctity of their bodies should be, at this tender age, at least equal to that afforded to other citizens." Whether you agree or not, comply with the laws of your state.

However, even if you do see the name of your state on the list, you've still made the laudable decision to forget about using corporal punishment for two extremely important reasons.

First, even legal corporal punishment can quickly become illegal child abuse. If that happens, you'll have crossed a statutory line and might find yourself subject to criminal prosecution. Just imagine that one of your kids has been defying you all day. You grab your yardstick and advance angrily toward him. Terrified, he tries to bolt. But you're too fast—you grab his arm and whack him on his legs with the yardstick, in front of your shocked class. Screaming, he tries to pull away, which only feeds your anger, and you whack him repeatedly, breaking the yardstick with a final devastating blow. Later, bruises are discovered on his legs. The principal calls you to his office. When you arrive, a police officer awaits. Just think—you could have calmly told your misbehaver, "You're going to the principal." Instead, you're the one visiting the principal.

FACT

It's interesting to note that, currently, seventeen countries have banned any use of corporal punishment directed toward children, whether by parents, teachers, or others. These "nonspanking" countries are Austria, Bulgaria, Croatia, Cyprus, Denmark, Finland, Germany, Greece, Hungary, Israel, Iceland, Italy, Latvia, Norway, Romania, Sweden, and Ukraine.

Second, suppose in the same hypothetical above, that the boy's father is telephoned at work. Furious, he races to the school and when he enters the principal's office—with you sitting there—and is informed of his son's injuries, he becomes enraged. He screams that he has never used corporal punishment at home because his own father was physically abusive. Suddenly, he grabs you by your coat, and before the police officer can react, delivers an uppercut to your jaw that you'll never forget. True, he's probably going to jail, but you're going to the hospital with a broken jawbone. Which is worse? And remember, all this happens in a state where corporal punishment is legal. You realize, far too late, that for a teacher the use of corporal punishment is never worth the serious risks that such disciplining entails.

Assault

When searching for definitions of particular criminal offenses such as assault, laymen tend to rely on legal dictionaries such as *Black's Law Dictionary,* originally written by Henry Campbell Black and published in 1891. Or they rely on Internet dictionaries such as Nolo's Legal Glossary (*www .nolo.com/glossary.cfm*). Although such dictionaries are often brilliant works of scholarship, attorneys and judges prefer whenever possible to get their legal definitions from federal or state case-law—the published decisions of judges. These definitions frequently carry more weight in the real world than dictionary definitions alone.

ALERT!

Be cautious about using online sources to further your knowledge of education law. Try to use recognized websites such as Wex, maintained by the Cornell Law School (*www.law.cornell.edu/topical.html*), and Findlaw (*http://public.findlaw.com*). Although new websites deserve a chance to establish themselves, use ordinary caution and triple check everything, every time.

Therefore, to define assault, turn to a federal case—*Harris v. United States*—decided by the United States Court of Appeals, Sixth Circuit, in 2005. The case's citation—the reference number you use to look up the case in reporters or case books—is 422 F.3d 322. The citation means the case is found in Volume 422 of *The Federal Reporter,* Third Series, page 322. When you look up the case, you find that the Court, referencing Ohio state law, defined assault as, "the willful threat . . . to harm or touch another offensively, [where that] threat or attempt reasonably places the other in fear of such contact." In other words, although some jurisdictions define assault as hitting, kicking, etc., most jurisdictions make clear that you're guilty of assault if you terrify a reasonable person into thinking you're about to wallop him.

No one is permitted to illegally assault another person, and teachers are not permitted to assault students. That is, you may not put a kid in reasonable fear that you're about to wallop him. Different fact patterns will show whether or not you're guilty of assault. For example, if one of your students whistles during a work period, you might thoughtlessly remark, "Joe, if you don't stop whistling I'll remove one of your fingers. Decide which one." The class laughs, including Joe. And, although your comment is crass and unprofessional, it might not rise to the level of assault. That's because neither Joe nor anyone else has any reasonable fear that you'll really get some scissors and lop off digits.

When you're furious, do the traditional thing—count slowly to ten. American consultant Richard Templar agrees with this advice in his book, *The Rules of Life:* "[G]et in the habit of counting to ten under your breath while you hope and pray that the feeling of impending rage will subside. It invariably does for me."

But suppose, in that same hypothetical, you suddenly stand up and slam your fist on your desk. Joe and the other kids freeze. You march toward Joe, grab the textbook he's using, raise it high above your head, and yell, "Joe, so help me, if you don't stop that freaking whistling, I'll bop you with this book!" Joe cringes in terror, holding up both hands to ward off an imminent blow. You grunt, toss the book onto his desk, and march back to your desk, leaving Joe trembling like a rabbit. Under this fact pattern, you might be guilty of assault. Joe's attorney, hired by Joe's parents the next day, might be able to show a jury that you threatened to harm Joe and he believed you. Loss of your teaching credential, your job, your money after losing a civil suit, and potential jail time—all of these may await you.

Remember all the strategies you've learned thus far for dealing with problems in the classroom? Use those, and any other intelligent tactics that you'll devise over the course of your career instead of wild, emotional, unprofessional stratagems such as putting kids in fear of an imminent beating. Never forget that professionalism could well be defined as "keeping your doggone temper under control at all times under all circumstances while on your job." A professional does not give in to the temptation to lose her temper, scream like a banshee, and loudly threaten people with thrashings.

In the sometimes high-stress world of teaching, you must remember that while others lose their minds you must be the one to stay even tempered and in control. Your students don't need a big, immature, hyper-emotional kid—they need a teacher. Do not make threats of violence, thereby setting yourself up for an assault charge. Instead, make professional promises: "Joe, if you don't stop whistling, I'll need to send you next door to write a behavioral essay. People are trying to work here." Nine times out of ten, Joe will say, "Sorry" and you'll have no further problems. Wasn't that easy? Remember, in your classroom-management toolkit, assault is a tool that's nowhere to be found.

Battery

In the case of *United States v. Stewart,* decided by the United States Court of Appeals, Sixth Circuit, in 2005, the Court, citing nineteenth century English jurisprudence, defined battery in this way: "[T]he unlawful beating of another. The least touching of another's person willfully, or in anger, is a battery; for the law cannot draw the line between different degrees of violence, and therefore totally prohibits the first and lowest stage of it; every man's person being sacred, and no other having a right to meddle with it, in any the slightest manner."

In other words, battery differs from assault because assault means you're putting people in fear of being whacked, whereas battery means that you actually whack them. And you don't have to administer a savage beating, either. Any unwanted or offensive touching constitutes a battery. Spitting on someone, blowing cigarette smoke in his face, kicking his car, shoving past him in anger—all of these, along with countless other acts, have been found by courts to constitute battery. Again, specific fact patterns will determine if you've committed battery or not.

For instance, none of the people who accidentally jostle each other on a crowded street are guilty of battery if all they're intending to do is reach their destinations. Likewise, if two students are fighting and you use reasonable force to separate them, courts have found that teachers in such situations are legally permitted to use appropriate force and therefore are not committing battery.

But if one of your students tells you, "Mrs. Doe, you're unfair!" and you slap her savagely in her mouth, that could constitute battery. Moreover, if a student says, "You never listen to me!" and you gently tickle her under her chin, saying sarcastically, "Aw, you're so cute when you're mad," that could well constitute battery, also. Never think that just because your act of unwanted or offensive touching is gentle that it automatically becomes legal or acceptable.

E-QUESTION

I teach huge twelfth graders. If one of them hits me and I hit back, is that battery?
No. The law permits anyone to use reasonable force, appropriate to the situation, to defend himself.

In real life, unlawful physical violence is battery, and battery is not permitted in any civilized society. Remember, you're not an ancient Viking warrior or an avenging cowboy, you're a professional educator, hired to nurture and guide society's precious children; act accordingly. Here's a classroom-management rule you can live by: Keep your hands to yourself at all times, unless sheer necessity forces you to do otherwise—to break up a fight, protect a child from injury, etc.—and never commit battery.

Molestation

No one is legally permitted to molest children; that is, to touch them sexually or induce them to engage in sexual intercourse. In the case of *Percy v. State of South Dakota,* decided by the United States Court of Appeals, Eighth Circuit, in 1971, the Court, citing South Dakota law, defined molestation in this way: "Any person who shall willfully and unlawfully commit any lewd or lascivious act upon or with the body, or any part of member thereof, of a child . . . with the intent of arousing, appealing to, or gratifying the lust or passion or sexual desires of such person, or of such child, shall be guilty of the crime of indecent molestation."

The majority of civilized human societies have made the collective decision long ago that children are emotionally incapable of making any kind of rational, informed, knowledgeable decision to engage in sexual intercourse. Therefore, all such societies prohibit children from engaging in sexual intercourse with each other or with adults.

FACT

Sexual predators and molestation apologists often argue that youngsters crave sex. However, the pervasive stereotype of the hormone-drenched adolescent is frequently proven patently false. In the 2003 book *Sexual Revolution* by sexual researchers Erica Jong and Jeffrey Escoffier, the authors assure readers that, "Many girls are still sincere and even lyrical about saving themselves for marriage."

The commonsense rationale behind this collective decision is that children do not possess sufficient experience, wisdom, understanding, or judgment regarding what sex really means for them. For instance, children cannot understand the full panoply of long-term consequences that sexual intercourse may entail, such as the real possibility of the transmission from an infected sex partner of dangerous sexually transmitted diseases (STDs). Children are equally incapable of genuinely comprehending the possibility that a pregnancy can often result from even a single act of sexual intercourse in those cases where young girls are currently menstruating.

Therefore, you've already been inculcated from an early age to understand and respect the sanctity of society's precious children. It's okay for parents to entrust their most valuable treasures—their children—to you for several hours each day because you are the kind of moral, ethical, well brought-up, law-abiding person who would never dream of violating the rights of children by tricking them into engaging in sexual intercourse.

Because you understand that you're one of the guardians of society's innocent children, you protect children from sexual predators to the best of your ability and you help students concentrate on what's important in their lives—gaining education. Kids aren't capable of giving themselves sexually with any kind of understanding because they haven't yet discovered exactly what their personality is, so they don't even know what they're proffering. Also, they haven't learned to distinguish truth tellers from liars—even you might not have perfected that skill yet—so they don't even understand what they're getting. Kids who don't even know that haircuts won't harm them are in absolutely no position to say that sex won't harm them.

FACT

Some child molesters even face capital punishment. Consider that in 2006, according to an article on the Jurist Legal News and Research website (*http://jurist.law.pitt.edu*), Oklahoma became the fifth state in America to permit capital punishment for child molesters convicted of multiple offenses. The other states imposing the death penalty on repeat-offending child molesters are Florida, Louisiana, Montana, and South Carolina.

Moreover, the harm that children suffer from being coerced into having early sex isn't limited solely to physical damage. In the article "Paedophilia: Plague or Panic?" in the December 2000 issue of *The Journal of Forensic Psychiatry and Psychology,* American psychologist Donald West warns, "Clinical evidence amply demonstrates that sexual molestation of children can cause immediate distress followed by severe, long-term psychological damage. . . ." And psychology professor James Mannon of DePauw University, Indiana, in his article "Domestic and Intimate Violence: An Application of Routine Activities Theory" from the Spring 1997 issue of *Aggression and Violent Behavior,* warns of the "long-term emotional and psychological damage suffered by victims of child sexual abuse."

In addition, even the molester himself may be required to suffer greatly after engaging in unlawful sexual intercourse with a child, because the criminal penalties nationwide for such malfeasance are often quite severe, including lengthy imprisonment and hefty fines.

But there's more. Just take a look at the federal Sexual Offender Act passed by the United States Congress in 1994. The statute is commonly referred to as Megan's Law, to honor seven-year-old Megan Kanka of New Jersey. In 1994, Megan was raped and murdered by a repeat sex offender who—unknown to the Kankas—lived just across the street. Megan's Law now requires convicted sex offenders to register with local authorities whenever they establish residence in a particular community. The law also requires authorities to make such residence information public, including posting it online. States determine the exact nature of the information that must be posted, but at a minimum it generally includes the offender's name, address, photograph, and details of his crimes.

There's even more. In the instructive case of *Kansas v. Hendricks*, decided by the United States Supreme Court in 1997, the Court outlined the steps whereby a state may commit a convicted child molester determined to have a "mental abnormality" to a psychiatric institution for an indefinite period of time.

Inappropriate and Illegal Relationships

Teachers must never come to work with the intention of flirting with, making sexually suggestive remarks to, or engaging in sexually suggestive actions with students or coworkers.

This doesn't mean that teachers who are single won't become attracted to professional colleagues whose interests mirror their own or that adult romantic relationships never blossom in the workplace. But you must be exceedingly careful. Just because you may desire a romantic relationship with a colleague does not mean that the colleague will reciprocate or will appreciate your attentions in the slightest. In fact, under certain circumstances you may be guilty of sexual harassment.

Courts have found that sexual harassment is sexual discrimination, and is prohibited under the federal Civil Rights Act of 1964. As the United States Court of Appeals, Second Circuit, explained in the 2002 case of *Jin v. Metropolitan Life*, "Title VII forbids an employer 'to discriminate against any individual with respect to his compensation, terms, conditions, or privileges of employment because of such individual's . . . sex.'" Because sexual harassment is sex discrimination, the law does not permit anyone to sexually harass a coworker.

But what is sexual harassment? In *Meritor Savings Bank v. Vinson*, the United States Supreme Court defined sexual harassment by citing the "Guidelines on Discrimination Because of Sex," a set of regulations written by the Equal Employment Opportunity Commission (EEOC), the federal agency created under the Civil Rights Act of 1964 to end workplace discrimination. The *Meritor* Court said sexual harassment included "[u]nwelcome sexual advances, requests for sexual favors, and other verbal or physical conduct of a sexual nature."

Moreover, there are two types of sexual harassment, as defined by the courts. One type is called *quid pro quo sexual harassment* and the other is *hostile environment sexual harassment.*

Regarding the first type, *quid pro quo* translates from Latin as "something for something." It was defined indirectly by the United States Court of Appeals, Seventh Circuit, in *Young v. Bayer.* The Court said that for the plaintiff (the harassed party) to successfully argue "the 'quid pro quo' theory of liability for a supervisor's harassment . . . the plaintiff [necessarily] alleges that the foreman threatened her with the loss of her job if she did not submit to his advances."

E-QUESTION

If an employee gives a coworker a birthday card, is that sexual harassment?
Sometimes. In *Bales v. Wal-Mart,* the U.S. Court of Appeals, Eighth Circuit, affirmed a lower-court verdict that the case's male defendant had harassed the female plaintiff—partly because he sent her a birthday card that could reasonably be interpreted as sexually suggestive.

The second type—hostile environment sexual harassment—was defined in the *Meritor* case as follows: "Title VII affords employees the right to work in an environment free from discriminatory intimidation, ridicule, and insult." And, where sexual harassment "has the purpose or effect of unreasonably interfering with an individual's work performance," such prohibited conduct creates "an intimidating, hostile, or offensive work environment."

But many times, an employee won't be the only one to suffer liability for his sexual harassment of a coworker. Often, the employee will also have the power to drag his employer down into the muck of liability. In the 2005 case of *Pollard v. DuPont*, the United States Court of Appeals, Sixth Circuit, ruled that if a plaintiff can show hostile environment sexual harassment perpetrated by a coworker, and if she can also show that the coworker's employer knew or reasonably should have known about the harassment, then the employer will be liable, too. In the *Pollard* case, the plaintiff repeatedly told her supervisors about a coworker's harassment, yet her bosses merely conducted a quickie investigation and imposed no punishments on the offender. The Court ruled in favor of the plaintiff.

The lessons from all this information seem to be quite clear:

- Always keep your working relationships with your coworkers professional and respectful.
- Do not engage in any behavior that might be interpreted as harassing or sexually suggestive.
- When told to back off, have the graciousness and simple decency to back off.
- Consult a lawyer if you have questions about the legality of your contemplated approaches.

Also, while you're considering the subject of inappropriate relationships, remind any colleagues who need reminding that the "dating game" never extends to students. You might think, "But everyone knows that. That's just ordinary common sense." And it should be; but consider the subject of flirting for a moment. If one of your colleagues is sliding down this path, pull him up. One of the definitions of flirting is an exchange of cutesy, sexually suggestive, risqué banter between two individuals who seem to be attracted to each other. Flirting also involves the deliberate use of gestures that can be interpreted sexually, such as licking one's fingers, running one's tongue across one's lips, conspicuously playing with one's hair, etc. Additionally, flirting may involve fleeting but purposeful touches, such as momentary leg or foot contact, touching another's arm or shoulder, etc.

If a colleague is absent mindedly or deliberately engaging in any such conduct with students, he needs to put an immediate end to it. And if he truly can't differentiate between potential dates and innocent, underage kids, then he needs to find another profession—today.

The Duty to Report Possible Child Abuse

Every state in the United States currently has laws mandating teachers must formally report cases of possible or confirmed child abuse. Generally, the process begins with the teacher having a discussion with the school nurse or the principal about a possible case of child abuse. The next step involves filing a formal written report with the nurse or principal. The nurse, principal, or other designee is then generally responsible for forwarding the report to the state's child-protective agency. Most of this procedural information will probably have been given to you beforehand, pursuant to your district's duty under state law to inform you of your responsibility to report child abuse.

Generally, state laws give you immunity from any criminal prosecution or any civil liability for reports that you make in good faith, which means reports based on a reasonable belief in the truthfulness of what you're saying. (Many states give immunity even in cases where you deliberately proffer a misleading or phony report.) The good-faith immunity you receive in all fifty states is sufficient to protect you from prosecutions or lawsuits.

As a matter of fact, if you do suspect child abuse yet say nothing, at that point you may well be subject to criminal prosecution under state reporting laws. Also at that point, civil lawsuits may become a real possibility if a child is subsequently injured—or worse—and it's learned that you could've filed a report and possibly prevented the tragedy. The impetus for your filing a child-abuse report might be that you have personally noticed cuts, welts, marks, etc., on a child that reasonably lead you to believe that child might be suffering physical abuse. Written or oral evidence of abuse, given to you by a child, may also spur you to file a child-abuse report.

If you do begin the process of filing such a report, remember two things: First, do your best to record statements and observations carefully. Second, try not to be tortured by moral qualms about what you're doing. If a child truly is being harmed, then it's not merely your legal duty, but your sacred responsibility as a teacher to put an end to such an outrage. Trust in the law, and protect your kids.

CHAPTER 14

Relationship Building

You should do everything ethically within your power to build lasting professional relationships with students, parents, colleagues, administrators, and the general community. Use the strategies presented in this chapter to show students and others that you care about teaching. Demonstrate to them that for you, teaching is not simply a job, but rather is the noblest profession of them all and one that is dear to your heart.

14

Students: *Show Them You Care*

Show students you care about them, because teaching isn't a profit-driven endeavor. Rather, teaching is a sacred calling that produces intelligent, productive citizens.

A great way to show students you care is to address them formally, as you've read earlier. Addressing students by titles and last names—"Miss Jones," "Mr. Chan"—demonstrates to students that you're according them the same respect they must accord you.

FACT

In the *Harry Potter* films, kids at the Hogwarts School of Witchcraft and Wizardry are addressed by titles and surnames—"Mr. Potter," for instance. That's because in Britain, students are routinely addressed in this respectful manner, even in primary grades. Give it a try.

You also show students you care by refraining from unnecessary touching. As you've learned, touches can be misinterpreted. Keep your hands to yourself, and show kids that you respect them enough not to inadvertently offend them with constant pawing.

"But kids need hugs!" you might protest. Maybe, but you're not the one who should hug them. Let parents hug; your job is to give kids the knowledge they need to compete successfully in life. Your students will respect you far more if you refrain from hovering and touching and grabbing.

Another way to build relationships with kids is to handle kids' delicate personal issues with discretion, tact, and compassion. For example, if a student's body odor eventually becomes so bad that her seatmates complain to you, help your little stinker maintain her dignity. Don't announce, "Jane Rank stinks, so I'm sending her to the bathroom to wash that funk off!" As the class roars with laughter, Miss Rank slinks from the room in disgrace. Now she's your sworn enemy, and the sensitive kids in class may judge you to be a cruel, heartless teacher.

Instead, take Miss Rank into the hallway while the other kids are working. Tell her she's a good person and add, "But your seatmates can't sit next to you anymore. Do you know why?" If she seems puzzled, say, "Because you need to wash a little. You're a nice girl, but you must keep clean. I'll send you to the nurse with a note and she'll speak to you, okay?" Then, immediately send her down. When she returns, she'll appreciate how tactfully you handled her situation.

In his book *Clinical and Forensic Interviewing of Children and Families*, psychiatrist Jerome Sattler lists child-abuse indicators, including this one: "Child is unwashed." Meaning, a foul-smelling child may be a victim of child abuse. Send the student to the nurse—discreetly—so the child knows you're her ally.

Another opportunity to get kids on your side arises during teacher-student conferences. Don't scream, "Jane Rank, you're disrespectful and lazy! Shape up or I'll make you wish you'd never been born!" Miss Rank is now either humiliated or furious, and is your newest enemy. It may be tempting to verbally slight a student who constantly disrupts your class; instead, tell her, "Miss Rank, you've got a great sense of humor and making people laugh can be fun. But when you horseplay during my lessons, you're keeping everyone from learning. I won't tolerate that. Your education is too important. Quiet down or I'll call your parents today for a conference."

Here are some rules for conducting a teacher-student conference: Mentally rehearse what you'll say beforehand so you don't skip anything. Keep classroom doors open so that passersby can see what you're doing. Don't shout—it's unprofessional. Keep your hands to yourself to avoid misunderstandings. And afterward, jot down a record of what was said.

You've now framed the discussion in the proper context: Jane Rank needs her education, and you'll make certain she gets it. The teacher-student conference is no longer about your supremacy, but about ensuring that she and the rest of your students receive a first-rate education.

Parents

When a parent arrives for a teacher-parent conference, show him you care about his child's academic success. Encourage him to see things intellectually rather than emotionally. Remember, "Parents who love too much are. . . unstoppable when it comes to their kids," warn therapists Laurie Ashner and Mitch Meyerson in their book *When Parents Love Too Much.* "They have an insatiable desire to protect their children." When a parent rushes in like a lion, use your genius to persuade him to depart like a lamb. Remember, lion tamers must control events.

ALERT!

Don't confer with parents who appear violent. If any parent—male or female—acts in a frightening manner, exit the classroom. It's better to flee now and apologize later than to risk conferring with a fool. After exiting, contact your principal immediately.

When the parent arrives for a conference, let him speak first. He may ramble about the alleged offenses you've perpetrated, but as long as he's not yelling or threatening, let him speak. Remember, your job is to serve the public—even the guy sitting before you, yakking about how unfair you are. Once he finishes, respond as calmly as possible. Explain that your only objective is to make sure his child and your entire class receives a proper education, and that you won't let the student waste instructional time daydreaming or disrupting. Praise the student's innate intelligence and add that you have total faith in his ability to excel magnificently.

However, you must also politely detail the student's misbehavior; then reiterate how intelligent he is. Ask the parent to talk to the student daily, reinforcing the necessity of paying attention and earning the highest possible grades. End the conference on a positive note. If you do these things, you might turn an incoming lion into an outgoing lamb.

Other Teachers

Treat teachers like colleagues, not like subordinates—and never like enemies. If you make friends of your colleagues they can offer marvelous assistance, including:

- Watching your class when you visit the restroom
- Being a buddy teacher and accepting misbehaving students
- Providing you with background information to help with particular
  students
- Attending one of your teacher-parent conferences when you want
  to present a united front
- Letting you vent about various problems
- Suggesting ways to improve your teaching methodologies

But if you make enemies of your colleagues, they'll shun you. And one
of the surest ways to make enemies is to engage in the worst behavior of
all—gossip. Take this mini quiz about gossip.

Gossiping may prove hazardous to my health because:
a. I may learn later that I've deeply hurt the person I've gossiped about.
b. The person I've gossiped about may spread rumors about me in
   retaliation.
c. The person I've gossiped about may kick me in my behind.
d. All of the above.

The answer is d.—all of the above. If you gossip about colleagues,
you've got only yourself to blame when someone plants a painful kick in
your butt. Do not gossip.

FACT

In Chinese, gossip is *bàng wén.* In French, it's *commérages.* In German,
klatsch. In Japanese, *zokuwa.* In Spanish, *chisme.* But in any language,
gossip can be defined as insulting slander, spread secretly behind a person's back to damage his reputation.

Of course, you can easily avoid gossip by simply never eating lunch with your colleagues, but this raises a crucial question: Should you eat alone or with the other teachers? Eating lunch with your colleagues is a great way to forge professional relationships; however, some teachers are so negative they ruin the entire meal. Whereas, if you eat in your room, you can quietly read a book—but you'll never form any relationships. Therefore, if you can build relationships while sharing meals, do so. But if you need a quiet lunchtime—and if you create other opportunities to bond with colleagues—then use your time for reading and reflection.

Administrators

Don't defy administrators—including the school board, which has the legal power to fire you. The quickest way to get fired is to disobey reasonable orders; that's insubordination. Just as your students must obey your orders, obey your superiors' orders—if those orders are reasonable.

E-QUESTION

Do I have to follow unreasonable orders?
Teachers' associations advise that if an administrator's nonsensical order isn't imminently dangerous, obey it, then immediately file a grievance—a written complaint—that the administrator has violated the law or the agreement between the district and association. You'll triumph in the grievance procedure by presenting an impartial arbitrator with compelling evidence.

In addition to obeying directives, forge relationships with administrators by volunteering to perform tasks that others dread. Recall that volunteers often gain immortal acclaim for their efforts. Therefore, volunteer to do a few difficult tasks. For example, if your principal sorely wants the Boy Scouts involved in your school but can't find anyone to make it happen, volunteer! Make phone calls and schedule an assembly for parents and Boy Scout representatives. You can do great things when you volunteer, and your principal may appreciate your efforts.

Perform Beneficial Tasks for Your School Board

Perform beneficial tasks for your school board and win their praise. To present your proposals in a huge district, your principal may have to help you penetrate the bureaucracy. But in small districts, one meeting may suffice. Run your proposals by your teachers' association and your principal to see if they have merit. Here are some suggestions:

- Arrange a dinner between board members and teachers' association officers.
- Present laudatory certificates from your teachers' association to board members.
- Propose instructional programs that may boost annual test scores.
- Propose cost-cutting programs that may save the district money.
- Disseminate school-board information and meeting dates to the community.

By helping your school board, you not only aid the district, you advance your students' interests, and ultimately, your own career.

Befriend Secretaries, Custodians, Techs, and Librarians

Befriend your school's secretaries, custodians, computer technicians, and librarians because these professionals can save you tons of work, if you'll simply treat them with respect.

For example, school secretaries can assist you professionally, including:

- Informing you precisely what time paychecks arrive each payday
- Expediting your supply order so your materials arrive more quickly
- Helping you complete complicated paperwork
- Giving you a heads-up when the principal is on the warpath
- Supplying you with updated information such as parents' contact information

In a like manner, your school's custodians are crucial to the running of a school. They can perform above and beyond the call of duty, including:

- Unlocking doors to let you into restrooms, offices, even your classroom if you lose the key
- Supplying you with multiple wastebaskets, even if most classrooms receive only one
- Scrubbing your sink and supplying you with tissues, even if such tasks aren't part of their job
- Occasionally helping you dispose of excessive amounts of trash
- Removing ugly carpet stains and scrubbing stains from floor tiles or wooden floors

In the same vein, computer technicians can often save your life. Their selfless assistance can include:

- Repairing your computer when the hard drive crashes
- Advising you personally on the best types of computers and peripherals to purchase
- Tutoring you on how to e-mail, record grades, take attendance, create folders, etc.
- Connecting the tangle of wires that connect CPUs to printers, scanners, etc.
- Rescuing wayward data you inadvertently delete

Finally, don't forget your school librarians, those highly trained professionals who can make your library trips easier. Their assistance can include:

- Helping with scheduling so that your class can visit the library
- Sending your kids written reminders that their library books will soon come due
- Accepting small groups of your students during another teacher's scheduled library time
- Acquainting you with new books that your students might enjoy reading
- Helping manage your class' behavior while they're in the library

In the end, it all comes down to mutual respect. If you respect others they'll probably respect and assist you. That's how you build professional relationships.

Utilize Friends, Family, Community, and PTA/PTSA

Get friends, family, and the community working for you. On field trips, for instance, you'll need several adult chaperones. Does your spouse have time that day to chaperone? What about your friends? Everyone has commitments, but it doesn't hurt to ask—and your friends might just reply, "I'd love to help." Community members are another untapped source of assistance. Certain parents may have access to the fifty clipboards you're desperately seeking. And many parents may be dying to help in class. Send a letter and find out if the community can supply your professional needs.

In particular, the Parent-Teacher Association (PTA) or Parent-Teacher-Student Association (PTSA), founded in 1897 in Washington, D.C., is a powerful child-advocacy organization with 23,000 chapters in the U.S. Join your school's PTA, and with your principal's approval approach them with professional requests. The PTA website states that the PTA is committed to providing "a quality education and nurturing environment for every child."

Participate in Your Teachers' Association

Decide if you'll join your local teachers' association, a recognized organization of teachers who elect representatives to improve working conditions and wages. The two largest national teachers' associations are the National Education Association (NEA), founded in 1857, with over 3 million members, and the American Federation of Teachers (AFT), founded in 1918, with over 1 million members. Every school district has local associations affiliated with one or both of these organizations. If you don't join your association, you'll have little input in its decisions—such as authorizations to strike, for example. But if you join, you'll be a voting member. Talk to your colleagues and association officers to decide.

CHAPTER 15

Cover Your Assessments

Become an exemplary teacher, the kind of high-minded professional who never discriminates against students because of ethnicity or gender and never mistreats students based on perceptions about sexual orientation. When you assess students equitably, you're covering your assessments, so to speak—also known as CYA. No one will be able to legitimately accuse you of discrimination because you'll scrupulously avoid such undemo-cratic, unprofessional behavior.

Assess Students Equitably

Incorporate time-honored precepts of universal human equality into your methodologies before you presume to teach any multiethnic, multiracial, multireligious class of children.

The easiest way to enhance your understanding of human-rights principles is to reread documents such as the Declaration of Independence, written in 1776 by the great American statesman (and eventual President) Thomas Jefferson, which declares, "We hold these truths to be self-evident, that all men are created equal. . . ."

FACT

You can also peruse the Universal Declaration of Human Rights, adopted in 1948 by the General Assembly of the United Nations, which states, "All human beings are born free and equal in dignity and rights. They are endowed with conscience and should act toward one another in a spirit of brotherhood."

In other words, outmoded notions of racial superiority, class superiority, gender superiority, or other ideas relegating people to subjugation and injustice have been branded obsolete by legislatures throughout history. Do you know a teacher who still subscribes to such precepts? Does he express these ideas to you through racist, sexist, or homophobic remarks?

Tell your friend that the teaching profession isn't for him. "Teachers must treat all with respect and do all they can to maximize appropriate opportunities for progression for all," says American educator John Butcher in his book *Developing Effective 16-19 Teaching Skills*. British educator Pamela Lomax adds in her book *Managing Better Schools and Colleges*: "I believe that pupils have the right not only to contribute to society but also to develop their own individual identities free from the preconceived stereotypes of their role in society. . . . I believe all students are equal in human terms."

If your friend isn't ready to embrace equal-rights concepts, he can't function as a teacher in our diverse, multicultural society. Suggest instead that he find a job where his prejudices won't cause as much damage as they would if he were to be unleashed in a classroom of innocent children.

Try to Create a Prejudice-Free Environment

Sometimes teaching can be a very difficult profession because there are aspects that are at the limits of your control. While you can maintain a level of discipline in your classroom through consistency and fairness, you can't control the uncontrollable. Prejudice and controversy will probably arise, especially in upper-level classes. Dealing with these uncertainties is one of the challenges of an effective educator.

Prejudice in the Classroom

Students come into your class from diverse backgrounds. Every student—and in fact, every person—has prejudices that they carry with them. As you teach, you will witness these prejudices surfacing and sometimes even causing problems within your class or the school. It is your job to keep your classroom as prejudice free as possible.

Your Reaction Sets the Tone

The first clue that students have to your staunch attitude against prejudice should be your initial reaction to any stereotypical or prejudicial statements that are voiced. For example, if a student says something derogatory about immigrants, your reaction should be firm, swift, and forceful. This does not mean that you should yell or become uncontrollable. Instead, with a serious expression, stare at the student in question and say something like, "That type of speech is not allowed in this classroom." You will have an impact.

Any form of prejudice harms the learning environment. Stereotypes and put-downs should be prohibited in your class, and you should set the example by making sure that you do not rely on stereotypes either.

The point is that you will need to be quick to stop offensive speech. If it gets out of hand, there will be hurt feelings and your classroom could become a battleground. This, of course, is to be avoided at all cost. Your classroom should be a safe haven for all students who feel that you welcome them despite their gender, religion, or ethnic background.

Freedom of Speech

The older the students you teach, the more likely they will be to argue with you concerning their right to voice their opinions. Students often bring up the Constitution and its protections for free speech. Point out to them that they do have the protection of the Constitution; however, according to the law, school is a special place. The Supreme Court has said that speech is not allowed that "materially and substantially" disrupts class. Any inflammatory speech against a group should be considered disruptive to the learning environment.

While your reaction should be swift and firm, it should be fair. Unless a student has a history of inappropriate speech, you should assume she made a mistake and did not realize the implications of her words. Use this opportunity to teach your students why the statement was inappropriate.

Remember, teachers must never say, write, or do things that are appallingly offensive to entire groups of children and their parents. For teachers, such unprofessional behavior simply has no place in the classroom.

Respect Local Practices and Traditions

Try to honor the ethnic, religious, and cultural practices of the community in which you work. This doesn't mean you have to do everything local residents do or believe everything they believe, but it does mean you have to demonstrate respect for other people's traditions. In fact, such respect might constitute a good definition of tolerance—namely, withholding judgment of other people's customs until you've made an effort to understand those customs.

For example, consider the historic African-American community of Harlem in Manhattan in New York City. If you're teaching in Harlem, realize that the global phenomenon of hip-hop music—rhythmic dance music coupled with spoken poetry—arose from Harlem in the 1970s, and is therefore revered by many residents as an original art form. Rather than dismissing hip-hop as uncouth, make an effort to listen to some vintage CDs by The Sugar Hill Gang and Public Enemy, and newer CDs by Kanye West, among others. You needn't embrace sexist or violent CDs; rather, ask your students which CDs contain social commentary, minus profanity or chauvinism. You might find that some of today's best poetry arises from young bards with roots in the very community where you're teaching.

E-QUESTION

Should I bring my family when I'm exploring the cultural landscape around my school?
Yes—if you talk to parents, colleagues, and administrators beforehand and gain sufficient information to convince yourself that such "acculturating" outings with your family will likely be safe, fun, and educational.

Or suppose you're teaching in Los Angeles, in an area called Little Tokyo, or Sho-tokyo as its Japanese-American residents call it. Try visiting the Union Center for the Arts Theatre, at 120 Judge John Aiso Street, and attend a theatrical performance by the East West Players acting troupe. The East West Players were established in 1965 by veteran Asian-American actors such as Mako (Mako Iwamatsu), best known for his portrayal of Admiral Yamamoto in the 2001 movie *Pearl Harbor*. The East West Players' Statement of Purpose reads: "To further cultural understanding between the East and West by employing the dual Oriental and American heritages of the East West Players." If you're willing, bring friends and see a performance so you can learn something about the people and traditions of the community where you're teaching.

The point of respecting local practices is not to try to become someone else, but to learn about other cultures. You don't have to go where you're not welcome or do anything you're uncomfortable with. But try talking to your students, reading new books, attending cultural festivals, eating new foods, and listening to new music. Perhaps the best statement regarding America's magnificent diversity was written by the American poet Walt Whitman in the preface to his poetry collection *Leaves of Grass*: "The United States . . . is not merely a nation but a teeming nation of nations." Think of the new nations you can explore, if you open your mind to a bit of cultural diversity.

Become Familiar with District Regulations

Become familiar with your district's written regulations, rules created by organizations to prohibit undesirable behavior or mandate desirable behavior. Regulations differ from statutes, which are laws passed by legislatures (elected lawmakers). Regulations proceed from statutes because statutes expressly authorize officials to create regulations.

You can get your district's regulations from your principal; they're usually contained in loose-leaf binders so that new regulations can continually be added. You can also find them online; get the website address from a colleague or your principal.

Your district's regulations cover a wide range of topics from building maintenance to employee performance, but the regulations you want to focus on are those prohibiting district employees from discriminating against students or other employees based on race, religion, gender, or sexual orientation.

Such antidiscrimination regulations are found in every district. The regulations generally state that they exist to ensure that employees obey state and federal statutes prohibiting unequal treatment. Regarding sex discrimination, there's usually a reference to Title IX of the federal 1972 Education Amendments, stating that no one shall, "on the basis of sex, be excluded from participation in, be denied the benefits of, or be subjected to discrimination under any education program or activity receiving federal financial assistance."

Such regulations generally go on to require:

- Equal education for all students, regardless of race, gender, sexual orientation, etc.
- A prohibition against banning student participation in school activities because of race, etc.
- Equal assessment, evaluation, and grading processes for students without regard to race, etc.
- Instructional materials and books free of bigotry and prohibited biases
- Guidance counseling free of discriminatory biases
- An educational environment free of harassment and discrimination

Contrary to the popular saying, these rules are not made to be broken. Every student deserves an equal education from a fair, even-handed, unbiased teacher.

Learn Something about Education Law

In an earlier chapter, you read detailed discussions about several specific legal principles relevant to the teaching profession. However, if you'd like to learn even more, then you've got to go out and get the information.

Go online and start hitting the legal websites. There are hundreds of really wonderful law-related websites, and no book could do them all justice. But here's a sampling of a few great ones:

- **AltLaw,** *http://altlaw.org,* is a free search engine that gives you access to more than 700,000 public-domain documents, including statutes and cases.
- **California Law,** *www.leginfo.ca.gov/calaw.html,* lets you search statutes in the twenty-nine California codes, which comprise the largest state legislative system in the United States.
- **Findlaw,** *http://public.findlaw.com,* is an invaluable resource listing countless state and federal statutes and cases, legal commentary, and attorney listings.

- **Findlaw Writ,** *http://writ.news.findlaw.com,* is an encyclopedic resource of legal articles written by eminent attorneys on myriad timely legal topics.
- **Law.Com Dictionary,** *http://dictionary.law.com,* is an exhaustive legal dictionary, part of the Law.Com website, where you can search by term, keywords, or alphabetic category.

You can also take one or more college courses to acquaint yourself with education law. Of course, a Juris Doctor (JD) is a graduate-level degree that takes three or more years of intensive study to earn. However, your goal isn't to become an attorney, but to become legally literate. Contact your local university as soon as you can to find out which legal courses they may offer specifically for laypersons and professional educators.

CHAPTER 16

Job Protection

Do everything ethically and legally necessary to safeguard your precious teaching job; not only because it's your family's livelihood but—equally as important—because if you're fired your students will lose a magnificent teacher. Certainly, teachers who are incompetent must be fired, but a teacher as gifted as you are should be retained at all costs, for your students' sake. Therefore, fight for your job whenever necessary.

Document Everything in Writing

Keep written notes regarding anything that occurs during the school year that might threaten your job. That way, you'll protect your job against any students, parents, teachers, or administrators who try to get you fired for petty, dishonest, or vindictive reasons.

Here's a case in point: During a student-teacher conference, you tell a student she must improve her math work. She retorts, "I hate you! You're so unfair!" Shocked, you remind the student that you will not tolerate such disrespect. After the student departs, write some notes while the meeting's fresh in your mind. A student this insolent probably has insolent parents as well, and they'll probably demand a meeting with the principal. Your notes will refresh your recollection before any such meeting. Take notes as follows:

- Write one page of notes, unless you feel more are absolutely necessary.
- Date your notes, because dates are crucial to refuting a variety of spurious charges.
- Write the name of the counseled student, conference time, location, and purpose.
- Record the most important topics discussed and actions taken.
- Record any other notes that might bolster your version of events.

No one, not even your principal, may read your notes (except for an attorney, if matters go that far). Your notes are strictly for your locked classroom filing cabinet or your home office.

Here's another instance where documentation might come in handy: One day, your principal calls you to his office and admits that he envies your superior education. Worse, he adds, "And I've heard you're forty! I wouldn't have hired you if I'd known you were so old!"

Afterward, jot down some notes about this disturbing meeting. Also, consider acknowledging the meeting by writing a letter and delivering it to your principal, while retaining a proof of delivery. If the conversation eventually becomes disputed, your letter might save your job. But note that events can escalate uncontrollably if you initially deliver an acknowledgment letter.

Before acknowledging any conversation, seek professional advice from your association.

FACT

If you want to keep your documents truly secure, save your dimes and buy a fireproof filing cabinet. The best cabinets are rated by Underwriters Laboratories (UL), a nonprofit testing facility, at Class 350—meaning your documents can actually survive a one-hour fire.

In short, don't assume that after you've had a rancorous conference everything will be fine. If a student is disrespectful during counseling, her subsequent tattling to her parents will probably be distorted. Or, if a parent is emotional during a conference, she'll probably contact your principal eventually. And if your principal reprimands you verbally, he'll probably do so in writing as well, and put the materials in your personnel file. Document everything to protect your job.

Make Teachers' Associations Work for You

Require your teachers' association to work hard to protect your job. After all, you're paying their salaries. Your association (with your consent) takes money from your paycheck to fund its operations, and many districts have agency fee rules requiring teachers to join the association or pay fees. Either way, you're paying, so make your association work for you.

Most local teachers' associations are affiliated with state associations, which are in turn affiliated either with the NEA or AFT. For instance, in California, NEA's state affiliate is the California Teachers' Association (CTA); likewise, CTA is currently affiliated with 1,100 local associations statewide.

One of your association's strongest job-protection weapons is the grievance, a written complaint seeking redress for an administrator's violation of your collective bargaining agreement or contract. The contract is negotiated between the association and the district and enumerates teachers' and administrators' rights. If an administrator violates your rights and threatens your job, the contract establishes grievance procedures to redress the violation.

Here's a situation where a grievance might arise: During an evaluation, your principal formally observes you twice then provides two glowing written reports regarding your teaching abilities. A week later, a student defies you when you ask him to stop talking during a lesson. He screams, "I'm not listening to you because you're crazy!" After such gross defiance, you're forced to invoke your legal rights, and you suspend the student. However, your principal hauls him back to your room, yelling, "Don't suspend kids on my watch! This is your second suspension in eight months!" He then orders the student back to class.

You can't be forced to join an association. Legally, an association must represent you whether you're a member or not. But realize that your colleagues may vehemently object to your using the association's services without becoming a member. You decide.

Your principal's actions are a flagrant contract violation, because every contract states that employees and administrators must obey all laws. If your state's laws let you suspend willfully defiant students, that's an unassailable right. And if the law says students can't return to class while suspended, absent your consent, your principal has violated the law and the contract by returning the student. However, don't be insubordinate! Don't tell your principal, "Don't return this kid to my class, idiot!" Now you're the one who's violated the contract, because all contracts prohibit insubordination. You'll swiftly find yourself fired over this issue.

Instead, you decide to simply drop the matter. But the next day, during your final evaluation conference, your principal hands you a final evaluation with an overall rating of "Unsatisfactory," despite two great observations. As a rationale, your principal has penciled in, "Excessive suspensions of students for trivial reasons."

You explain to your principal that by punishing you for exercising your rights he's violating the contract. You ask him to destroy the evaluation and write one based on observations, but he refuses. You bring your association representative to a subsequent meeting, and after you both fail to dissuade him, you decide to file a grievance because unsatisfactory final evaluations can get you fired. You file your grievance immediately because all contracts contain a timeline requiring you to file your grievance within a certain number of days.

Any insubordination toward administrators can get you fired, but be particularly cautious about verbalizing incitements to violence. Your words then become subject to the "imminent lawless action" test created by the United States Supreme Court in the 1969 case of *Brandenburg v. Ohio* (395 U.S. 444). If you fail the test, unemployment awaits.

You meet with your association representative and ask her to complete a grievance form per the contract, while both of you keep a careful eye on the timeline. When completing the grievance form, your representative doesn't elaborate unnecessarily because she'll have time to fully state your case later. The grievance form generally requests the following information:

- Your name, position, and school
- Enumerated contract provision(s) violated
- Nature of the grievance
- Remedy you're requesting
- Your signature and your representative's signature

Your contract specifies what happens next. Usually, your representative submits copies of the grievance to your principal and the district. The principal then has a certain number of days to respond in writing. If he still refuses to destroy the evaluation, per the contract, other grievance meetings are scheduled. When all steps are exhausted and you've gotten no satisfaction, your representative can ask your association to fund an arbitration—a hearing involving a mediator who hears evidence and renders a binding decision. The district and your association furnish advocates to argue their cases and if your advocate prevails, you'll get your remedy.

Survive Teacher Evaluations

Make a great impression on your principal during an evaluation and you'll protect your job. Evaluations, where an administrator observes you teach then writes observation reports, plus a final evaluation, are required by state law. The principal's comments are based on whether you've met professional standards such as those promulgated by the nonprofit National Board for Professional Teaching Standards.

Advance preparation is the key to successful evaluation observations. Schedule a conference with your principal before any observation and bring a list of questions regarding her expectations. Your questions might include the following:

- Do you prefer extensive use of technology such as PowerPoint presentations?
- Do you prefer a more traditional approach without undue reliance on technology?
- Do you condone extensive use of teacher-made materials?
- Do you prefer reliance on textbooks and publisher-supplied materials?
- Would you prefer a lesson where students work cooperatively or individually?
- Would you prefer a lesson incorporating whole-group and small-group instruction?
- Would you prefer an orthodox or unorthodox lesson?
- Would you prefer students to exhibit creativity or a mastery of traditional academics?
- How much of the lesson-period do you want devoted to student assessment?

Also, ask colleagues for tips on impressing administrators during observations. Next, attend district or association seminars such as "Perfect Lesson for Observations." After conferring with colleagues and attending seminars, write two lesson plans and ask your principal to select one. After receiving her input, promptly give her your correctly formatted lesson plan.

Next, practice your presentation beforehand with your students. Revise anything that doesn't work. Remind your students that you'll teach this lesson again, as a review. That way, when you reteach it during your observation your kids are less likely to yell, "Didn't we already do this?"

Finally, the night before an observation, eat a good meal and get some sleep. Above all, don't be afraid. As the great English statesman Edmund Burke wrote in a 1756 treatise, "No passion so effectively robs the mind of all its powers of acting and reasoning as fear." Be well prepared, courageous, and great.

Join Your District's PAR Program

Participate in your district's PAR Program—the Peer Assistance and Review Program. Every district has a similar program, created by state statutes to help teachers become more competent educators. Yes, teachers who receive an unsatisfactory rating on a final evaluation must join PAR; but there shouldn't be any stigma if you join voluntarily—it's just teachers helping teachers. If you request peer assistance, colleagues and administrators should applaud your initiative. Your participation in PAR can reacquaint you with the high standards that are the hallmarks of your profession.

Your district's PAR coordinator can meet with you prior to an observation to discuss an administrator's expectations. After the observation, she can review a checklist of your professional strengths and flaws. State statutes prohibit peer reviews from being used by administrators; these documents are for your self-improvement only. If you work diligently with your PAR coordinator, you'll probably notice an improvement in your teaching.

Strikes and Job Actions

Don't participate in job actions and strikes—unless you and your local teachers' association have rigorously followed the law beforehand and have met all conditions precedent to taking such drastic job-protection actions.

For your purposes, a strike is a collective action by a majority of your association's teachers, or bargaining unit members, who vote to withhold their labor because the district has not met your association's contract-negotiation demands.

Strikes result from a breakdown of the collective bargaining process, established by state law to ensure that associations and districts bargain in good faith to craft a contract covering salaries, hours, and working conditions. However, if negotiations reach an impasse, both sides declare a stalemate and admit that further negotiations will prove fruitless in the short term.

After a declaration of impasse, states generally implement fact-finding procedures, where a mutually acceptable fact finder tries to uncover information that may help both sides break the logjam. Thereafter, both sides may agree to submit the matter to mediation, where a mutually acceptable mediator attempts to resolve the dispute. However, even after the mediator renders her decision, a local association may call for a strike-authorization vote from the membership anyway (if the association operates within a state where such strikes are lawful).

ALERT!

Learn whether your state's statutes proscribe strikes by public employees deemed vital to public health and welfare, such as nurses, firefighters, and teachers. If your state doesn't permit public-employee strikes, don't strike. This admonition isn't a moral or political judgment; it's just a warning that if you break the law, you can land in jail.

Also, even if your association operates in one of the twelve states currently permitting public-employee strikes, if your contract contains a no-strike clause, your association is barred from striking. Instead, it has agreed to be bound by an arbitrator's final decision. However, absent such a clause and additional legislation specifically barring teachers from striking, an association in a strike state is generally not barred from voting to authorize a strike.

Job actions are similar to strikes because employees withhold labor during contract negotiations to gain better terms. However, job actions involve unorthodox tactics as well as a partial, rather than a complete, withholding of labor. So for example, an association might urge its members to follow a work-to-rule strategy during contract negotiations, where teachers forego the countless hours of free work they donate to their districts each year and instead follow all workplace rules to the letter—leaving and arriving precisely on time, using lunchtime to eat instead of grading papers, etc. Additionally, an association might organize a sickout, where teachers phone in sick en masse to disrupt district operations.

E-QUESTION

Which states currently allow public employees to strike?
Public employees are allowed to strike in the following states: Alaska, California, Hawaii, Idaho, Illinois, Montana, Minnesota, Ohio, Oregon, Pennsylvania, Vermont, and Wisconsin.

On the one hand, such job actions can prove very effective; on the other hand, if the district views them as underhanded or even illegal, management can penalize or fire employees who engage in them. You and your association must weigh the costs and benefits of job actions carefully before utilizing such tactics.

Lawyers: Generally a Last Resort

Ask your association for advice about retaining a lawyer if you reach a point in your career where you feel a lawyer is required to protect your job. You may have reached such a conclusion for a number of salient reasons. Perhaps you've gone through a grievance process, only to lose at the eleventh hour because of an arbitrator's failure to properly interpret the evidence before him. Or perhaps an administrator has discriminated against you and now you feel the courts are your sole recourse. Or perhaps a student has made a false accusation against you so you require the services of a criminal defense lawyer. For these and many other valid reasons, you're convinced it's time to go to court.

Get counseling from your association first. If they can help you, even up to providing a skilled advocate to argue your grievance before an arbitrator, let them handle it. Why? Simple economics: Lawyers are extremely expensive because their analytical and oratorical skills are prized by laypersons seeking justice. Therefore, discuss the matter with your association first; if they agree that you need a lawyer, let them counsel you on the options for paying for one.

One option for circumventing huge legal bills is to find a lawyer who accepts a contingent fee; that is, if she wins your civil action—say a suit for wrongful termination or sexual harassment—and collects damages, she'll get paid from that fund.

Of course, contingent fees only apply to civil cases—suits seeking money damages for unjust injury. In a criminal case—say if you're charged with molestation—your association may agree to pay to represent you. Remember, they do their job when they protect your job.

CHAPTER 17

Extra-Curricular Duties

Perform your extra-curricular duties—those tasks that are generally performed outside of your classroom—as conscientiously as you perform your in-class duties. Regard all extracurricular duties as sacred responsibilities. You never have to compromise your principles; if an extracurricular task isn't immoral or illegal, then even if it isn't one of your favorite activities, complete your assignment to the best of your professional ability.

Yard Duty

Many contracts contain provisions requiring teachers to do yard duty. This means that you and your colleagues watch over students during specified times and in specified areas such as the athletic field, multipurpose room, crosswalks, etc. Your obligation is to safeguard students and keep their activities orderly.

Some of your colleagues may regard yard duty as a waste of preparation time, and there's some merit to that objection; teachers need every available moment to prepare lessons. However, the counter argument is that student safety trumps all other considerations.

FACT

In Great Britain, pedestrian crossings are highly visible. Zigzag white lines precede the crosswalk for several yards, warning drivers to reduce speed. Next, white stripes mark the crosswalk itself, giving rise to the fanciful name zebra crossing. Finally, flashing amber Belisha beacons appear at both ends of the crosswalk, alerting drivers that pedestrians may be present.

Imagine the rage a parent will surely feel when your principal calls her one afternoon to say that her child has been hit by a car in the crosswalk near the school. "But she was only grazed," adds the principal, "and the paramedics say you can collect her—right after they've bandaged her leg."

"How could this happen?" demands the angry parent. "Was *anyone* supervising the crosswalk?"

"Well . . . the teacher who was supposed to be on yard duty was . . . elsewhere."

This dreadful accident might never have happened if the assigned teacher had been on duty. After she's summoned to meet parent and child in the principal's office, the teacher admits, "I'm sorry, I forgot my yard duty! But it interferes with my schedule, so it's hard to make time for it."

By now, the parent is so furious that she immediately escorts her child from the office so that she can retain a lawyer as soon as possible. She intends to sue the district for negligence, a civil action that arises when someone fails to do a thing any reasonable person would have done. In this case, a teacher was assigned to watch the crosswalk—yet she couldn't even be bothered to show up. As a result, a child was injured. After the parent is awarded substantial money damages in court, the negligent teacher is fired. Make certain that teacher isn't you.

Staff Meetings

Show up promptly for all after-school staff meetings. Take notes, stay awake, and pay attention to everything. You might think staff meetings are boring, but it's one of your extracurricular duties, so attend. Don't go AWOL because most principals circulate a sign-in sheet during meetings or instruct a secretary to scan the room and write the names of missing teachers.

ALERT!

School staff meetings fall into a category of meetings called recurring meetings, where you and the rest of the staff meet at regular calendar intervals, generally once a month. Staff meetings are always announced well ahead of time, and your principal expects you to attend consistently so that important information can be disseminated to you.

If you routinely sleep in staff meetings or skip them altogether you'll occasionally miss important news and debates. For example, suppose that during a meeting several teachers propose that when the kids finish state-mandated testing, their scratch paper should be graded based on how well the kids have copied the problems and solved them. Other teachers ask whether state law permits such a thing. A debate begins—and because you're awake, you're lucky enough to be part of it.

After a lively exchange, the consensus seems to be that the test-administration manual forbids students from copying problems and forbids scratch paper from being graded by the state. Therefore, the staff decides that teachers shouldn't grade scratch paper, either. The thought occurs to you, "That was no waste of time—that was an exciting, problem-solving staff meeting."

Chaperoning a School Dance

Don't confuse the kids' fun with your fun when the principal asks you to chaperone a school dance. During the dance you might be tempted to boogie with the kids, but remember that the French word *chaperon* means the hood that falconers cover their birds' heads with to keep them calm. You're trying to ensure that students' high-octane energy doesn't explode into misbehavior. You do this by walking, talking, and keeping order. Step back from the fun and remember that it's irresponsible to dance when you're supposed to be chaperoning.

You serve a vital protective function as a chaperone because kids have sometimes suffered harm at social functions. For instance, in 1999, two visiting fifteen-year-old British girls said they were raped at a party held in the resort town of Mammoth Lakes, California. The girls said they were given liquor prior to their ordeal. Keep your eyes open.

Protect the kids by patrolling everywhere in the building where the dance is being held. Don't linger anywhere too long because you're trying to keep an eye on everybody. Visit all parts of the room so that if a kid in an isolated corner needs help you can come running.

You're not there to spoil the kids' fun, but you are there to prevent misbehavior. Enlist the help of other teacher-chaperones if necessary. Take chaperoning seriously: Watch over everyone, mediate arguments, discourage inappropriate dancing, and encourage all the kids to dance and have fun.

Graduations and Awards Ceremonies

If you're asked to participate in graduation programs or awards ceremonies, drive to the venue at least one hour early. Otherwise, you'll probably end up battling hundreds of cars for precious parking spaces, increasing the chance of being late for your assigned duty, whether it's ushering, speaking onstage, distributing awards, etc.

Be cheery and helpful at these events. The crowds of family members and friends will be confused about where to go, so carry maps, programs, etc., in order to answer questions intelligently. Remember that many attendees will be elderly, so escort them inside and let them be seated early, if your principal consents. Familiarize yourself with the facility so that when people ask about restrooms, seating, etc., you'll know the answer.

E-QUESTION

What should I do if I'm late for the ceremony and can't find parking?
Don't arrive late! Otherwise, remind yourself, "I only need one parking space, not two," and patiently cruise around the entire parking lot, or the entire block, until you find a space. You can also call your principal on your cell phone to request assistance.

If your principal has asked you to announce students' names at the podium, study your name list carefully. If a name gives you trouble, find your colleagues and ask them for the correct pronunciation. Write it phonetically beside the name and memorize it. For instance, if you see, "Tadeusz Kosciuszko," ask the student's teacher, who'll tell you, "Tah-DOOSH KOSH-choo-shko." Jot down the pronunciation and practice it.

Once you're at the podium, project your voice: "Ladies and gentlemen, my name is Jane Doe, and I'm honored to announce the next fifteen students who will graduate from Washington Elementary!" Don't forget that this is a once-in-a-lifetime event for the proud families involved. Make it as unforgettable as possible.

The Power of Festivals, Sales, and Bazaars

Utilize the power of school-wide festivals, sales, and bazaars to bring much-needed money to your school and help you bond with the community.

School bazaars can offer saleable items from pies to T-shirts, but one of the most lucrative types of sales is the garage sale. In a garage sale, the community brings unwanted household items to school, where everything will be securely stored for an upcoming weekend sale. Worthless junk should be discouraged, but all reasonable items should be accepted. The community's generosity can be stimulated if the principal distributes receipts for the items—with monetary amounts to be estimated by the donators—showing that all accepted items are tax deductible.

The beauty of such sales is that on the sale day, students and community members buy back everything they've donated! You and your colleagues can assist during the sale, either as draftees or as volunteers. You can also hunt for bargains yourself, all the while getting to know community members and their kids. In the end, your school may have raised sufficient funds to buy new books, equipment, and more.

One of the oldest types of bazaars is the wet market, an outdoor bazaar selling fresh meats and produce. Wet markets are cleansed by being thoroughly sprayed with water, hence the name. Your school bazaar should be considerably easier to manage—a few carnival booths, a few food stands, and no water hoses required.

Your school can also combine the garage sale with a bazaar, where parents sell baked goods, T-shirts, and other items. Raffle tickets can also be sold, with prizes going to the winners. Booths can be erected where kids who purchase tickets can try their hand at bean-bag tosses and other fun activities. Candy, popcorn, and drinks can also be sold. The point of these activities is not just to raise money, but to build rapport between the community and the school. The hours you volunteer to this extracurricular activity can help you build invaluable community relationships.

Hold a Class Party

Offer a party to your students as a reward for good grades. If your kids meet the academic challenges you set for them, keep your promise and throw a party.

Of course, you'll need permission from your principal first. If she says that parties may only be held in the multipurpose room, never in classrooms, follow her instructions. If she says that certain foods can't be brought, pass those instructions along to your kids.

The cheapest way to put together a party is to send a letter to parents, with the principal's approval, asking parents to prepare a plate of nonperishable items such as fruit snacks, cookies, crackers, chips, pretzels, cupcakes, candy, etc., and juice boxes. Such fare might not be wholly nutritious, but it's fun! Ask parents to place all items on a large paper plate, wrap it securely, and have students bring it to school. You'll marvel at the culinary variety and your kids will enjoy critiquing each other's plates.

You might want to be extremely cautious about letting your kids bring any foods that need to be warmed up, such as chicken, beef, pork, fish, casseroles, soups, etc. These kinds of foods are delicious, but if improperly cooked or stored, they can also harbor pathogenic bacteria—microorganisms that can cause diseases. Stick with nonperishable items.

In your letter, also ask parents to let their kids bring appropriate CDs, if the parents screen them and if they're willing to risk any damage or loss. If you supply a CD player, the kids can dance under your careful supervision. Class parties—although they involve lots of extra work—are a great opportunity for you and your students to get to know each other as human beings.

Field Trips: A Class Bonding Opportunity

Use field trips—school-sponsored journeys to educational sites outside the school—as an opportunity to share exciting extracurricular experiences with your students. Certainly, the work's hard and the hours can be brutal—you might get home at 9 P.M., for instance—but you also might give your kids a learning adventure they'll never forget. Museums, theatres, zoos, and much more offer you a chance to laugh with your kids and discover new sights with them.

Always pay attention to safety if you want to enjoy a successful field trip. Carry a notepad and pen with you to write down information such as:

- The first and last name of every kid in your assigned group
- The number of the bus to which you'll be returning later
- The names of parent volunteers who are accompanying your group
- Important times, such as the hour when everyone must return to the bus
- Meeting places and times where groups will rendezvous

Also, carry a small backpack stocked with essential items, including:

- Completed field-trip slips for every kid in your group, with emergency phone numbers
- Plastic water bottles
- Breakfast bars and fruit snacks
- A first-aid kit
- Lots of resealing plastic bags—there's always a use for these little guys

Additionally, stay sharp during your field trip so that you don't make blunders. A common error is to lead students across an intersection on a green light, and when the light turns red, allow students to continue pouring into the intersection. That's an accident begging to happen. Also, teachers sometimes fail to count the kids in their assigned group, with the result that a kid wanders off and isn't found for hours. Another error is for buses to depart without a teacher counting every student. When someone yells, "Jen's missing!" the bus has to turn around and retrieve her.

Of course, as with school dances, make certain you recall your primary duty during extracurricular outings—to keep kids safe. Parents are depending on your professionalism to protect their children. Stay alert, don't allow problems to develop, and regularly count your students to make sure no one's missing.

Treat field trips as an extracurricular duty where you might learn nearly as much as your students, perhaps giving all of you something to write about and talk about for many months.

Class Newspapers or Websites

Consistently produce a high-quality class newspaper or maintain a class website to provide students with a place to showcase their creative writing, drawing, and technological super skills. A newspaper can easily be written and formatted using your classroom computers, and sent for printing to the school's best laser printer (pages to be hand stapled later). To generate articles, students can be assigned to interview each other in pairs, then write about each other's academic or personal achievements. Moreover, a class newspaper is an excellent forum for your students to express their viewpoints on local, state, national, and even global issues.

E-QUESTION

How do I set up a class website?
Persuade your principal to buy content management system (CMS) software that allows you, your students, your colleagues, and school administrators to utilize passwords to upload bulletins, articles, essays, stories, poetry, artwork, and more to a custom website. The software is user friendly and will guide you every step of the way.

However, be aware of the legal limitations courts have imposed on what you and your students may say in your newspaper or website. The United States Supreme Court, in the 1969 case of *Tinker v. Des Moines,* ruled that students' First Amendment free-speech rights are constitutionally guaranteed, but if the speech causes disruption, administrators and teachers can regulate or proscribe it. So, if your students encourage their peers to jeer the principal at the upcoming school assembly for failing to build a skate park at your school, that kind of speech probably won't be legally protected. It's always prudent to let your principal sneak a peek at any material that's going into a newspaper or onto a website.

CHAPTER 18

A Discussion of Private Schools

So far, the discussions and information in this book have focused entirely on the public educational system. However, a parallel system of private schools also exists—educational institutions that aren't operated by governments or funded by taxpayers, but instead are financed by means of tuition—money paid by students' parents directly to the schools. If you're interested in teaching in a private school, study the information in this chapter carefully so you can make an informed decision.

Teachers' Rights: Public Versus Private Schools

The most significant legal right that public-school teachers have historically enjoyed, and private-school teachers have not, is sovereign immunity, whereby governmental entities and their employees have traditionally received immunity from lawsuits arising from torts, or civil wrongs, committed by government employees.

Of course, in virtually every state the ancient doctrine of sovereign immunity has been amended by statutes expressly waiving immunity. In Virginia, for example, the Virginia Torts Claims Act declares that Virginia "shall be liable for claims of money . . . on account of . . . personal injury or death caused by the negligent or wrongful act or omission of any employee. . . ."

However, this statute only applies to the Virginia state government—not to its agents, such as public schools and public-school teachers. If a Virginia parent wants to sue a school district, the parent will have to sue the Virginia state government itself, utilizing a cause of action called vicarious liability, where the state becomes responsible for the negligence of its agencies.

FACT

Even if a parent can prove that a district negligently caused injury to her child, state statutes generally cap recoverable damages at approximately $100,000–$250,000. To circumvent such arbitrary caps and recover meaningful damages, the parent would probably have to prove gross negligence—a willful and wanton neglect of a legal responsibility.

Or consider the state of Illinois. There, the Tort Immunity Act says that although the state government may be sued, "public employees" such as public-school teachers cannot be sued for injuries caused by failure to properly supervise school activities.

But such immunity does not apply to private schools or their teachers. In the 1979 case of *Cooney v. Society of Mt. Carmel*, the Illinois Supreme Court ruled that merely because private schools "serve the public good" does not "transform such schools from private into public entities." This ruling was referenced in another Illinois Supreme Court case, 1998's *Henrich v. Libertyville High School,* where the court again declined to attach the protections of the Tort Immunity Act to private schools.

In fact, in the 2002 Illinois Supreme Court case of *Brugger v. Joseph Academy,* the court ruled that in a situation where a student was injured after a private-school teacher required her to play dodge-ball—though she had a doctor's note of excuse—the Tort Immunity Act didn't protect the school from being sued.

Therefore, if you want to teach in a private school, consider carefully the difference in the degree of legal protection that your state affords public-school teachers and private-school teachers.

The Issue of Uniforms

Many public-school and private-school students are required to wear school uniforms. The majority of public schools, in lieu of uniforms, generally adopt dress codes specifying permissible student clothing. But most private schools require students to don standardized uniforms. Uniforms vary in style but frequently consist of black or dark-colored slacks, white dress shirts, and neckties for boys; and dark slacks or skirts and white blouses for girls. Suit jackets for boys and girls are also frequently worn.

ALERT!

If you feel that students should be required to wear uniforms, and you're drawn to private schools because of their uniform requirements, be aware that in 2001, the National Association of Elementary School Principals (NAESP) reported that 21 percent of all American public schools had begun to mandate school uniforms for their students.

If you share the widely held view that school uniforms influence students' academic success, then you probably agree with noted law professor David Altheide, who wrote in his book *Terrorism and the Politics of Fear*: "School uniforms . . . convey the institutional values of the school."

Therefore, private schools' uniform requirements might appeal to you more than the sartorial freedom offered by public schools. Many eminent academicians find uniforms appealing, as well. For example, psychologist Dewey Cornell notes in his book *School Violence*: "Even President Clinton, in his 1996 State of the Union Address, endorsed the concept of school uniforms as a way to improve student behavior and reduce gang violence. . . . Regardless of setting, school uniforms are thought to encourage more polite and civil behavior among students and to focus their attention on schoolwork."

At the same time, even if uniforms are an important issue for you, note that entire public school districts nationwide are also mandating uniforms. One of the first districts to require uniforms was the Long Beach Unified School District (LBUSD) in the city of Long Beach, California. LBUSD began its experiment with uniforms in 1994, and has since reported that suspensions have decreased by nearly 35 percent and assault-and-battery complaints have decreased by nearly 70 percent. While these encouraging trends might not actually be linked to the district's adoption of uniforms, the connection seems compelling nevertheless. Other public-school districts with uniform requirements include the School District of Philadelphia (SDP), encompassing Philadelphia, Pennsylvania. The District's website *(www.phila.k12.pa.us)* reminds parents that, "All School District of Philadelphia students are required to wear a uniform." Therefore, even if you've decided that any students you teach will have to wear uniforms, with a bit of research you might find a public school district that meets your requirements.

Scholarships

Public schools are free, democratic institutions supported by taxpayers; private schools are enterprises that charge tuition or fees that parents pay for their children's care and instruction.

Tuition at some of the world's finest private schools can be impressive, such as the $54,000 per year that parents currently pay at the venerable Eton (the King's College of Our Lady of Eton beside Windsor), in Berkshire, England. In the United States, the renowned Andover (the Philips Academy Andover) currently charges $37,000 per student. Often, many talented students who wish to attend such prestigious private schools but who lack sufficient funds must earn scholarships, or grants of money from charitable foundations, the federal government, etc. A scholarship can pay part or all of a private school's tuition and/or boarding fees, depending on the amount awarded.

Numerous private-school scholarships are available to kids nationwide, with much of the money generously provided by the schools themselves. For instance, schools belonging to the National Association of Independent Schools (NAIS), a Washington, D.C., based association of 1,300 independent schools, awarded some $960 million in financial aid to deserving students.

Scholarships are often designed to increase the private-school enrollment of minority students, who have been traditionally underrepresented in such schools. If you are excited by the idea of encountering as many ethnicities and cultures as possible in your classroom, you might be more attracted to public schools than to private schools. As a general rule, public schools attract a somewhat more diverse clientele than private.

The Black Student Fund (BSF), established in 1964 in Washington, D.C., is a scholarship program specifically addressing the needs of minority youth. According to the BSF's website (*www.blackstudentfund.org*), 99 percent of BSF aid recipients complete high school and 97 percent go on to attend college.

According to the website of the National Center for Education Statistics (NCES) (*http://nces.ed.gov/index.asp*), the percentage of minority students attending public schools nationwide—kindergarten through twelfth—was 58 percent as of 2005–2006. During that same academic year, the NCES reports in its landmark 2008 study "Characteristics of Private Schools in the United States" that only about 25 percent of private-school students were minorities. If you're searching for the most diverse student populations possible, you might wish to explore the career opportunities available in the public educational system before moving on to the private sector.

The Merits and Demerits of Boarding Schools

Boarding schools provide students not merely with full-time academic instruction, but with meals and full-time living quarters, as well. The boarding school becomes a home away from home for students, and for the teachers who frequently live with them. Typically, teachers are assigned as housemasters to oversee students who reside in the school's houses or dormitories. Each house might feature a library, dining hall, chapel, study rooms, and bedrooms.

If you crave the unique professional opportunity to become intimately familiar with your students' individual personalities, career goals, and academic needs, a boarding-school teaching position might satisfy your requirements.

E-QUESTION

What's the world's oldest boarding school?
The oldest boarding school in the United States is West Nottingham Academy (WNA) in Colora, Maryland, established in 1744 and still going strong. However, Winchester College in Hampshire, England, was established in 1382 by the Bishop of Winchester, and is currently administered by the eminent Dr. Ralph Townsend.

However, if you're the kind of teacher who likes to hurriedly pack up at the end of a long, stressful day and drive down to the lake for two hours of freshwater fishing, boarding school might not be your best option. Boarding schools require teachers to supervise students day and night, until lights out or bedtime. Your job comes to resemble parenting as much as teaching, as you fulfill your duties as housemaster, counselor, after-hours tutor, sports coach, chaperone, chauffeur, etc.

Therefore, do some research before making a career decision; read authoritative books, articles, and studies on the boarding school way of life and talk to representatives of boarding schools, as well as to alumni, to decide whether a boarding-school teaching position is for you.

The Pros and Cons of Religious Schools

Private religious elementary and secondary schools, also called parochial schools, deliver not only academic instruction, but religious instruction as well.

According to a 1994 report by the National Center for Educational Statistics (NCES) titled "Private Schools in the United States: A Statistical Profile, 1993–94," the majority of religious schools nationwide are administered by the Catholic Church. Serving some 3 million students in over 8,000 schools as of 1994, Catholic parochial schools operate under the supervision of the church's many dioceses or local administrative districts and dominate the religious-school landscape.

Increasingly, though—and this is also according to the NCES's 1994 report—the number of non-Catholic Christian religious schools has increased significantly, and as of 1994 such schools comprised approximately 40 percent of the nation's religious schools, serving over 600,000 students. The report noted, "Religion is an especially important facet of these schools, as attested by the responses [to an NCES survey] of principals, 80 percent of whom indicated that religious development was among the . . . most important educational goals of their school. . . ."

FACT

The 2004 book *Urban Issues: Selections from the CQ Researcher* by the editors of the Congressional Quarterly, makes the cogent observation that, "schools operated by Christians, Jews, Muslims, or other faiths . . . serve primarily religious purposes. Furthermore, a United Church of Christ minister is quoted as saying, "Religious schools exist to promote faith."

Therefore, if you're thinking about working in a parochial school, you might want to examine whether your personal beliefs are compatible with the specific religious tenets taught at the school where you're hoping to interview. Such a compatibility of beliefs might not seem absolutely essential to you, but your prospective principal might raise the issue, and might ask if you're comfortable with the school's doctrines. If you can't honestly answer yes, then the principal might consider you a less-than-perfect match for his school.

Are Charter Schools the Future?

Charter schools are a fascinating hybrid of public schools and private schools. They're taxpayer-supported public schools, but they're operated by individuals or private corporations under a charter or grant of permission from a state or school district, allowing them to experiment with innovative methodologies and sidestep various bureaucratic regulations. In return, the charter school is expected to improve students' academic performance and raise standardized test scores.

Since the first charter-school statute was enacted by the Minnesota legislature in 1991, and the second was enacted by California in 1992, charter-school laws have been adopted in the District of Columbia and in forty of the United States.

ALERT!

If you've got your heart set on working in a charter school, then be especially careful about where you decide to live, because ten states currently carry no statutes on their books authorizing the creation of charter schools. The ten nonchartering states are Alabama, Kentucky, Maine, Montana, Nebraska, North Dakota, South Dakota, Vermont, Washington (state), and West Virginia.

If you're in love with the idea of charter schools and you've decided that a charter school would be the perfect place for you to advance your teaching career, you should know that charter schools do sometimes fail, just like private schools. Currently, over 10 percent of all schools chartered nationwide since 1991 have ceased operations.

Also, regarding the enhancement of students' academic performance—the reason why charter schools were created—a 2003 report compiled by researchers Howard Nelson, Bella Rosenberg, and Nancy Van Meter of the American Federation of Teachers (AFT), titled "Charter School Achievement on the 2003 National Assessment of Educational Progress," concluded that charter-school kids perform about as well statistically on standardized tests as public-school kids. The AFT report was publicly excoriated in 2000 by Caroline Hoxby, an economics professor at Harvard University, who said that the report's reliance on the test scores of only 6,000 students invalidated the published conclusions.

However, a 2006 report by the National Center for Education Statistics (NCES) titled "A Closer Look at Charter Schools Using Hierarchical Linear Modeling," concluded that the measurable academic performance of charter-school students in mathematics and reading was somewhat lower than the performance of public-school students. This report has also been criticized as flawed, most notably by the Washington, D.C. based Center for Education Reform, a conservative nonprofit corporation established in 1993 to promote charter schools and other educational reforms.

Research a charter school carefully before signing on, because some former proponents of charter schools point to an unintended consequence: decreased job security for teachers. A former charter-school booster, Pennsylvania Representative Mark Cohen, has been quoted as saying, "The evidence to date shows that the high turnover of staff undermines [charter] school performance more than it enhances it. . . ."

Charter schools have also been criticized for interfering with longstanding societal aims of fostering racial integration. University of Georgia sociology professor Linda Renzulli and sociologist Vincent Roscigno offered evidence in their 2007 article "Charter Schools and the Public Good," published in the Winter issue of the journal *Contexts,* that charter schools are serving to solidify racial segregation. Thus, as with private schools in general, if your ambition is to teach a diverse, multicultural group of kids, research charter schools carefully.

CHAPTER 19

Organizing School Clubs and Sports Teams

An excellent way to have fun with your students is to organize and supervise one or more clubs or sports teams. When you take the time to guide youngsters in these kinds of exciting extracurricular activities, you'll be constantly reminded of a wonderful truth: The reason you became a teacher is that when you do fun, wholesome things with kids, you reap endless joy and stay eternally young.

Solicit Students' Ideas for Clubs and Teams

If you're ready to start an after-school club or sports team, ask your students for ideas—but make sure you've got paper and pen, because kids can come up with endless suggestions when it comes to having a little fun.

Here's one example: Do you know what Japanese *animé* is? It's the most popular style of cartoon animation in the world. As reported in the March 30, 2008 issue of Osaka's *Mainichi Newspaper,* animé may have originated in Japan as early as 1917 with a short cartoon titled "Namakura Gatana." Directed by filmmaker Junichi Kou'uchi, the cartoon featured a samurai using a new sword. Since then, thousands of popular animé films, television series, and video games have captured kids' attention worldwide, including such current favorites as *Naruto, Pokémon*, and the *Kingdom Hearts* video-game series. If one of your kids—or you—suggests starting an after-school gathering of animé fans, you'll probably be inundated with suggestions from your enthusiastic students as to activities, meetings, rules, field trips, etc. for their new Animé Club.

FACT

According to *Newtype,* a widely read Japanese magazine dedicated to animé, the most-watched animé cartoon in Japan is *The Melancholy of Haruhi Suzumiya.* Known in Japanese as *Suzumiya Haruhi no Yūutsu,* this popular television series follows the exploits of a high school girl who learns she has the superhuman ability to bend the universe to her will, for good or evil.

How about a chess club? You might not think chess is that popular with kids, but you'd be wrong. The annual World Junior Chess Championship, for instance, sponsored by the World Chess Federation or Fédération Internationale des Echecs (FIDE), has been held since 1951 for players under twenty years old. As of 2007, it attracts over 100 competitors and thousands of youthful spectators from the United States, Russia, China, India, Vietnam, Egypt, Israel, and dozens of other nations. Add to that the World Youth Chess Championship, an annual kids' competition that even includes children under eight years old. The 2007 tournament held in Turkey, and the brilliant victories of Ivan Popov and Valentina Gunina, were witnessed by thousands of eager kids and their parents. If you can sponsor an after-school chess club, your club might be flooded with as many participants as you can handle.

Another suggestion your kids might offer is a debate team. Kids are bursting with strong opinions, and they love to argue. Since you don't allow pointless arguing in the classroom, why not put their genius for repartée to good use in an after-school debating club? Debate is a popular activity, as evidenced by the huge crowds that attend the annual World Schools Debating Championships, a competition for high-school kids that attracts teams from approximately thirty-five countries. A sixteen-year-old member of the 2002 U.S. International Debate Team summed up the feelings of many competitors when she told reporters from the Honolulu Star-Bulletin, "It's like the Olympics. I'm so thrilled and honored." If your kids request a debate team, help them turn their dream into a reality.

ALERT!

Don't take on more after-school responsibilities than you can reasonably handle, and don't create clubs or teams if you don't know what the heck you're doing. You want kids to have fun, but more importantly, you want them to be safe. For example, don't sponsor judo or karate teams if you know nothing about these difficult-to-master sports.

Regarding athletic teams, does your school have a drill team, cheer squad, field-hockey team, foosball team, ice-hockey team, judo team, karate team, lacrosse team, skateboard team, soccer team, or volleyball team in addition to the traditional baseball, basketball, and football teams found in virtually every school? If not, and if you have sufficient expertise and talent to coach kids in any of these sports, consider organizing after-school teams. Get as many ideas from the kids as possible so you can sponsor a team that will have wide appeal.

Publicize Your Club or Team

Your first step in creating a club or team is to make an appointment with your principal then sit down with her to pitch your idea. You don't have to jump up and down in your seat with enthusiasm; you just have to show your principal that you're knowledgeable and prepared. Once your principal gives you the go-ahead to create your club, start publicizing it.

If you know for a fact that all the students in your school are mature and trustworthy, then after careful consultation with your principal and your family members you might consider posting your classroom telephone number, classroom e-mail address, and home telephone number and address. But if you have any doubts at all, never publicly post this information.

Your students will be eager to help in this area. You'll need posters to stick on hallway walls as well as on windows and doors throughout the school. Enlist students who are interested and who possess skill to design images, logos, and imaginative fonts, telling the world that a community service club, bible club, math club, guitar club, or drama club has finally come to your school. Ask the kids to use bright colors and bold artwork to convey a sense of excitement. At a minimum, the poster should contain the following information, written legibly:

- The club's or team's purpose or reason for being
- Your name, as the sponsoring teacher, along with your teaching position and room number
- The room where the club will regularly meet
- The weekday and time when the club meets and the frequency of meetings
- Proposed fun activities such as possible field trips, presentations, guest speakers, etc.
- A nicely written exhortation not to miss such a fun, unique club
- A cordial invitation to parents to contact you with any questions

You'll also want to help your kids create eye-catching 8½" × 11" flyers, which can also be posted throughout the school, but which are primarily designed to be distributed to as many students as possible to read and then take home to their parents. The flyers can mirror the posters, with many of the same design elements, plus the information kids need to get excited about the club and consistently attend its meetings.

Finally, make sure that for at least one week prior to the first scheduled meeting of your new club the students or administrators who read daily announcements over the public-address system include a catchy announcement about your club. Have the kids write something well ahead of time and deliver it promptly to the announcers in the office.

Maintain Professionalism

Maintain the same high standards of professional conduct during your after-school club meetings that you maintain every day in your regular classroom. An after-school club is certainly an opportunity to have some fun, but it's not an opportunity to become inappropriately over familiar with any of your club attendees, for any reason. Especially when you're coaching a sport, a great deal of physical contact is to be expected; nevertheless, try to make sure all such contact is necessary and appropriate.

E-QUESTION

What other ideas might kids come up with for after-school clubs or teams?
The list is practically inexhaustible. The kids might suggest a gourmet cooking club, academic decathlon team, Girls Club, Boys Club, stamp-collecting club, bowling team, fashion-design club, comic-book club, equestrian club, computer club, book-discussion club, future-leaders club, multicultural club, and more.

Also, maintain the same high behavioral expectations for your after-school kids as you do for your classroom kids. You are meeting to form a club that might remain popular for decades, ideally. You're not meeting to break school rules, argue violently, and generally go nuts. When arguments begin, moderate the discussions so kids don't start screaming. When fundamental disagreements arise, stop debate at some point and put the matter to a group vote or simply use your veto power as a teacher to quash unsafe or unworkable ideas. You want the kids to have a little freedom, but don't forget that you're a mentor in this situation and your job is to use your adult-level knowledge and experience to help the kids have some good, clean fun.

The First Meeting

Your first step, once you've called your club's or team's first meeting to order, is to ask each kid to take a moment to introduce himself by stating his name, interests, etc. Try to get even the shy kids to say something—at least their names, if nothing else. You don't have to ask the kids to stand up; keep this part of the meeting really friendly and informal.

FACT

The Boys & Girls Clubs of America (BGCA), established in 1860, is a nationwide nonprofit organization consisting of 4,000 independent clubs, all of which seek to actively assist kids and "promote and enhance the development of boys and girls by instilling a sense of competence, usefulness, belonging, and influence," according to the BGCA website *(www .bgca.org).*

Next, distribute an agenda—a printed sheet of items you'd like to discuss with the kids. Yes, the use of an agenda might seem awfully formal, but you don't necessarily have to discuss how you'll usher in an era of global peace. You just want to have a few talking points so the conversation doesn't degenerate into a pointless verbal free for all.

One of your first agenda items will be a brief information session where you explain how often the club will meet, dues that the kids will need to pay, and so forth. Next, explain your overall vision for the club or team. Let the kids know if the club will meet daily, weekly, or otherwise. If you've started a chess club, will you and the kids be playing just for fun or will they compete during the school year to determine an ultimate champ? Or will you take the kids to official tournaments so that they can compete with kids from other schools? Decides such issues beforehand then talk to the kids.

ALERT!

Note that the Animé Expo is generally held only in three venues: The greater Los Angeles, California, metropolitan area; the greater New York City, New York, metropolitan area; and the Tokyo, Japan, metropolitan area. So if your club members want to attend, all of you might need to make timely travel and hotel arrangements.

Next, solicit ideas or objections regarding the vision you've outlined for the club or team. If there's general disapproval or the kids just want to voice their own ideas, ask for alternative ideas then let the kids vote, if necessary. Write some of their ideas on the whiteboard or on large chart paper. (You might be surprised to discover that their ideas are even better than yours!) Then, if you trust democracy sufficiently, let everyone vote on the four or five ideas that you feel are reasonably sound. Once the kids have voted on their suggestions, tally the results and incorporate the winning ideas into your plans.

After presenting your vision and letting the kids vote on alternative ideas, you might next hold a group election for club officers, if you think officers will be necessary to facilitate the club's operations. Here are a few suggestions for club officers:

- A president to help you call club meetings to order and introduce each meeting's agenda
- A vice president who can take over the president's duties when the president is absent
- A secretary to briefly record what's discussed and what's resolved

Finally, promise each other you'll do some really fun things on a regular basis and one spectacularly fun thing each school year. So, if you've founded an animé club, you could show one hour of a high-quality, appropriate animé movie during each meeting then have a round-table discussion afterward, if there's time. Then, every July when the annual Animé Expo rolls around, the club could decide to put its pennies together so every member can attend.

End your first meeting and every subsequent meeting on a positive note. Thank the kids for coming and express your sincerest wishes that this club will be not only educational, but fun.

Money-Collection Issues

Collecting money from kids for club activities is an extremely serious business and must be handled in a businesslike manner. Don't dump everyone's money into an old shoebox without keeping any records and expect to remember later on who gave what and how the money's supposed to be spent.

Instead, buy a serviceable receipt book, which generally contains a few hundred pages of NCR (no carbon required) paper. Just press down hard while you write and the interaction of dry chemicals on the sheets of paper will produce an instant copy. Carefully fill out each receipt for each kid, then gently tear out the receipts along their perforations and distribute them. The copies left behind form a book with a record of all cash or checks paid and receipts given out.

If you want to be a bit more high tech, you can use your classroom computer to issue electronic receipts or e-receipts, which in this case simply means that you type receipt information when a kid pays you, then print the kid a receipt. Depending on your typing and computer skills, this may be much faster for you than writing by hand.

Each time you issue a receipt, immediately lock the money away in a small portable strongbox or safe, to which only you, as the adult in charge, possess the key or numeric combination or both. Put the safe away in a locked cupboard after all money has been collected. When the meeting eventually ends, unlock the cupboard and take the safe home.

One more thing: Remember that holding money for a specified purpose is a sacred trust, not to be violated, upon your honor. If you're collecting money to buy movie tickets, make certain you use the money to buy movie tickets. If you're collecting money to buy uniforms, make certain you buy uniforms. Don't do anything that might violate your students' trust.

Discipline and Nonparticipation Issues

Run your club or team just like you run your class: Don't tolerate violence, bullying, disrespect, defiance, discrimination, or any other inappropriate misbehavior. Don't allow the kids to bring pornography, weapons, tobacco, alcohol, or controlled substances to club meetings. Also, don't allow kids to play with iPods, PSPs, DSs, or other portable gadgets that might distract everyone from the business at hand during meetings. You want your kids to have fun, but they can listen to iPods any time; during meetings, it's time to focus on why they're here—to celebrate their shared love of a particular interest, issue, or activity.

If certain kids simply won't cooperate, warn them that they're facing expulsion from the club then talk to their parents if all else fails. Finally, carry through on your threat if it becomes necessary, and ask them to leave the club. A bit of temporary pain will make for a much more enjoyable club experience for all the other cooperative students.

CHAPTER 20

What to Do During Emergencies

To keep your students safe during emergencies, you must exercise a sufficient amount of control so your kids will suffer no harm. You don't have to become a screaming, red-faced demon; but by the same token, you absolutely must be firm, clear-headed, and thoroughly in command of the precious human beings whose welfare has been entrusted to you. You can take proper command of emergency situations by being properly prepared and knowing what to do before an emergency develops.

20

Snow Days

Snow days are a form of weather-related cancellation when a school or other organization is forced to shut down temporarily due to the onset of problematic, clearly unsafe, or even life-threatening weather.

If you live in an area where five feet of snow is a common wintertime occurrence, your district might not announce a one-day shutdown just because a little snow is falling. Indeed, snow-prone districts are more likely to be located in cities or towns that have sufficient snow plows to keep roads reasonably clear. Also, such districts routinely add additional days to the end of each academic year—beyond the number of days their state requires—to use as snow days. If the snow days aren't needed, the kids get a little extra instruction at year's end; and if snow days are needed, they're available for immediate usage.

However, if you live in an area where it's warm seven months of the year and the idea of snowfall in winter is a little farfetched, if a snowstorm hits your district is likely to declare a snow day and shut down the schools. Where snow isn't expected, snow-clearing equipment is in short supply or nonexistent. Nor have additional snow days been factored into the school year; therefore teachers and students will eventually have to make up all snow days.

FACT

Any district will declare a snow day if blizzards render the roads impassable. Even in a place like Monmouth County, New Jersey, where winter snowstorms are a way of life, two snow days were declared on May 13 and 14, 2007, when blizzards turned roads into an "ice skating rink," according to the local *Atlantic Herald* newspaper.

If it's snowing when you wake up in the morning, check your favorite radio station or television news program to learn if there is an official announcement of a snow day for your district. If you hear nothing and you've received no phone calls from your school, check your school's website on your home computer. If you still see nothing, assume the schools are open and get moving; but drive carefully—your students need you in one piece.

Under a different scenario, if everyone's at school on a particular day and the weather gradually worsens to the point where your district declares a snow day, stay calm—even if you get snowed in. Certain jobs, such as teaching, require employees to carefully weigh the safety of other people against their own safety. You've got kids who are depending on you to get them through the snow day unharmed; if you panic, who will safeguard your students? If you run away screaming, who will parents trust to protect their children?

Maintain your cool. If your school becomes snowed in, realize that the outside world is doing everything it can to get you and the kids out safely; but you'll have to be patient. If you're required to stay overnight with the kids, cheer up. Realize that you're a hero and you're doing more for your fellow humans than most people get to do in a lifetime.

Fires

Keep your students under firm control if the fire alarm sounds and no drills have been announced. Assume the emergency is real and calmly ask your kids to line up so they can walk to their evacuation station—usually on the athletic field. As they're hustling to line up, grab your roll sheet, a clipboard with paper, and your medical box. Then, remind the kids that they've practiced many times and if they'll follow your directions they'll be safe. Lead the kids outside single file, but before closing the door, scan the room to ensure that you've left no child behind.

Be aware of a tradition that requires you to grab the American flag if a fire breaks out; but remember also that the kids come first. If you can safely snatch the American flag as everyone exits, do so. But if it's not feasible to bring the flag, just forget it and get your kids to safety.

Have your class walk single file briskly, but not haphazardly, along their familiar emergency route toward their evacuation station. If you ever had doubts about where your station was located, you've since practiced walking to it many times so that now, during a real fire, you lead your kids straight to safety. Or, if your school requires students to line up for buses that will transport them to safety, line those kids up and let the buses whisk all of you away.

Whether you're standing on the field or you're on the bus, take roll as quickly as possible. Note if anyone's missing, then ask your students if anyone's injured, following up with a quick visual check. Don't touch kids in sensitive or inappropriate areas unless, in your professional judgment, it seems absolutely necessary to do so. When an administrator comes by to check on your status, inform him at once if you have any missing or injured students. Constantly remind your kids that they must not horseplay, shove, argue, use cell phones unnecessarily, or get separated from the group. They must obey your instructions and those of valid authority figures such as other teachers, administrators, firefighters, paramedics, and police.

Earthquakes

Keep your students safe from earthquakes. Earthquakes generally occur when the Earth's tectonic plates—sections of the Earth's crust that float over magma or molten rock—suddenly move after a release of built-up pressure. Earthquakes can last for an instant, causing relatively minor damage, or for over a minute, causing severe damage.

The force of an earthquake can be measured using the Richter scale, a measurement system invented in 1935 by American physicist Charles Richter. At the low end of the scale, a measurement of less than 2.0 indicates a barely perceptible tremor; while on the scale's high end, an earthquake measuring 9.8 or above signifies total destruction.

If an earthquake strikes during school hours, don't tell your students to stand in a doorway. Instead, order them to get under their desks for protection from falling debris and flying shards of glass. Kids should crouch in a fetal position facing away from windows and lace their fingers across the backs of their necks to protect their spinal columns from injury. Remind the kids to stay under their desks until instructed otherwise by you, an administrator, or emergency personnel. Ask your kids to count quietly to sixty—most earthquakes don't last a full minute and the counting can be calming. You should get under your desk for sixty seconds, too, because if you're incapacitated you can't help anyone—and your kids really need you at this point.

Your school's earthquake preparedness policy or rules for surviving an earthquake may require you to escort your kids to the athletic field as soon as the initial tremors cease. Before you do this, carefully check for injured students.

If you have students who are bleeding, get rubber gloves from your medical kit and use paper towels to apply pressure to the wound to stanch the bleeding. Apply bandages afterward. If any student appears so badly injured she can't walk, use your classroom phone to call the principal to the scene. If you can't get through, use your cell phone to dial 911. Tell the dispatcher your name and give him the information he requests. Ask for an ambulance to be dispatched immediately. Try not to move students with possible spinal-cord injuries.

E-QUESTION

Must I abandon a badly injured student in the classroom?
If your school's policy requires it, have everyone wait with the injured student until help arrives. However, if you're required to leave the injured student and rescue the majority who can still walk, march your students to the field. Trust that medical professionals will soon assist the injured child.

If the classroom doorway isn't blocked or inoperable, grab your medical kit and your roll sheet and lead your students to the field, where there's less likelihood they'll be injured by glass and debris. Have the kids sit down at their evacuation station while you take attendance. Finally, wait for further instructions from administrators about procedures allowing parents to pick up their children and take them home.

Hurricanes or Tornadoes

Protect your students in the event of a hurricane or destructive windstorm; or a tornado, an enormous whirling cone of devastating winds.

Unlike earthquakes, advance warning can often be provided prior to the onset of a hurricane or tornado. The National Weather Service (NWS), a government weather-forecasting organization, currently operates 122 weather-forecast offices nationwide and can issue repeated hurricane and tornado warnings via radio and television stations and over the Internet *(www.nws.noaa.gov)*.

FACT

When the NWS issues a Hurricane Watch (HWA) for a coastal region, a hurricane is forecast within thirty-six hours. Seagoing vessels indicate HWAs by hoisting one red flag with a black square. A Hurricane Warning (HWW) means a hurricane is forecast within twenty-four hours. Seagoing vessels indicate HWWs by hoisting two red flags with black squares.

Because of advance warnings for hurricanes and tornadoes, your school should be able to implement its emergency plan for wind-related disasters. Part of the plan will direct you to evacuate your students in an orderly manner so their parents can take them to a secure shelter. Next, you may receive instructions for battening down equipment, boarding up windows, securing classrooms, etc. After that, you may need to use a phone tree or list of people to call in case of emergencies to receive further directives. Finally, you'll be directed to get to a secure shelter yourself, as soon as possible.

The NWS's Storm Protection Center (SPC), a forecasting agency focusing on thunderstorms and cyclones, will issue a Tornado Watch (TOA), indicating that climatic conditions favor the creation of tornadoes. A Tornado Warning (TOR), on the other hand, means that a tornado is imminent and that everyone needs to get to a secure shelter immediately. Again, follow your school's emergency plan for evacuating your students, securing equipment and classrooms, making phone calls, and leaving to find a secure shelter.

Attacks and Lockdowns

Do your best to shield your students during a lockdown or state of emergency announced by an administrator over the public-address system, where students and school personnel must remain in locked rooms to defend against armed attackers. Exit doorways are also locked.

As with earthquakes and other disasters, it's a good idea for students to get under their desks to receive some protection in the event of weapons fire.

Lockdowns can be just as terrifying as natural disasters, but you mustn't forget that you have a responsibility to keep your children safe. The world doesn't expect you to be Wonder Woman or Iron Man, but it does expect you to fulfill your responsibilities. Because you're a human being, you might quake with terror when a gunman assaults the peace and good order of your school; nevertheless, you must master your fear for the sake of your kids.

FACT

The four deadliest school massacres in U.S. history were the 1927 Bath School bombings in Bath, Michigan, with forty-five people killed; the 2007 Virginia Polytechnic Institute shootings, with thirty-two people killed; the 1966 shootings at the University of Texas at Austin, with fourteen people killed; and the 1999 Columbine High School shootings in Columbine, Colorado, with thirteen people killed.

Avoid standing too close to windows where assailants are more likely to spot you. Consider whether to turn off the classroom lights, since the darkness might cause an assailant to pass by your classroom. Try to keep your kids quiet to prevent the possibility of attracting an assailant's attention with noise. And wait for an all-clear signal via the public-address system or rescue by law enforcement before unlocking your classroom door.

In the end, you'll have to use your own judgment to decide how you and your kids are going to come through the lockdown unscathed. Therefore, no one can tell you with complete certainty, "This is the only appropriate course of action when a gunman is on the loose, threatening your kids." Many courses of action have saved many lives in different ways. In the 1999 Columbine High School mass shooting spree, for example, shooters Eric

Harris and Dylan Klebold killed numerous students while sparing others, reportedly based on statements the students may have made. Use your common sense and your sense of professional responsibility to keep your kids safe; that's all anyone can ask.

How to Handle Medical Emergencies

In any emergency, if medical professionals are overwhelmed with calls, you might have no choice but to administer basic first aid to kids who need it. Initially, for any unconscious kids, remember the ABCs of Basic Life Support: Airway, Breathing, and Circulation. First, help a victim breathe by carefully lifting her chin and tilting her head back, unless you suspect a neck injury. Second, put your ear by her nose to listen for breathing. Third, put your ear to her chest or hold her wrist to check for a heartbeat or pulse, indicating normal blood circulation.

ALERT!

Don't move an injured or unconscious student's head if you suspect she has suffered neck trauma. If your suspicions are correct and you move her head anyway, you might be responsible for greater injury than she has already suffered, including paralysis. Unless you believe there's no choice, let trained medical professionals treat her.

Take the following steps for anyone over the age of one year old:

1. Assess that it is safe to approach the fallen person.
2. Attempt to wake the person by rubbing your knuckles firmly against the sternum (breastbone) and shouting, "Are you okay?"
3. If the person fails to rouse, immediately call 911 or shout for help, depending on your situation. If there is an AED available, also shout for someone to bring it.
4. If the person becomes conscious, is moaning, or moves, do not start CPR.
5. Call 911 if the person is not able to speak or appears confused. If the person does not wake, begin CPR and use an AED, if available.

If a student isn't breathing, you may have to administer emergency CPR or cardio-pulmonary resuscitation. The steps for performing CPR are:

1. Open the airway using the head-tilt, chin-lift method—one hand on the forehead, fingers of the other hand under the bony part of the lower jaw, near the chin. Tilt the head back, gently lift the jaw, making sure not to close the mouth or push on soft parts beneath the chin. Avoid lifting the neck in the case of spinal injury.
2. Check for normal breathing by putting your ear to the person's mouth and turning your head to look for chest movement while listening for air flowing through the mouth or nose and trying to detect breath on your cheek. A person with periodic gasping is most likely in cardiac arrest and needs CPR.
3. If there are no signs of breathing, pinch the nose; make a seal over the mouth with your mouth and give the person a breath strong enough for you to see the chest rise. When the chest falls, repeat the rescue breath once more for a total of two breaths. If available, use a CPR mask as a barrier between your mouth and the person's mouth that you are rescuing. The above three steps are called rescue breathing.
4. Begin chest compressions by placing the heel of your hand in the middle of the chest, over the lower half of the breastbone at the nipple line. Place your other hand on top and lace your fingers together (heel of one hand on chest; heel of the other hand on top of that hand) and compress the chest about 1"–2". Allow the chest to recoil completely and then perform thirty compressions, a rate of 100 compressions per minute.
5. After thirty chest compressions, immediately repeat the two rescue breaths. Open the airway with head-tilt, chin-lift again. This time, go directly to rescue breaths without checking for breathing again. Give one breath, making sure the chest rises and falls, then give another.
6. Perform the cycle of thirty compressions followed by two breaths for about two minutes. Then stop and recheck for breathing. If the person is not breathing, continue chest compressions and rescue breaths.

Continue this cycle until he's revived or medical professionals arrive.

If a kid is bleeding profusely, wear rubber gloves, then get a wad of gauze from your medical kit and press it firmly to the wound until the bleeding stops. If the pad becomes blood soaked, press another pad on top of it and continue stanching the bleeding. When the bleeding stops, wrap a bandage around the wound, but not so tightly that it impedes circulation. Finally, await the assistance of medical professionals. For more in-depth information on first-aid procedures, read *The Everything® First Aid Book*.

FACT

AED is a small electronic device used to deliver an electric shock in an attempt to disrupt or stop abnormal electrical activity in the heart. The AED will automatically diagnose any cardiac arrhythmia when attached to an unconscious person. When you see one of these lethal rhythms, you can then treat the person with the AED electrical therapy or a shock (defibrillation) to re-establish a normal and effective rhythm. You can learn how to use an AED in many first-aid and CPR classes.

Choking

When monitoring special events or lunch periods you may also encounter a choking emergency. Choking occurs when an object gets stuck in the throat and partly or completely blocks the airway. Signs of choking include:

- Pointing to throat, hands crossed on throat (universal sign of choking)
- Gasping or coughing
- Signs of panic
- Difficulty speaking
- Red face that steadily turns blue
- Loss of consciousness

When you suspect a student is choking, ask her, "Are you choking?" If the student is able to answer you, don't do anything because it's likely she will free the food or object on her own. In the case of actual choking, the person will not be able to talk and you need to help them. Call 911 if the person can't talk, make noise, or breathe well or is unconscious, then perform the Heimlich maneuver as outlined below. If the person is unconscious, lay her on her back, check her mouth for any visible obstruction, and try to dislodge it using a finger sweep. If you are unable to do so, begin mouth-to-mouth resuscitation and CPR. Continue to check inside her mouth for any signs of the foreign body as the chest compressions of CPR may dislodge it.

Never slap any person on the back you think might be choking. A baby who is crying, has a strong cough, and appears to be breathing well should be placed in a sitting position and allowed to finish coughing. Never stick your fingers down a baby's or anyone else's throat in an attempt to remove an object while they are coughing, as you run the risk of pushing the object further into the airway.

Heimlich Maneuver

The Heimlich maneuver (pronounced "Hi-mlick") is a technique whereby you administer abdominal thrusts to yourself or another person who is choking. The Heimlich maneuver is recommended for use in clearing a blocked airway in conscious adults and children over the age of one. The act of abdominal thrust lifts the diaphragm and forces air from the lungs, similar to a coughing action, so that the foreign body in an airway may be moved and expelled.

The steps to perform the Heimlich maneuver on a choking person are:

1. Stand behind the person, wrap your arms around the waist, and tip the person slightly forward.
2. Make a fist with one hand and place it slightly above the navel.
3. Grasp your fist with your other hand and press forcefully into the abdomen with quick, upward thrusts, using force as if you were attempting to lift the person up.
4. Continue the thrusts until the foreign body is dislodged.

CHAPTER 21

Alternative Careers in the Education Field

Teaching is the noblest profession on Earth. However, the education field encompasses many other noble professionals such as school psychologists, speech therapists, school nurses, and school administrators. If you're interested in exploring these admirable career options, you're to be commended. Some of these professionals earn far more than teachers and have more opportunities for advancement. Study this chapter to learn what the future might hold for you if you're considering alternatives to teaching.

An Administrative Career

If you want to faithfully educate all of the children in your district; if you want to support your district's hardworking, heroic teachers with all your heart; if humility, honesty, open-mindedness, and integrity are character traits instilled in you by years of valuable experience; and if you want to listen to teachers and kids and learn from their remarkable wisdom you should seriously consider becoming a principal.

FACT

In virtually all U.S. public schools, the principal denotes a school's primary educator and financial manager. However, in many independent schools in the United States, the principal is called the head of school. In Great Britain, principals are referred to as headmasters, headmistresses, or head teachers. In Scotland, in particular, principals are often called rectors.

Psychoanalysts Bruce Sklarew, Stuart Twemlow, and Sallye Wilkinson lament in their 2004 book *Analysts in the Trenches: Streets, Schools, War Zones*: "Some principals seem . . . to operate as dukes and duchesses, conscious of their absolute power and demanding complete loyalty and obedience from their subordinates. . . . Such persons appear to be overburdened by the demands of their positions, and, like others so over-involved in the minutiae of their jobs, they are not truly in control. They are critical, judgmental, and regarded coldly by their staffs."

These incisive authors are reminding you that principals exist to wholeheartedly support teachers and kids, not vice versa. If you don't plan on supplying teachers with the funds, equipment, materials, facilities, training, and support they require to do their all-important jobs, then you shouldn't plan on becoming a principal.

"Good principals . . . realize that retaining good teachers is essential because experience counts. . . . Research demonstrates that teachers with more experience plan better, apply a range of teaching strategies, understand students' learning needs, and better organize instruction. Good principals understand this research," says educator Jeffrey Ganz in his 2005 book

What Every Principal Should Know About Instructional Leadership. In other words, for schools to serve children, principals must serve teachers. Principals must encourage, nurture, treasure, and respect their teachers so teachers can teach.

ALERT!

Good principals realize that good teachers are the school. Poor principals delude themselves into thinking they are the school. When self-centered, self-serving principals are absent for a day, many teachers and students in his school are apt to remark, "So what?" But when teachers are absent, the kids and staff notice and wait expectantly for the teacher's return.

A 2007 study by the Teacher Recruitment and Retention Task Force of South Carolina reported that many teachers leave the profession because of adverse working conditions which include:

- Unsupportive administration
- Lack of empowerment by administration
- Expectations by district or school administrators to work days off contract without pay

All of these factors are well within the purview of a caring, sincere principal. If you're ready to address these types of issues and make certain you serve teachers by giving them everything they need to do their jobs, then here's how you can become a principal.

First, you've already done the really hard work. You've earned a bachelor's degree from an accredited university in a field that you love, and as you already know, that field doesn't necessarily have to be education. You've also earned a teaching credential or teaching license, a certificate from the state authorizing you to teach. Moreover, you've taught full time for at least three consecutive years.

Next, re-enroll at your alma mater or gain acceptance to some other fine university to begin your post-graduate studies in educational administration. If you choose a new university, make certain its college of education is accredited by the National Council for Accreditation of Teacher Education (NCATE) as well as by your state's teacher-credentialing agency.

Finally, when you've completed your courses, earned your degree, and passed the required state examination to earn your administrative credential, you'll be on your way to realizing your dream of becoming a dedicated, compassionate principal.

School Psychologist

If you make the commendable decision to become a school psychologist, you'll be entering a profession whose members practice educational psychology (the study of how teachers teach and how kids learn) to help students resolve personal and educational difficulties. School psychologists also employ clinical psychology, where the scientific study of the mind is used to help students resolve psychological problems. School psychologists help kids by talking to them and, most importantly, listening to their responses.

As a school psychologist, you'll be assisting students who are striving to improve their mental health and become productive citizens. You'll speak not only with the students but with their parents and teachers as well to gain insight into the nature of students' psychological dysfunction, if any, as well as proper courses of treatment.

You'll also be measuring and assessing students' learning abilities through the use of intelligence tests such as the Stanford-Binet Intelligence Quotient Test, the Universal Nonverbal Intelligence Test, and the Woodcock-Johnson 3 Test, among others.

Students with learning disabilities or physical handicaps will also come within your purview, because these children may require special guidance and assistance as they make their way through the educational system. Disabled students were given the legal right to a free, appropriate public education, along with every other kid in America, when the United States Congress passed the Individuals with Disabilities Education Act (IDEA) in 1975.

Under the IDEA, disabled children may attend school in the "least restrictive environment" that meets their educational needs; in other words, in a normal, mainstream classroom. As a school psychologist, you'll help these kids gain the maximum benefit from your school's educational programs.

To become a school psychologist, you don't necessarily have to attain a doctorate, although many school psychologists do spend upward of seven years in graduate school earning their Educational Doctor degrees, Doctor of Philosophy degrees, or Doctor of Psychology degrees.

All prospective school psychologists must become familiar with the work of Lightner Witmer, a psychologist who, in 1896, established a children's clinic in Philadelphia, Pennsylvania—the first one devoted to the practical application of psychology. Witmer also started a boarding school for troubled students in 1908 and is regarded as a founder of the discipline of school psychology.

Instead, you can begin working as a school psychologist by gaining acceptance to a university's college of education and spending upward of four years earning your Master of Science degree, Master of Education degree, Master of Arts degree, or Educational Specialist degree.

You'll also need to take additional courses and pass your state's exam in order to earn your School Psychology Credential (the certificate's exact title varies from state to state)—that is, your state license granting you permission to practice psychology. Clear these professional hurdles and you'll become a highly trained, highly qualified, state-licensed school psychologist, ready to help children of all ages overcome their personal difficulties and enjoy unparalleled educational success.

Speech Therapist

If you choose to become a speech therapist, a speech-language pathologist, or a speech and language therapist, you'll be joining the speech-language pathology profession, a dedicated group of school-based caregivers who treat students with problems related to speech, vision, and hearing. Such cognitive difficulties can unnecessarily impede kids' educational progress, but thanks to speech therapists and others, kids can frequently overcome their impairments and enjoy wonderful academic success.

When you work as a speech therapist, you'll help kids overcome numerous impediments and strengthen their ability to:

- Pronounce and articulate words
- Understand the syntax and phonetics of language to facilitate correct usage
- Employ appropriate physiognomy and general body language
- Read with self-assurance and confidence and create effective written compositions

You'll give your assigned students regular practice routines designed to correct problems and enhance each kid's ability to make themselves understood. You'll also utilize a variety of professional tools such as Blissymbolics, pictographic communication symbols developed by Australian language-expert Charles Bliss, to help people with cerebral palsy communicate. Other tools can include laptop computers, speech-producing devices, sign language, and stroboscopes used to inspect vocal cords.

To become a speech therapist, you'll spend upward of three years earning your graduate-level master's degree in speech-language pathology from an accredited university, plus additional coursework for your credential. You'll then need to pass the state examination to earn your Clinical Rehabilitative Services Credential (again, the certificate's exact title varies from state to state). Once you've completed all your requirements and have your degree and credential in hand, you'll be ready to join the proud ranks of speech therapists who consistently make a significant difference in children's lives.

School Nurse

A school nurse, like any nurse, is a selfless health-care professional who either assists doctors or patients directly in protecting and improving their health. As a school nurse, you'll be advocating for patients' welfare; treating injuries and illnesses; working to prevent the spread of disease or the proliferation of unnecessary accidents; effectively organizing patients' records and casework; and communicating with teachers, parents, and administrators regarding health-related matters.

FACT

The advocacy group for the 45,000 school nurses currently working in the United States is the National Association of School Nurses (NASN), founded in 1979. According to the NASN website's mission statement (*www.nasn.org*), "The National Association of School Nurses improves the health and educational success of children and youth by developing and providing leadership to advance school nursing practice."

To become a school nurse, gain acceptance to an accredited university with a college of health and human services or some similarly named college. Then, enroll either in the college's department of nursing, its department of health science, or a similarly named department; a university guidance counselor will direct you to the correct department and undergraduate-level program for school nursing. Thereafter, you'll spend upwards of four years taking courses to earn your Bachelor of Science in Nursing degree and your Health Services Credential. After you pass your state's exam and gain your credential, you'll be ready to administer to the overall health needs of countless grateful students throughout your school-nurse career.

District-Office Positions

If you're hoping to move up in the world you can always apply for any one of numerous office and staff positions, working directly for the district in your local district headquarters or one of its satellite offices (if your district is that large).

But perhaps you'd like to focus on the highest administrative position available in any school district: superintendent of schools, often referred to as the superintendent or chief school administrator. The superintendent is answerable to the local school board, the group of elected officials who set policy and decide funding issues for your school district.

The superintendent is hired by the board and has many responsibilities, both to the board and to the district as a whole. If you want the job, understand that you'll be the chief executive officer of what can be a mammoth governmental enterprise if you manage a large urban area with thousands or even hundreds of thousands of students, plus tens of thousands of teachers and other district employees.

Even if you superintend a small district, you'll still find yourself in charge of what may be one of the biggest organizations and the biggest employer in your town or region.

Either way, you'll ultimately be given countless responsibilities and you'll be required to make countless decisions, including many of the following:

- Drawing up annual budgets for board approval
- Overseeing the building of new school-site facilities
- Making hiring and firing recommendations to the board
- Making certain the district is in compliance with local, state, and federal laws
- Instilling a sense of team spirit and collegiality between teachers and administrators
- Putting board policies regarding curriculum, new technologies, discipline, etc., into practice

If you want to be a district superintendent, you'll probably be asked to provide evidence that you have many, or all, of the following qualifications:

- A Bachelor's degree from an accredited university in Education or other recognized field
- A valid teaching credential issued by a state credentialing agency
- Several years of successful, verifiable, full-time teaching experience
- A Master's or Doctorate from an accredited university in Education or other recognized field
- A Master's degree in Business Administration or related field from an accredited university
- A Juris Doctor degree in Law, from an accredited university

- An impressive resume listing compelling experience, education, and specific qualifications
- Numerous glowing letters of recommendation from administrators, teachers, parents, etc.

A Total Career Change?

The intent of this book is to provide you with current, usable information so you can manage your classroom to the best of your ability, enjoy professional success, and have a little fun with your students. But it's possible that this book may actually have overwhelmed you with its discussions of specific classroom-management issues, methodologies, and strategies.

Certainly, there are thousands of alternative careers in the world. You might even make more money and gain more societal prestige if you decide to work as an engineer, doctor, lawyer, scientist, nurse, businessperson, writer, or thousands of other honest trades.

Having acknowledged all that, don't forget—and this can't be repeated too many times—that teaching, for all its travails and sacrifices, frequently seems to have the magical effect of keeping many teachers young at heart. Mentally compare your teaching colleagues with other professionals whom you know and you may be surprised to see that teachers seem to be somewhat younger, more energetic, more open minded, and more interested in current events and new ideas than a lot of other professionals.

That's what happens when you teach: The kids' youthful energy rubs off on you. And it happens every day. Good luck, and may you decide to continue working in this most magnificent of professions for the rest of your days.

APPENDIX A

Additional Resources

Books

Adams, Henry. *The Education of Henry Adams*. NuVision Publications, 2007.

Adedeji, Adebayo. *Towards a Dynamic African Economy: Selected Speeches and Lectures, 1975–1986*. Routledge, 1989.

Altheide, David. *Terrorism and the Politics of Fear*. AltaMira Press, 2006.

Ashner, Laurie and Mitch Meyerson. *When Parents Love Too Much: Freeing Parents and Children to Live Their Own Lives*. Hazelden, 1997.

Barkow, Jerome. *The Adapted Mind: Evolutionary Psychology and the Generation of Culture*. Oxford University Press, 1995.

Beattie, John and LuAnn Jordan. *Making Inclusion Work: Effective Teaching Practices for All Teachers*. Corwin Press, 2006.

Burton, Robert. *The Anatomy of Melancholy*. Vernon Hood & Sharpe, 1806.

Butcher, John. *Developing Effective 16-19 Teaching Skills*. Routledge Falmer, 2004.

Church, Ellen Booth and Karen Miller. *Learning Through Play: A Practical Guide for Teaching Young Children*. Teaching Resources/Scholastic, 1990.

Cornell, Dewey. *School Violence: Fears Versus Facts (Landmark Essays)*. Lawrence Erlbaum Associates, 2006.

Crosby, Brian. *The $100,000 Teacher. A Solution to America's Declining Public School System*. Capital Books, 2003.

Dahl, Roald. *Matilda*. Viking Kestrel, 1988.

Dickens, Charles. *A Christmas Carol*. Prestwick Publications, 2005.

Donoghue, Mildred, Ruane Hill, Allen Koenig, and Henry Clay Lindgren. *Educational Psychology in the Classroom: Educational Psychology Today*, 1967.

Duffell, Nick. *The Making of Them: The British Attitude to Children and the Boarding School System*. Lone Arrow Press, 2000.

Editorial Staff of the Congressional Quarterly. *Urban Issues: Selections from the CQ Researcher*. CQ Press, 2004.

Editorial Staff of LexisNexis. *Deering's California Desktop Code Series (Family Code Including Enactments Through the End of the 2005–2006 Legislature)*. LexisNexis, 2006.

Epstein, Lawrence and Steven Mardon. *The Harvard Medical School Guide to a Good Night's Sleep*. McGraw-Hill, 2006.

Escoffier, Jeffrey and Erica Jong. *Sexual Revolution*. Running Press, 2003.

Ganz, Jeffrey. *What Every Principal Should Know About Instructional Leadership*. Corwin Press, 2005.

Garner, Bryan. *Black's Law Dictionary, Eighth Edition*. Thomson West, 2004.

Giles, Herbert. *Gems of Chinese Literature*. Dover, 1965.

Groves Sr., Eric. *The Anti-War Quote Book*. Quirk Books, 2008.

Groves Sr., Eric. *Butt Rot and Bottom Gas*. Quirk Books, 2007.

Groves Sr., Eric. *Divine Baby Names*. Sellers Publishing, 2008.

Gyatso, Geshe Kelsang. *How to Solve Our Human Problems: The Four Noble Truths*. Tharpa Publications, 2005.

Hall, Olive and Beatrice Paolucci. *Teaching Home Economics*. John Wiley, 1961.

Hirsch, Eric Donald, Joseph H. Kett, and James S. Trefil. *The Dictionary of Cultural Literacy*. Houghton Mifflin, 1988.

Horace. *The Odes*. Princeton University Press, 2005.

Janus, Samuel and Cynthia Janus. *The Janus Report on Sexual Behavior*. Wiley, 1994.

Kinsella, Kate, et al. *Prentice-Hall Literature: Timeless Voices, Timeless Themes*. Prentice-Hall, 2002.

Lao-Tzu. *The Way of Lao-Tzu*. Bobbs Merrill, 1963.

Lomax, Pamela. *Managing Better Schools and Colleges*. Multilingual Matters Limited, 1991.

Lustberg, Arch. *How to Sell Yourself: Using Leadership, Likeability, and Luck to Succeed.* Career Press, 2008.

Martin, Kingsley. *Critic's London Diary: From the New Statesman, 1931–1956.* Secker & Warburg, London, 1960.

McGinnis, Alan Loy. *Bringing Out the Best in People: How to Enjoy Helping Others Excel.* Augsburg Fortress Publishers, 1985.

Mester, Cathy Sargent and Robert Tauber. *Acting Lessons for Teachers.* Praeger Publishers, 2006.

Millbower, Lenn. *Training with a Beat.* Stylus Publishing, 2000.

Miller, Leonard and Leonard Dunsmoor. *Principles and Methods of Guidance for Teachers.* International Book Company, 1949.

Myers, John E. B. *Myers on Evidence in Child, Domestic, and Elder Abuse Cases.* Aspen Publishers, 2005.

O'Dell, Scott. *The Island of the Blue Dolphins.* Yearling, 1971.

Overmeyer, Mark. *When Writing Workshop Isn't Working: Answers to Ten Tough Questions, Grades 2–5.* Stenhouse Publishers, 2005.

Rafferty, Max. *What They Are Doing to Your Children.* New American Library, 1966.

Rath, Tom and Donald Clifton. *How Full Is Your Bucket?* Gallup Press, 2004.

Reeve, William David. *Mathematics for Secondary School: Its Content and Methods of Teaching and Learning.* Holt, 1954.

Rice, Ann Smith, Paulena Nickell, and Suzanne M. Tucker. *Family Life Management.* MacMillan, 1986.

Sattler, Jerome. *Clinical and Forensic Interviewing of Children and Families: Guidelines for the Mental Health, Education, Pediatric, and Child Maltreatment Fields.* Jerome M. Sattler, Publisher, 1997.

Select Committee on Children, Youth, and Families, U.S. House of Representatives. *Investing in Families: A Historical Perspective.* Government Printing Office, 1992.

Shakespeare, William. *Hamlet (The New Folger Library Shakespeare)*. Washington Square Press, 2003.

Shakespeare, William. *The Merchant of Venice (The New Folger Library Shakespeare)*. Washington Square Press, 2004.

Shakespeare, William. *A Midsummer Night's Dream (The New Folger Library Shakespeare)*. Washington Square Press, 2004.

Shakespeare, William. *Romeo and Juliet (The New Folger Library Shakespeare)*. Washington Square Press, 2004.

Shakur, Assata. *Assata: An Autobiography*. Lawrence Hill Books, 2001.

Sklarew, Bruce, Stuart Twemlow, and Sallye Wilkinson. *Analysts in the Trenches: Streets, Schools, War Zones*. The Analytic Press, 2004.

Smith, Tara. *Moral Rights and Political Freedom*. Rowman & Littlefield Publishers, Inc., 1997.

Sprenger, Marilee. *Learning and Memory: The Brain in Action*. Association for Supervision & Curriculum Deve, 1999.

Suzuki, David. *The Sacred Balance: A Visual Celebration of Our Place in Nature*. Greystone Books, 2004.

Templar, Richard. *The Rules of Life: A Personal Code for Living a Better, Happier, More Successful Life*. Reuters Prentice Hall, 2006.

Thoreau, Henry David. *Walden*. Time, Inc., 1962.

Turiel, Judith Steinberg. *Beyond Second Opinions: Making Choices about Fertility Treatment*. University of California Press, 1998.

Whitman, Walt. *Leaves of Grass*. Oxford University Press, 2005.

York, Phyllis, David York, and Ted Wachtel. *Toughlove*. Doubleday, 1982.

Websites

AltLaw Legal Search Engine
http://altlaw.org

Black Student Fund
www.blackstudentfund.org

Boys & Girls Club of America
www.bgca.org

California Law
www.leginfo.ca.gov/calaw.html

California State University, Long Beach
www.ced.csulb.edu

Cartoon Network Rescuing Recess
www.cartoonrecessweek.com/experts_say.html

Findlaw
http://public.findlaw.com

Forms and Testing, Mrs. Perkins, First Grade
www.mrsperkins.com/testing.htm

Great Dreams Native American Culture
www.greatdreams.com/native.htm

Jurist Legal News and Research
http://jurist.law.pitt.edu

Law.Com Dictionary
http://dictionary.law.com

National Association of School Nurses
www.nasn.org

National Center for Education Statistics
http://nces.ed.gov/index.asp

National Weather Service
www.nws.noaa.gov

Nolo's Legal Glossary
www.nolo.com/glossary.cfm

School District of Philadelphia
www.phila.k12.pa.us

Sloan Consortium, e-learning Advocates
www.sloan-c.org/resources/index.asp

Wex, Cornell Law School
www.law.cornell.edu/topical.html

Employment-Discrimination Information for Selected States

Alabama *www.dhr.state.al.us/eeo/default.asp*

California *www.dfeh.ca.gov*

Florida *http://fchr.state.fl.us*

Georgia *www.dhr.state.ga.us/Departments/ DHR/0102.pdf*

Hawaii *www.state.hi.us*

Illinois *www.state.il.us/dhr*

Kansas *www.ink.org/public/khrc*

Massachusetts *www.state.ma.us:80/mcad*

New York State *www.nysdhr.com*

Ohio *www.state.oh.us/crc*

Texas *http://tchr.state.tx.us*

Glossary of Essential Teaching Terms

ABCs of Basic Life Support

In first aid, the ABCs of basic life support indicate Airway, Breathing, and Circulation; first, a victim should be helped to breathe by lifting her chin and tilting her head back, unless a neck injury is suspected; second, breathing should be listened for; third, a heartbeat or pulse should be checked for, indicating normal blood circulation.

adjuvant instructional time

Additional time slots before and after a teacher's daily instructional time when she prepares lessons and gets ready to teach.

administrator

An educational leader within a school district, including the superintendent, as well as each of the principals and assistant principals at the school sites.

agency fee

A contract-negotiated rule requiring teachers to join the local teacher's association or pay fees.

agenda

A student planner or plan book used by students to record assignments and by teachers to communicate with parents on a regular basis.
A printed sheet of items that will be discussed at a meeting.

answer key

A list of correct answers, keyed to a specific test, to be used for grading.

arbitration

A hearing involving a mediator who hears evidence and renders a binding decision.

back-to-school night

An event held on an evening near the start of the school year where parents visit their children's teachers to view classrooms, examine schoolwork, and confer with teachers.

bazaar

A school fundraising event where parents sell baked goods, T-shirts, and other items.

bilingual education

A process where limited-English speakers or non-English speakers are taught in English and in a primary home language—generally Spanish in the United States.

boarding school

A school that provides students not merely with full-time academic instruction, but with meals and full-time living quarters as well.

buddy teacher

A teaching colleague, usually working in a neighboring classroom, who you can send misbehaving students to for brief time-outs.

bulletin board

An area of classroom wall space that can provide lively and appropriate decoration or showcase student work or display timely school-related information.

business casual

The business-casual look for men generally consists of tasteful polo shirts, pleated slacks, and comfortable yet presentable shoes. For women, the business-casual look is generally quite similar to that of the men, except that tasteful, below-the-knee shorts or tailored skirts are often substituted for full-length slacks.

career portfolio

A collection of documents that highlight educational and professional achievements, used by savvy adults to attain promotions or raises.

cephalagia

Headaches sometimes experienced by students perhaps necessitating a trip to the school nurse.

chaperone
A teacher or other responsible adult assigned to a school dance or other social function to safeguard kids and prevent inappropriate behavior.

charter school
Taxpayer-supported public schools operated by individuals or private corporations under a charter or grant of permission from a state or school district allowing them to experiment with innovative methods and sidestep bureaucratic regulations.

child sexual molestation
Also called child sexual abuse; a child experiences unwanted, degrading, and emotionally harmful sex talk, embracing, touching, kissing, or even intercourse, forced upon her or him by an adult or another child.

chorditis
A medical condition where vocal chords get inflamed, usually from shouting, and which can temporarily cause loss of voice.

classroom management
A personal toolkit of policies, actions, and words a teacher uses to keep her classroom functioning smoothly.

classroom meeting area
A bit of classroom space set aside for the purpose of holding intimate teacher-class discussions regarding timely and important issues.

classroom suspension form
A form, generally containing a lengthy essay to be copied, used for sending a student out of the classroom due to nonstop goofing and disruption.

clinical depression
An ongoing psychiatric disorder which debilitates and saddens some children to such a degree that they cannot competently function in school.

collective bargaining agreement or contract
The contract is negotiated between the association and the district and enumerates teachers' and administrators' rights.

collective bargaining process
Procedures established by state law to ensure associations and districts bargain in good faith to craft a contract covering salaries, hours, and working conditions.

content management system (CMS)
Software that allows you, your students, your colleagues, and school administrators to utilize passwords to upload bulletins, articles, essays, stories, poetry, artwork, and more to a custom website.

cooperative learning
Students work in pairs or small groups to advise and assist one another in order to complete an assignment.

copy master
An original document used for making copies for student use.

corporal punishment
The use of spanking or other physical coercion to induce students to behave properly.

CPR
Cardio-pulmonary resuscitation, where the heartbeat and respiration of a nonresponsive victim are restored through chest compressions and breathing into the victim's mouth.

cross-curricular teaching
Also called interdisciplinary teaching, a master teacher's attempts to enliven lessons by lifting a particular concept from its narrow academic field and relating it to other academic fields.

cubbies
Orderly classroom storage compartments where students may store personal belongings or classroom supplies.

cumulative file
Also known as a cum (pronounced "kyoom"), a comprehensive record containing a student's photograph, contact information, health data, grades, teachers' comments, and other personal information.

depression

A bleak state of mind characterized by listlessness, hopelessness, and deep sadness and often arising in children due to molestation or extreme environmental factors.

detention slip

A form used by teachers to assign chronically misbehaving students to serve a certain number of minutes after school, either in a teacher's classroom or elsewhere.

discipline

A set of ethical procedures and rules whereby you appropriately control your students, enabling them to learn.

dress code

The set of rules indicating which clothes students may and may not wear.

drill

A practice run through, held periodically at a school site to help ensure that students and staff will be trained in competently dealing with a real emergency if one should arise.

duck-and-cover

A type of emergency drill where students duck under their desks and cover the backs of their necks with their interlaced fingers, in the event of an attack or other catastrophe.

dyscalculia

A mathematical disability where students experience trouble understanding mathematical tasks such as memorization of math-facts tables, telling time, counting money, etc.

dysgraphia

A specific type of writing disability or physiological problem inhibiting a student's ability to write competently.

earthquake-preparedness policy

A school's emergency rules that will help ensure students will survive an earthquake.

e-mail

Electronically transmitted messages or "mail" from one computer to one or more outlying computers.

emancipation

The court-ordered, legal separation of a child from his parents.

emergency kit

Also called a medical box, medical kit, or med-kit. A clear plastic box containing adequate amounts of basic emergency medical supplies such as bandages, etc.

evaluation

A state-mandated assessment where an administrator observes you teach, then writes observation reports and a final evaluation.

extracurricular duties

Tasks that a teacher generally performs outside of her classroom.

fair-use doctrine

Under United States copyright law, a legal doctrine allowing teachers to photocopy and use copyrighted materials such as textbooks for educational purposes without securing permissions from writers and publishers.

FAPE

A legally mandated free and appropriate public education for all disabled students, a right often unfairly denied in the past.

field trip

A school-sponsored journey to educational sites outside the school.

floater

A teacher who doesn't have her own classroom, but moves from room to room in a school, educating students.

focus box

A piece of technology that lets your classroom computer display documents and animated presentations directly to your classroom TV.

glossophobia
The fear of speaking in public.

good faith
Acting based on a reasonable belief in the truthfulness of what you're doing and saying.

graphical user interface
A bundle of powerful capabilities found in word-processing software allowing you to import graphic elements such as clip art, pictures from the Internet, pictures from your computer, etc., into your documents.

grievance
A written complaint that the administrator has violated the law or the agreement between the district and association.

gross negligence
A willful and wanton neglect of a legal responsibility.

hall pass
A tear-off form that a teacher fills out when a student needs to leave the classroom.

home learning
Also called homework, where students complete exercises at home to reinforce what was taught at school.

honor
One's heartfelt love of what is good, just, and right, including good manners, courteous behavior, and treating others as you wish to be treated.

html
HyperText Markup Language, used to create computer-accessible documents for the world wide web network of linked documents.

IDEA
The Individuals with Disabilities Education Act, passed in 1975 by the U.S. Congress, where disabled students were given the legal right to a free, appropriate public education.

IEP

An individualized education program, also called an individualized education plan, a personalized instructional program created for disabled students under the Individuals with Disabilities Education Act (IDEA), passed by the United States Congress in 1975.

impasse

Both sides in contract negotiations declare a stalemate and admit that further negotiations will prove fruitless in the short term.

in loco parentis

A Latin legal term meaning "in place of parents," indicating that within the school setting teachers substitute for parents in many ways.

in-service

A district-sponsored seminar to disseminate information for professional growth.

insubordination

Rude, unprofessional, insulting, or inappropriate behavior directed from a teacher toward an administrator, often resulting in the employee's termination.

Internet

Also called the Information Super-Highway, a planet-spanning network of billions of computers, all sharing information.

intranet

A local network set up to handle e-mail traffic in your school or district.

irony

A strangely amusing disconnect between what is and what ought to be.

job action

Similar to a strike because employees withhold labor during contract negotiations to gain better terms; but a job action involves unorthodox tactics as well as a partial, rather than a complete, withholding of labor.

learning center

An area consisting of a table and some chairs where students can engage in self-directed educational enrichment using the supplemental educational materials provided.

learning disability

A physiological problem which can interfere with a student's speech, hearing, or information-processing skills; therefore, affecting his overall ability to learn.

LEP

A term created by the United States Department of Education to identify students who are learning the English language. A somewhat more modern and widely accepted abbreviation is an ELL, or English-language learner.

lockdown

A state of emergency announced by an administrator over a school's public-address system; students and school personnel must remain in locked rooms as protection against armed attackers.

maintenance-work request form

A check-off sheet to inform custodial personnel that a classroom requires cleaning or restocking of supplies or specific repairs.

master teacher

A professional designation created by the American Board for Certification of Teacher Excellence (ABCTE), a nonprofit organization established in 2001 dedicated to "increasing the supply of highly qualified teachers essential for achieving student success."

material term

In a written agreement, a term which the drafter considers extremely important.

memorandum form

A customized, teacher-created form a teacher uses to send messages to colleagues, administrators, and other staff.

memorializing

Reducing a conversation to a letter and mailing the letter to one of the participants in the conversation.

molestation

The unlawful and inappropriate touching of children for sexual purposes.

mp3 player

A handheld device such as the Apple iPod Nano that can store huge amounts of digital audio data.

multilanguage bilingual education

Where non-English speakers attend classes with English speakers in order to gain assistance and encouragement from peers.

multimedia cart

A wheeled, portable trolley well stocked with modern audio-visual equipment.

navigating the classroom

When a student leaves his assigned seat with the teacher's permission to walk about the classroom to accomplish a specific purpose.

negligence

A civil action arising when someone fails to do a thing which any reasonable person would certainly have done.

nonapology apology

Different from a sincere apology, in that the person apologizing tries to make the recipient feel that she is far too sensitive in regards to the original slight.

no-strike clause

A provision in an association-district contract barring collective bargaining members from striking, both sides agreeing instead to be bound by an arbitrator's final decision.

online learning

Also called electronic learning or e-learning, where college-level courses are offered to teachers online to facilitate professional growth.

overhead projector

An optical device for showing enlarged images on a white screen to facilitate instruction.

PAR

Your district's Peer Assistance and Review Program, created by state statutes to offer guidance and assistance to teachers to help them become more competent educators.

parent conference

A face-to-face meeting, generally arranged by a teacher, between a teacher and a parent to discuss a student's academic and/or behavioral progress.

password

An individual code a student uses to gain access to a website.

pattern disruption

A term used by comedians to indicate laughter arising from the disruption of familiar patterns of images, objects, and ideas.

pedagogue

A teacher of young children.

phone tree

A list of people to call in case of emergencies to receive further directives.

positive reinforcement

Where a student who exhibits a desired behavior instantly receives a reward for that behavior to induce a repetition.

preparation period

Also called a planning period, this is a teacher's time slot for planning lessons, grading papers, copying papers, etc.

preplanning
The planning a teacher engages in before students arrive, such as writing lesson plans, procuring materials and equipment, etc., to get the classroom ready to receive students.

presentation program
Computer software allowing teachers to create and present lessons to students using the classroom computer and television.

principal
The chief educational leader of a school in charge of budgeting, teacher evaluation, and academic instruction.

private schools
Educational institutions funded by tuition rather than taxpayers.

professional growth
The accumulation of professional information and training subsequent to graduation and employment by completing a certain number of hours in college classes.

PTA
The Parent-Teacher Association, or Parent-Teacher-Student Association (PTSA), founded in 1897 in Washington, D.C., is a child-advocacy organization with 23,000 U.S. chapters.

reading rewards program
A reading program that assigns a certain number of points to particular books, which are then awarded to students who successfully read the books and pass computer quizzes keyed to the books.

recess
A time slot set aside for students to temporarily exit the classroom and enjoy approved recreational activities.

recurring meeting
A particular type of meeting held at regular calendar intervals, generally once a month.

regulations
Rules created by organizations to prohibit undesirable behavior or mandate desirable behavior.

restitution
Restoring a person to "wholeness" who has been damaged in some way.

scanner
A machine that converts text or graphics into computer information.

scholarship
A grant of money from charitable foundations, the federal government, etc.

school board
The elected overseers of a school district in charge of hiring and firing, district finances, and setting the district's policies.

screencast
Where prerecorded computer data can be played on your computer just like a movie using a DVD; or the information can be streamed to your computer over the Internet.

search engine
A website that enables you to search the world wide web for information.

sick days
Days provided by state statute or contract that a teacher may utilize in the event of illness or matters of personal necessity.

sickout
During contract negotiations, teachers phone-in sick en masse to disrupt district operations.

snow day
A form of weather-related cancellation where a school or other organization is forced to shut down temporarily due to the onset of problematic, clearly unsafe, or even life-threatening weather.

sovereign immunity

A legal doctrine giving governmental entities and their employees immunity from lawsuits arising from *torts,* or civil wrongs, committed by government employees.

standard business attire

For men, a suit-jacket, slacks, dress shirt, necktie, and dress shoes. For women, a suit-jacket, blouse or knit top, a tasteful skirt, panty hose, and dress pumps or flats.

statute

A state or federal law enacted by legislatures.

strike

A collective action by a majority of your local association's teachers or bargaining unit members, who vote to withhold their labor because the district has not met the association's contract-negotiation demands.

student conference

A face-to-face meeting, generally called by a teacher, between the teacher and one of her students to discuss academic and/or behavioral issues.

student portfolios

A set of file folders, one for each student, arranged alphabetically by students' last names, to hold graded and recorded work.

substitute teacher

Also called a sub, a temporary teacher who fills in for a regular classroom teacher when the teacher is indisposed.

substitute teacher's notebook

A binder full of indispensable information such as emergency lesson plans, etc., for use by a substitute teacher when the regular classroom teacher is absent.

supply order form

A checklist used to quickly reorder essential classroom supplies.

suspension form
A form used by a teacher for serious disciplinary problems when other forms of discipline have failed or when a student commits a particularly egregious offense.

sustained silent reading
Also called SSR, a class period where students read quietly.

synchronous conferencing
Technologies that allow students and online course instructors to confer with each other over the Internet.

talking books
Prerecorded novels and nonfiction books read by professional actors or the authors themselves.

tardiness
When a student arrives late to class.

tardiness letter
Mailed to the parents of those students who arrive chronically tardy.

teacher's aide
A person who assists you with the many classroom-management tasks you'll face each day as a teacher.

teachers' association
A recognized organization of teachers who elect representatives to improve employee working conditions and wages.

teacher's pet
A commonly used slang term indicating a student who is perceived by other students as receiving unfairly favorable treatment from a teacher.

teaching credential
A state-issued license, granted for a lifetime or a specific time period, permitting a person to teach specific subjects and grade levels within the state.

tickler file
Invented by businessperson David Allen for holding twelve monthly folders and thirty-one daily folders, all containing tasks to be timely completed.

timeline
A contract requirement that you file a grievance within a certain number of days.

timetable
A document showing preplanned activities and designated times for those activities.

tort
A civil wrong committed by government employees or anyone else.

transitional bilingual education
Where students are taught in their own language for a few years then moved into mainstream English-only classes.

transparency
A piece of clear plastic with educational material drawn, written, or printed on it, designed to be projected onto a screen using an overhead projector.

tuition
Fees that parents pay to private schools for their children's care and instruction.

username
A student's real name, or a fanciful moniker, used to gain access to a website.

vicarious liability
A legal doctrine that says the state is responsible for the negligence of its agencies.

voicemail
A complex answering-machine system which uses a series of recordings to shunt telephone messages to your classroom.

walkabout
When a teacher walks around a school campus prior to the arrival of students to become familiar with the facilities and traffic patterns of a school site.

word processing
Using your classroom computer, along with word-processing software, to type and print professional-looking documents.

word wall
An area of classroom wall space to display sentence strips or word cards featuring useful vocabulary words the class has learned.

work-to-rule strategy
During contract negotiations, teachers forego the hours of free work they donate to their districts each year and instead follow all workplace rules to the letter—leaving and arriving precisely on time, using lunchtime to eat instead of grading papers, etc.

world wide web
Generally referred to by its call letters—www—the world wide web is a network of linked documents accessible by modem and computer.

writing disability
A physiological problem inhibiting a student's ability to write competently.

yard duty
A professional responsibility where teachers watch over students during specified times and in specified areas such as the athletic field, multipurpose room, crosswalks, etc.

zero tolerance
A policy and attitude permitting absolutely no amount of proscribed misbehavior.

Sample Student Contact Form

When trying to contact parents, most teachers would agree that it is far better to have too much information than to not have enough. It is interesting how many times a teacher's records proves to be more thorough than those kept by the building's administration. This is because parents fill out the contact cards that are filed in the office, and students fill out the ones kept by the classroom teacher. Unsurprisingly, kids tend to be far more forthcoming with teachers about the ways in which their parents can be contacted than they are about anything regarding themselves!

STUDENT INFORMATION

Name _____

                Last   First   Middle

_____   _____

                D. O. B.   Sex

Address _____

                Street   Apt #   City

_____

                County   State/Prov.   Zip/Postal Code

Lives with: ❏ Mother   ❏ Father   ❏ Both   ❏ Other _____

Medical Conditions _____

_____

_____

PARENT CONTACT INFORMATION
Primary Parent/Guardian

Name _____

                Last   First   Middle

E-mail _____

Address _____

                Street   Apt #   City

_____

                County   State/Prov.   Zip/Postal Code

_____

                Cell Phone   Work Phone   Home Phone

Other Parent

Name _____

               Last   First   Middle

E-mail _____

Address _____

               Street   Apt #   City

_____

               County   State/Prov.   Zip/Postal Code

_____

               Cell Phone   Work Phone   Home Phone

EMERGENCY CONTACT INFORMATION

Name _____

               Last   First   Middle

E-mail _____

Address _____

               Street   Apt #   City

_____

               County   State/Prov.   Zip/Postal Code

_____

               Cell Phone   Work Phone   Home Phone

Doctor's Name _____

                                                   Office Phone

Preferred Hospital _____

                                                   Hospital Phone

OTHER IMPORTANT STUDENT INFORMATION:

Sample Substitute Lesson Plan

Since you must assume that the substitute teacher covering your classes for you on any given day will likely be a stranger to your classroom, it is in your best interest to make your substitute lesson plan as concrete as possible. Break down processes, such as transitions, for which you might only use shorthand when writing out your own plan

TASK/ACTIVITY	TIME FOR EACH TASK/ACTIVITY
ENTRY TASK	**5 to 10 minutes**
Have students answer the following warm-up question (written on the board): "Name the factors that caused the Kingdom of Israel to split into two separate and distinct successor states by 922 B.C."	
INDIVIDUAL ACTIVITY	**10 minutes**
Have students individually take time in class to review flashcards of geography terms for upcoming test on the geography of the Ancient Mediterranean Sea Region.	
SMALL GROUP ACTIVITY	**5 to 10 minutes**
Have students break into their regular small groups, where their group leaders will facilitate a discussion of the warm-up question. Expect kids to exchange answers and add to their own.	
LARGE GROUP ACTIVITY	
Lead the class in discussion of the warm-up question, laying out the factors in detail, expanding on them as needed, over the course of the discussion.	
CLOSING EXERCISE	**5 to 10 minutes, as needed, and as time allows**
Verbal comprehension check. Ask, "Let's recap: what did we learn today?" Write out student responses on overhead projector and review them with the class. Assign tomorrow's reading assignment for tonight's homework.	
ADDITIONAL NOTES:	

Sample Emergency Substitute Lesson Plan

Since there is no telling where or when you'll have an actual emergency over the course of your school year, it is in your best interest that you focus your lesson plan on skill development, rather than content exploration. After all, it doesn't do your classes much good if your emergency lesson plan covers the ins and outs of cell division and replication if you covered that in November, and (it now being April) the students are studying biological classification. Here is an example of a type of lesson that lends itself well to being used as your emergency lesson.

TASK/ACTIVITY	TIME FOR EACH TASK/ACTIVITY
ENTRY TASK	**5 to 10 minutes**
Write a warm-up answer to the question, "What is geography?"	
INDIVIDUAL ACTIVITY	**25 minutes**
Hand out geography terms packet. Students are to work on this independently.	
SMALL GROUP ACTIVITY	**10 minutes**
Compare geography terms packet answers with other members of their small group.	
LARGE GROUP ACTIVITY	
N/A	
CLOSING EXERCISE	**5 to 10 minutes, as needed, and as time allows**
Review what students learned today. Unfinished portion of the geography terms packet is homework.	
ADDITIONAL NOTES:	

Index

teacher evaluations and, 197
using computers, 109–11
VCRs, DVD players, and CD
    players, 37–38, 117–18
voicemail, 113–14
Textbook shortage, 91–93
Time management, 7–9. *See also*
    Everyday routines; Forms;
    Lesson planning; Organizing
    adjuvant (additional)
        instructional time activities,
        7–8, 15, 16–18
    categories of time and, 7
    as critical classroom-
        management domain, 2
    daily schedule and, 15–19
    defined, 7
    delegating responsibility and,
        129–32
    digital PDA for, 19, 20
    grading papers and, 21–24

harnessing power of volunteers,
    132–33
instructional minutes and, 18,
    19, 128
instructional time activities,
    8–9, 15, 18–19
personal organizer for, 19–20
planning periods and, 43
reasonable approach to, 9
Tornadoes, 234
Traditions, respecting, 187–89

U

Uniforms, 213–14

V

VCRs, DVD players, and CD
    players, 37–38

Voicemail, 113–14
Volunteers, using, 132–33

W

Websites, as resources, 254
Websites, for class, 210

Y

Yard duty, 203–4

THE EVERYTHING SERIES!

BUSINESS & PERSONAL FINANCE

Everything® Accounting Book
Everything® Budgeting Book, 2nd Ed.
Everything® Business Planning Book
Everything® Coaching and Mentoring Book, 2nd Ed.
Everything® Fundraising Book
Everything® Get Out of Debt Book
Everything® Grant Writing Book, 2nd Ed.
Everything® Guide to Buying Foreclosures
Everything® Guide to Fundraising, $15.95
Everything® Guide to Mortgages
Everything® Guide to Personal Finance for Single Mothers
Everything® Home-Based Business Book, 2nd Ed.
Everything® Homebuying Book, 3rd Ed., $15.95
Everything® Homeselling Book, 2nd Ed.
Everything® Human Resource Management Book
Everything® Improve Your Credit Book
Everything® Investing Book, 2nd Ed.
Everything® Landlording Book
Everything® Leadership Book, 2nd Ed.
Everything® Managing People Book, 2nd Ed.
Everything® Negotiating Book
Everything® Online Auctions Book
Everything® Online Business Book
Everything® Personal Finance Book
Everything® Personal Finance in Your 20s & 30s Book, 2nd Ed.
Everything® Personal Finance in Your 40s & 50s Book, $15.95
Everything® Project Management Book, 2nd Ed.
Everything® Real Estate Investing Book
Everything® Retirement Planning Book
Everything® Robert's Rules Book, $7.95
Everything® Selling Book
Everything® Start Your Own Business Book, 2nd Ed.
Everything® Wills & Estate Planning Book

COOKING

Everything® Barbecue Cookbook
Everything® Bartender's Book, 2nd Ed., $9.95
Everything® Calorie Counting Cookbook
Everything® Cheese Book
Everything® Chinese Cookbook
Everything® Classic Recipes Book
Everything® Cocktail Parties & Drinks Book
Everything® College Cookbook
Everything® Cooking for Baby and Toddler Book
Everything® Diabetes Cookbook
Everything® Easy Gourmet Cookbook
Everything® Fondue Cookbook
Everything® Food Allergy Cookbook, $15.95
Everything® Fondue Party Book
Everything® Gluten-Free Cookbook
Everything® Glycemic Index Cookbook
Everything® Grilling Cookbook
Everything® Healthy Cooking for Parties Book, $15.95
Everything® Holiday Cookbook
Everything® Indian Cookbook
Everything® Lactose-Free Cookbook
Everything® Low-Cholesterol Cookbook

Everything® Low-Fat High-Flavor Cookbook, 2nd Ed., $15.95
Everything® Low-Salt Cookbook
Everything® Meals for a Month Cookbook
Everything® Meals on a Budget Cookbook
Everything® Mediterranean Cookbook
Everything® Mexican Cookbook
Everything® No Trans Fat Cookbook
Everything® One-Pot Cookbook, 2nd Ed., $15.95
Everything® Organic Cooking for Baby & Toddler Book, $15.95
Everything® Pizza Cookbook
Everything® Quick Meals Cookbook, 2nd Ed., $15.95
Everything® Slow Cooker Cookbook
Everything® Slow Cooking for a Crowd Cookbook
Everything® Soup Cookbook
Everything® Stir-Fry Cookbook
Everything® Sugar-Free Cookbook
Everything® Tapas and Small Plates Cookbook
Everything® Tex-Mex Cookbook
Everything® Thai Cookbook
Everything® Vegetarian Cookbook
Everything® Whole-Grain, High-Fiber Cookbook
Everything® Wild Game Cookbook
Everything® Wine Book, 2nd Ed.

GAMES

Everything® 15-Minute Sudoku Book, $9.95
Everything® 30-Minute Sudoku Book, $9.95
Everything® Bible Crosswords Book, $9.95
Everything® Blackjack Strategy Book
Everything® Brain Strain Book, $9.95
Everything® Bridge Book
Everything® Card Games Book
Everything® Card Tricks Book, $9.95
Everything® Casino Gambling Book, 2nd Ed.
Everything® Chess Basics Book
Everything® Christmas Crosswords Book, $9.95
Everything® Craps Strategy Book
Everything® Crossword and Puzzle Book
Everything® Crosswords and Puzzles for Quote Lovers Book, $9.95
Everything® Crossword Challenge Book
Everything® Crosswords for the Beach Book, $9.95
Everything® Cryptic Crosswords Book, $9.95
Everything® Cryptograms Book, $9.95
Everything® Easy Crosswords Book
Everything® Easy Kakuro Book, $9.95
Everything® Easy Large-Print Crosswords Book
Everything® Games Book, 2nd Ed.
Everything® Giant Book of Crosswords
Everything® Giant Sudoku Book, $9.95
Everything® Giant Word Search Book
Everything® Kakuro Challenge Book, $9.95
Everything® Large-Print Crossword Challenge Book
Everything® Large-Print Crosswords Book
Everything® Large-Print Travel Crosswords Book
Everything® Lateral Thinking Puzzles Book, $9.95
Everything® Literary Crosswords Book, $9.95
Everything® Mazes Book
Everything® Memory Booster Puzzles Book, $9.95

Everything® Movie Crosswords Book, $9.95
Everything® Music Crosswords Book, $9.95
Everything® Online Poker Book
Everything® Pencil Puzzles Book, $9.95
Everything® Poker Strategy Book
Everything® Pool & Billiards Book
Everything® Puzzles for Commuters Book, $9.95
Everything® Puzzles for Dog Lovers Book, $9.95
Everything® Sports Crosswords Book, $9.95
Everything® Test Your IQ Book, $9.95
Everything® Texas Hold 'Em Book, $9.95
Everything® Travel Crosswords Book, $9.95
Everything® Travel Mazes Book, $9.95
Everything® Travel Word Search Book, $9.95
Everything® TV Crosswords Book, $9.95
Everything® Word Games Challenge Book
Everything® Word Scramble Book
Everything® Word Search Book

HEALTH

Everything® Alzheimer's Book
Everything® Diabetes Book
Everything® First Aid Book, $9.95
Everything® Green Living Book
Everything® Health Guide to Addiction and Recovery
Everything® Health Guide to Adult Bipolar Disorder
Everything® Health Guide to Arthritis
Everything® Health Guide to Controlling Anxiety
Everything® Health Guide to Depression
Everything® Health Guide to Diabetes, 2nd Ed.
Everything® Health Guide to Fibromyalgia
Everything® Health Guide to Menopause, 2nd Ed.
Everything® Health Guide to Migraines
Everything® Health Guide to Multiple Sclerosis
Everything® Health Guide to OCD
Everything® Health Guide to PMS
Everything® Health Guide to Postpartum Care
Everything® Health Guide to Thyroid Disease
Everything® Hypnosis Book
Everything® Low Cholesterol Book
Everything® Menopause Book
Everything® Nutrition Book
Everything® Reflexology Book
Everything® Stress Management Book
Everything® Superfoods Book, $15.95

HISTORY

Everything® American Government Book
Everything® American History Book, 2nd Ed.
Everything® American Revolution Book, $15.95
Everything® Civil War Book
Everything® Freemasons Book
Everything® Irish History & Heritage Book
Everything® World War II Book, 2nd Ed.

HOBBIES

Everything® Candlemaking Book
Everything® Cartooning Book
Everything® Coin Collecting Book
Everything® Digital Photography Book, 2nd Ed.

Everything® Drawing Book
Everything® Family Tree Book, 2nd Ed.
Everything® Guide to Online Genealogy, $15.95
Everything® Knitting Book
Everything® Knots Book
Everything® Photography Book
Everything® Quilting Book
Everything® Sewing Book
Everything® Soapmaking Book, 2nd Ed.
Everything® Woodworking Book

HOME IMPROVEMENT

Everything® Feng Shui Book
Everything® Feng Shui Decluttering Book, $9.95
Everything® Fix-It Book
Everything® Green Living Book
Everything® Home Decorating Book
Everything® Home Storage Solutions Book
Everything® Homebuilding Book
Everything® Organize Your Home Book, 2nd Ed.

KIDS' BOOKS

All titles are $7.95
Everything® Fairy Tales Book, $14.95
Everything® Kids' Animal Puzzle & Activity Book
Everything® Kids' Astronomy Book
Everything® Kids' Baseball Book, 5th Ed.
Everything® Kids' Bible Trivia Book
Everything® Kids' Bugs Book
Everything® Kids' Cars and Trucks Puzzle and Activity Book
Everything® Kids' Christmas Puzzle & Activity Book
Everything® Kids' Connect the Dots
        Puzzle and Activity Book
Everything® Kids' Cookbook, 2nd Ed.
Everything® Kids' Crazy Puzzles Book
Everything® Kids' Dinosaurs Book
Everything® Kids' Dragons Puzzle and Activity Book
Everything® Kids' Environment Book $7.95
Everything® Kids' Fairies Puzzle and Activity Book
Everything® Kids' First Spanish Puzzle and Activity Book
Everything® Kids' Football Book
Everything® Kids' Geography Book
Everything® Kids' Gross Cookbook
Everything® Kids' Gross Hidden Pictures Book
Everything® Kids' Gross Jokes Book
Everything® Kids' Gross Mazes Book
Everything® Kids' Gross Puzzle & Activity Book
Everything® Kids' Halloween Puzzle & Activity Book
Everything® Kids' Hanukkah Puzzle and Activity Book
Everything® Kids' Hidden Pictures Book
Everything® Kids' Horses Book
Everything® Kids' Joke Book
Everything® Kids' Knock Knock Book
Everything® Kids' Learning French Book
Everything® Kids' Learning Spanish Book
Everything® Kids' Magical Science Experiments Book
Everything® Kids' Math Puzzles Book
Everything® Kids' Mazes Book
Everything® Kids' Money Book, 2nd Ed.
Everything® Kids' Mummies, Pharaoh's, and Pyramids Puzzle and Activity Book
Everything® Kids' Nature Book
Everything® Kids' Pirates Puzzle and Activity Book
Everything® Kids' Presidents Book
Everything® Kids' Princess Puzzle and Activity Book
Everything® Kids' Puzzle Book

Everything® Kids' Racecars Puzzle and Activity Book
Everything® Kids' Riddles & Brain Teasers Book
Everything® Kids' Science Experiments Book
Everything® Kids' Sharks Book
Everything® Kids' Soccer Book
Everything® Kids' Spelling Book
Everything® Kids' Spies Puzzle and Activity Book
Everything® Kids' States Book
Everything® Kids' Travel Activity Book
Everything® Kids' Word Search Puzzle and Activity Book

LANGUAGE

Everything® Conversational Japanese Book with CD, $19.95
Everything® French Grammar Book
Everything® French Phrase Book, $9.95
Everything® French Verb Book, $9.95
Everything® German Phrase Book, $9.95
Everything® German Practice Book with CD, $19.95
Everything® Inglés Book
Everything® Intermediate Spanish Book with CD, $19.95
Everything® Italian Phrase Book, $9.95
Everything® Italian Practice Book with CD, $19.95
Everything® Learning Brazilian Portuguese Book with CD, $19.95
Everything® Learning French Book with CD, 2nd Ed., $19.95
Everything® Learning German Book
Everything® Learning Italian Book
Everything® Learning Latin Book
Everything® Learning Russian Book with CD, $19.95
Everything® Learning Spanish Book
Everything® Learning Spanish Book with CD, 2nd Ed., $19.95
Everything® Russian Practice Book with CD, $19.95
Everything® Sign Language Book, $15.95
Everything® Spanish Grammar Book
Everything® Spanish Phrase Book, $9.95
Everything® Spanish Practice Book with CD, $19.95
Everything® Spanish Verb Book, $9.95
Everything® Speaking Mandarin Chinese Book with CD, $19.95

MUSIC

Everything® Bass Guitar Book with CD, $19.95
Everything® Drums Book with CD, $19.95
Everything® Guitar Book with CD, 2nd Ed., $19.95
Everything® Guitar Chords Book with CD, $19.95
Everything® Guitar Scales Book with CD, $19.95
Everything® Harmonica Book with CD, $15.95
Everything® Home Recording Book
Everything® Music Theory Book with CD, $19.95
Everything® Reading Music Book with CD, $19.95
Everything® Rock & Blues Guitar Book with CD, $19.95
Everything® Rock & Blues Piano Book with CD, $19.95
Everything® Rock Drums Book with CD, $19.95
Everything® Singing Book with CD, $19.95
Everything® Songwriting Book

NEW AGE

Everything® Astrology Book, 2nd Ed.
Everything® Birthday Personology Book
Everything® Celtic Wisdom Book, $15.95
Everything® Dreams Book, 2nd Ed.
Everything® Law of Attraction Book, $15.95
Everything® Love Signs Book, $9.95
Everything® Love Spells Book, $9.95
Everything® Palmistry Book
Everything® Psychic Book
Everything® Reiki Book

Everything® Sex Signs Book, $9.95
Everything® Spells & Charms Book, 2nd Ed.
Everything® Tarot Book, 2nd Ed.
Everything® Toltec Wisdom Book
Everything® Wicca & Witchcraft Book, 2nd Ed.

PARENTING

Everything® Baby Names Book, 2nd Ed.
Everything® Baby Shower Book, 2nd Ed.
Everything® Baby Sign Language Book with DVD
Everything® Baby's First Year Book
Everything® Birthing Book
Everything® Breastfeeding Book
Everything® Father-to-Be Book
Everything® Father's First Year Book
Everything® Get Ready for Baby Book, 2nd Ed.
Everything® Get Your Baby to Sleep Book, $9.95
Everything® Getting Pregnant Book
Everything® Guide to Pregnancy Over 35
Everything® Guide to Raising a One-Year-Old
Everything® Guide to Raising a Two-Year-Old
Everything® Guide to Raising Adolescent Boys
Everything® Guide to Raising Adolescent Girls
Everything® Mother's First Year Book
Everything® Parent's Guide to Childhood Illnesses
Everything® Parent's Guide to Children and Divorce
Everything® Parent's Guide to Children with ADD/ADHD
Everything® Parent's Guide to Children with Asperger's
        Syndrome
Everything® Parent's Guide to Children with Anxiety
Everything® Parent's Guide to Children with Asthma
Everything® Parent's Guide to Children with Autism
Everything® Parent's Guide to Children with Bipolar Disorder
Everything® Parent's Guide to Children with Depression
Everything® Parent's Guide to Children with Dyslexia
Everything® Parent's Guide to Children with Juvenile Diabetes
Everything® Parent's Guide to Children with OCD
Everything® Parent's Guide to Positive Discipline
Everything® Parent's Guide to Raising Boys
Everything® Parent's Guide to Raising Girls
Everything® Parent's Guide to Raising Siblings
**Everything® Parent's Guide to Raising Your
        Adopted Child**
Everything® Parent's Guide to Sensory Integration Disorder
Everything® Parent's Guide to Tantrums
Everything® Parent's Guide to the Strong-Willed Child
Everything® Parenting a Teenager Book
Everything® Potty Training Book, $9.95
Everything® Pregnancy Book, 3rd Ed.
Everything® Pregnancy Fitness Book
Everything® Pregnancy Nutrition Book
Everything® Pregnancy Organizer, 2nd Ed., $16.95
Everything® Toddler Activities Book
Everything® Toddler Book
Everything® Tween Book
Everything® Twins, Triplets, and More Book

PETS

Everything® Aquarium Book
Everything® Boxer Book
Everything® Cat Book, 2nd Ed.
Everything® Chihuahua Book
Everything® Cooking for Dogs Book
Everything® Dachshund Book
Everything® Dog Book, 2nd Ed.
Everything® Dog Grooming Book

Everything® Dog Obedience Book
Everything® Dog Owner's Organizer, $16.95
Everything® Dog Training and Tricks Book
Everything® German Shepherd Book
Everything® Golden Retriever Book
Everything® Horse Book, 2nd Ed., $15.95
Everything® Horse Care Book
Everything® Horseback Riding Book
Everything® Labrador Retriever Book
Everything® Poodle Book
Everything® Pug Book
Everything® Puppy Book
Everything® Small Dogs Book
Everything® Tropical Fish Book
Everything® Yorkshire Terrier Book

REFERENCE

Everything® American Presidents Book
Everything® Blogging Book
Everything® Build Your Vocabulary Book, $9.95
Everything® Car Care Book
Everything® Classical Mythology Book
Everything® Da Vinci Book
Everything® Einstein Book
Everything® Enneagram Book
Everything® Etiquette Book, 2nd Ed.
Everything® Family Christmas Book, $15.95
Everything® Guide to C. S. Lewis & Narnia
Everything® Guide to Divorce, 2nd Ed., $15.95
Everything® Guide to Edgar Allan Poe
Everything® Guide to Understanding Philosophy
Everything® Inventions and Patents Book
Everything® Jacqueline Kennedy Onassis Book
Everything® John F. Kennedy Book
Everything® Mafia Book
Everything® Martin Luther King Jr. Book
Everything® Pirates Book
Everything® Private Investigation Book
Everything® Psychology Book
Everything® Public Speaking Book, $9.95
Everything® Shakespeare Book, 2nd Ed.

RELIGION

Everything® Angels Book
Everything® Bible Book
Everything® Bible Study Book with CD, $19.95
Everything® Buddhism Book
Everything® Catholicism Book
Everything® Christianity Book
Everything® Gnostic Gospels Book
Everything® Hinduism Book, $15.95
Everything® History of the Bible Book
Everything® Jesus Book
Everything® Jewish History & Heritage Book
Everything® Judaism Book
Everything® Kabbalah Book
Everything® Koran Book
Everything® Mary Book
Everything® Mary Magdalene Book
Everything® Prayer Book

Everything® Saints Book, 2nd Ed.
Everything® Torah Book
Everything® Understanding Islam Book
Everything® Women of the Bible Book
Everything® World's Religions Book

SCHOOL & CAREERS

Everything® Career Tests Book
Everything® College Major Test Book
Everything® College Survival Book, 2nd Ed.
Everything® Cover Letter Book, 2nd Ed.
Everything® Filmmaking Book
Everything® Get-a-Job Book, 2nd Ed.
Everything® Guide to Being a Paralegal
Everything® Guide to Being a Personal Trainer
Everything® Guide to Being a Real Estate Agent
Everything® Guide to Being a Sales Rep
Everything® Guide to Being an Event Planner
Everything® Guide to Careers in Health Care
Everything® Guide to Careers in Law Enforcement
Everything® Guide to Government Jobs
Everything® Guide to Starting and Running a Catering
    Business
Everything® Guide to Starting and Running a Restaurant
**Everything® Guide to Starting and Running
    a Retail Store**
Everything® Job Interview Book, 2nd Ed.
Everything® New Nurse Book
Everything® New Teacher Book
Everything® Paying for College Book
Everything® Practice Interview Book
Everything® Resume Book, 3rd Ed.
Everything® Study Book

SELF-HELP

Everything® Body Language Book
Everything® Dating Book, 2nd Ed.
Everything® Great Sex Book
**Everything® Guide to Caring for Aging Parents,
    $15.95**
Everything® Self-Esteem Book
Everything® Self-Hypnosis Book, $9.95
Everything® Tantric Sex Book

SPORTS & FITNESS

Everything® Easy Fitness Book
Everything® Fishing Book
Everything® Guide to Weight Training, $15.95
Everything® Krav Maga for Fitness Book
Everything® Running Book, 2nd Ed.
Everything® Triathlon Training Book, $15.95

TRAVEL

Everything® Family Guide to Coastal Florida
Everything® Family Guide to Cruise Vacations
Everything® Family Guide to Hawaii
Everything® Family Guide to Las Vegas, 2nd Ed.
Everything® Family Guide to Mexico
Everything® Family Guide to New England, 2nd Ed.

Everything® Family Guide to New York City, 3rd Ed.
**Everything® Family Guide to Northern California
    and Lake Tahoe**
Everything® Family Guide to RV Travel & Campgrounds
Everything® Family Guide to the Caribbean
Everything® Family Guide to the Disneyland® Resort, California
    Adventure®, Universal Studios®, and the Anaheim
    Area, 2nd Ed.
Everything® Family Guide to the Walt Disney World Resort®,
    Universal Studios®, and Greater Orlando, 5th Ed.
Everything® Family Guide to Timeshares
Everything® Family Guide to Washington D.C., 2nd Ed.

WEDDINGS

Everything® Bachelorette Party Book, $9.95
Everything® Bridesmaid Book, $9.95
Everything® Destination Wedding Book
Everything® Father of the Bride Book, $9.95
Everything® Green Wedding Book, $15.95
Everything® Groom Book, $9.95
Everything® Jewish Wedding Book, 2nd Ed., $15.95
Everything® Mother of the Bride Book, $9.95
Everything® Outdoor Wedding Book
Everything® Wedding Book, 3rd Ed.
Everything® Wedding Checklist, $9.95
Everything® Wedding Etiquette Book, $9.95
Everything® Wedding Organizer, 2nd Ed., $16.95
Everything® Wedding Shower Book, $9.95
Everything® Wedding Vows Book, 3rd Ed., $9.95
Everything® Wedding Workout Book
Everything® Weddings on a Budget Book, 2nd Ed., $9.95

WRITING

Everything® Creative Writing Book
Everything® Get Published Book, 2nd Ed.
Everything® Grammar and Style Book, 2nd Ed.
Everything® Guide to Magazine Writing
Everything® Guide to Writing a Book Proposal
Everything® Guide to Writing a Novel
Everything® Guide to Writing Children's Books
Everything® Guide to Writing Copy
Everything® Guide to Writing Graphic Novels
Everything® Guide to Writing Research Papers
Everything® Guide to Writing a Romance Novel, $15.95
Everything® Improve Your Writing Book, 2nd Ed.
Everything® Writing Poetry Book